WALKING
CAPE ANN

with **Ted Tarr**

WALKING CAPE ANN
WITH TED TARR
EXPLORING THE TRAILS OF ROCKPORT, GLOUCESTER, ESSEX AND MANCHESTER-BY-THE-SEA WITH A FAVORITE NATIVE SON.

by

Helen Naismith

Ten Pound Island Books
Gloucester, Massachusetts
1994

ISBN 0-938459-08-2

Printed in the United States of America

Book & Map Design: Dorian Sweet - Grand Tableau Design

For
My daughter, Kathi

Acknowledgments

In writing this book, I received much encouragement and help along the way from many familiar with Cape Ann's rich history, both on land and sea, as well as those knowledgeable about its flora and fauna, and others who simply enjoy walking the scenic trails throughout its four townships. All felt a book of this type was long overdue.

With sincere gratitude, I wish to acknowledge those who shared in this effort: Steve Rask and his fine research staff at the Rockport Public Library; Ellen Nelson, who performs the same friendly service at the Cape Ann Historical Society Association; Ed Becker, Executive Director of the Essex County Greenbelt Association; Gail Halloran, Forest and Park Supervisor at Halibut Point State Park and Reservation; U. S. Coast Guardsmen at the Gloucester Station; Diana Stockton, Executive Director of the Essex Ship Building Museum; Ann Sheinwald, Chairman of the Rockport Rights-of-Way Committee; Boston meteorologist Bob Copeland, formerly with Channel 5; bird watcher Frances Ruggles; and Bill Frost whose expertise in many areas made this a better book, as did the editorial assistance of Rae Francoeur, Peter Coley, Dennis Schaefer and Ted Tarr, who also outlined the maps. I also want to thank Sue MacNeil, my friend, for encouragement and moral support.

And a special tribute is due those far-sighted, dedicated individuals who seek to protect natural resources by preserving open spaces and trails, thus allowing walkers of today and future generations to enjoy the beauty of this very special place known as Cape Ann.

TABLE OF CONTENTS

INTRODUCTION

Walking Cape Ann with Ted Tarr every Sunday morning has become one of my greatest pleasures since returning to New England from Atlanta several years ago. Having been a walking enthusiast for many years (brisk evening jaunts along the Chattahoochie River were among my favorites), I was delighted to find the walking group which Ted has been leading for 20 years. These two-hour explorations include informal talks on plants, birds and local history, and are usually determined by weather conditions and seasonal interest. A summer walk along the oceanside Atlantic Path (from Pigeon Cove to Halibut Point), the fragile beauty of fall in the Manchester Woods, the windswept dunes at Wingaersheek in the off season, and the winter mystique of Ravenswood, are among the enchanting nature trails explored each week.

A direct descendant of Rockport's first family, the Richard Tarrs who settled this land in 1690, Ted has been walking its many trails since he was a young boy—picking blueberries with his mother, swimming in the quarries (when it was permitted), and hiking with childhood friends. After college (with a degree in research biology) came a stint in the military, followed by worldly travels, but his heart never left his native New England. After working in other states as a consultant in land management, he returned to Rockport, where he has served for many years as selectman and civic leader. Like generations of his forebears, he plays a vital role in the life of his community, generously giving of his time and energy to maintain a balance between progress and preservation. When he's not attending to business at Town Hall or the State House, he's clearing public trails, fighting fires, tending his beautiful flower garden, or delivering Meals-on-Wheels to shut-ins.

This book is a narrative of walks taken with Ted over a one-year period. After exploring its network of meandering trails, I'm sure you'll become as captivated by the many faces of Cape Ann as I have. Unfortunately, it was not possible to walk every pathway during this past year because an unusually severe winter kept us out of the woods for weeks at a time. All the trails described here are open to the public. Maps are included to enable visitors to enjoy the area's wilderness and rocky coastline. The legend noted on each map points out interesting sites and scenes along the way.

Readers are encouraged to learn about these and other interesting trails listed in the Appendix, including Boston's famous Emerald Necklace, a seven-mile walk through nine contiguous parks, and the Bay Circuit, a 200-mile outer arc of scenic routes along the eastern Massachusetts landscape.

A word of caution: The conditions of Cape Ann's greenspaces vary: some are wide, flat surfaces, others are steep, winding and rocky. All are slippery when wet. Always walk with a companion and take a trail map when walking unfamiliar routes. Dress according to the weather and wear comfortable walking shoes.

To all, we extend a warm invitation to join us on Sunday morning. We meet at 10 o'clock at Whistlestop Mall on Railroad Avenue—year-round. There's much to see and enjoy along Cape Ann's historic trails. Plan a walk with us soon.

Helen Naismith
Rockport, Massachusetts
July 1993

Ravenswood

Ravenswood Park - Gloucester

It was unseasonably cold the July 4th weekend I joined Ted and his band of walking enthusiasts for the very first time at the Whistlestop Mall on Railroad Avenue in Rockport.

How many will be with us today? I wondered aloud when I was introduced to the friendly, outgoing walkmaster that brisk July morn.

"We usually have 25 to 30 every Sunday during good weather" he responded, adding with a touch of humor that I would come to know as wit personified. "In the dead of winter, we're down to 12 nuts."

On this day, we loaded ourselves into cars and drove to Gloucester, past the oceanside statue of the Fisherman's Memorial, dedicated to Cape Ann fishermen lost at sea, and continued west on Western Avenue about four miles to Ravenswood Park. This beautiful 600-acre forest was deeded to the Ravenswood Park Trust, the legacy of Samuel E. Sawyer, one of Gloucester's leading benefactors. Widowed and childless at the time of his death in December 1889, the philanthropist accompanied his bequest with a sizable endowment for the preservation of this mystical, enchanted primeval forest. (Another valuable gift from this generous civic leader was a 1764 Georgian mansion which has been modernized into the Gloucester Public Library; here, too, he thoughtfully left a handsome sum for its long-term upkeep.) The Ravenswood endowment has since been exhausted, and the park has recently come under the jurisdiction of the Trustees of Reservations, a private statewide organization which seeks out and preserves beautiful places for public use.

The main gate into the park is set back a little into the woods, alongside a small, wooden chapel, recently renovated into a private residence for the park superintendent. A small paved area off to its side provides free parking for 12 cars. Open from sunrise to sunset seven days a week year round, Ravenswood offers five miles of meandering trails through a beautiful natural forest of untouched New England woodlands. The trails are both easily trod (broad, dirt and gravel, or narrow, soft pine-needle flooring) and challenging (single-file, rigorous footpaths over rocks and marshy terrain).

As we walked the Valley Road, a wide gravel roadway leading into the dark woodlands, Ted began to lecture on the subject he loves most—the rich, textured landscape of Cape Ann, ancestral home of the Tarr family since 1690. He described the nuances of ecology and the make-up of the region, taking the time to explain in detail the characteristics and qualities of plants and trees and the means by which they arrived in this forested wilderness. A tremendous glacial force shattered Cape Ann millions of years ago, leaving in its wake the valleys, drumlins and streams we now call "charming," "picturesque" and "beautiful." Having the good fortune to live amid this groundswell of geological dynamics, at times I feel as though I'm walking the ledge of civilization when, in fact, I'm only following in the footsteps of many like-minded travelers who have wondered about our time and place in this polarized universe.

The trail into Ravenswood offered a sampling of what the good earth, undaunted by modern technology, continues to yield: wintergreen (tea berries), hairycap moss, bracken fern, mapleleaf viburnum and wild sarsaparilla. White-blossomed mountain laurel, which usually peaks here in mid-June, hovering witch hazel trees (resembling Atlanta's famous dogwoods), and towering Canadian hemlocks deepened the senses of our nature-loving group as we hiked deeper into the woods. Hemlock looper, a devastating disease which destroyed many of the older hemlocks in Manchester's beautiful woodlands about 20 years ago, did not seem to encroach on Ravenswood.

MAGNOLIA SWAMP

From the wide gravel roadway, we turned left onto Rockingstone Path, a narrow footpath which twisted and turned through the dense forest, winding into Magnolia Swamp. Along the trail, we came to a large boulder which, as Ted demonstrated, could be rocked slightly with a little push. As we continued toward the swamp, we passed through luxuriant, waist-high cinnamon ferns. Plowing through the lush, green thicket, we were soon stopped short—not to smell the roses, but the delicately scented blossoms of a lone magnolia virginiana, commonly called sweet bay. Overshadowed by hemlock, beech and maple, this little gem manages to survive in this fortuitous environment—but just barely. Its creamy petals were smaller than those found in the South. In warm climates this romantic tree, so prevalent in southern culture, is evergreen and enjoys a much longer flowering season than in New England. In the damp hollows of Ravenswood, it is deciduous and blooms only a few weeks in early summer. Too, the southern magnolia towers proud and stately on expansive lawns and other open places. The wild New England variety is small and shrub-like. In Ravenswood's dark, damp forest, its northernmost boundary, the magnolia was bent and misshapen under a canopy of hemlocks and large hardwood trees. During an earlier period, this lovely tree (from which the Magnolia section of Gloucester takes its name) was more prevalent, but annual strippings of flowers and branches have placed it on the state's endangered-species list.

"This sort of vandalism will probably cause the trees to be extirpated before many years," wrote Wilson Flagg, a noted Cape Ann naturalist, in 1872. His words could not have been more prophetic.

Continuing on, Ted pointed out the partridgeberry, sometimes called "twinberry," the starflower, and off to our right, growing out of a huge rock, a pretty green polypody fern.

"The build-up of dust, pine needles and other fallen woodlife entrapped by lichen provides rich soil for the fern to take root and germinate into the beautiful plant you see there now," he explained.

Approaching a small brook flowing into a swampy marsh, we noticed a stand of domestic lilies ready to burst forth into bloom; and a little further on, we came upon a soft ground covering of "goldthread," so called, as Ted demonstrated, because of the color of the plant's root. Removing the soil clinging to it, he revealed its delicate roots which appeared as thin gold threads attached to tender green leaves. According to Indian folklore, this plant is helpful in healing stomach ailments.

Also covering the ground along the trail were Indian cucumbers in flower. This unique plant is beautifully formed, having a long slender stem with two whorls of luxurious growth. Encircling its lower stem are six or seven graceful, outstretched green leaves. About three inches higher are four delicate white petals with star-shaped seed clusters. Growing alongside this lovely native plant, velvety emerald green moss lay in the shade of spreading red and white oaks. Tall white pines looked on nearby. In the days of early colonization, many trees from Cape Ann forests were marked with the king's broad arrow for use in the English navy—jointed oaks for the hull and straight pine for masts. One such timber fortunately escaped His Majesty's ax. Carved into the wrinkled bark of an ancient Gloucester pine the words "King's Pine" are still readable, noting its designation for the monarch's fleet. But, for some reason, it was not meant to be. This towering white pine has remained standing for three hundred years overlooking the port city of Gloucester. How old it was at the time of branding, no one knows.

The "wolf tree" tells another interesting tale about this species. The reason for its unusual name remains a mystery, but its growth characteristics were explained by Ted. "The white pine's multi-trunks are caused by the pine bud worm killing the tree's main leaders. When the main trunk dies, growth continues through smaller trunks formed along branches. Usually these trees are dominant in open sun, reforesting cleared areas which indicate their recent history."

THE HERMIT OF RAVENSWOOD

The trail wound around Bond Hill where Ted told us about a fascinating creature of the wild—a man named Mason A. Walton, known as the Hermit of Ravenswood. It was during the last quarter of the nineteenth century that this quiet, gentle man waded into the stream of Gloucester history. But I'll let Harvard naturalist Frank Bolles, author of *From Blomidon to Smoky*, introduce him.

"I have a friend who lives alone, summer and winter, in a tiny hut amid the woods. The doctors told him that he must die, so he escaped from them to nature, made his peace with her, and regained his health. To the wild creatures of the pasture, the oak woods, and the swamps he is no longer a man, but a faun; he is one of their own kind, shy, alert, silent. They, having learned to trust him, have come a little nearer to men."

An unnamed traveler, writing in *Pleasure Drives Around Cape Ann* in 1896, had this to say about Gloucester's hermit: "for years he has lived in these dense woods far from all habitation, cultivating the friendship of birds, squirrels, woodchucks, spiders and other natives which claim this spot their home. No more interesting place to visit (on foot) is there than this of hermit Walton's and no more intelligent person to converse with can be found."

For 33 years Walton lived alone in the Ravenswood forest, writing many newspaper and magazine articles on the animals and birds that visited his dooryard. He was considered an authority on ornithology by experts in the field. From his book *A Hermit's Wild Friends*, one gets a glimpse of his keen intellect and gentle sensitivity. He kept a daily journal and throughout these writings often refers to his little wilderness pals by name: Satan was a mischievous raccoon, Bismarck a feisty red squirrel, and Wabbles a very special song sparrow. Very special, indeed. For 26years, Wabbles returned to the little Ravenswood cabin every summer from his winter home in southern rice fields—three years in a row on April 13— waking the hermit at daybreak with his loud singing. Today a bronze plaque mounted on a huge boulder marks the spot on Bond Hill where the hermit's home once stood, reminding passers-by of the tender, scholarly man who lived life to his heart's content among his animal friends.

The decision to walk the trails of Ravenswood on a misty morning in mid-October was dictated by weather conditions. It had rained several days during the week and the woods were still wet and soggy. Knowing Cape Ann's trails as well as he does, Ted felt that the broad gravel roads of Ravenswood would keep us relatively dry while we viewed the changing autumn landscape.

On this day there was lots of gorgeous fall foliage among the broad-leafed hardwoods, their rain-soaked leaves covering the wide entrance road. "These roads were raked daily when endowment funds were available," Ted said.

Continuing along the Old Salem Path, we looked down an embankment upon patches of yellowing royal fern clustered among golden beech and red maples. Nearby the pretty red-flowering rosettes of the hobblebush, a showy viburnum called the American wayfaring tree, were fading into muted ivory.

Large boulders dotted the landscape. "The glacier went back and forth in this area several times," Ted said, pointing out the rocky debris left in its wake, clearly visible through the open land beneath a forest of gray birch.

"Hardwoods need sun in forested areas. They provide shade for hemlocks."

Our walk continued—past a vernal pond on our right, an open vista to our left, crimson sumac in the distance. Along the way, Ted narrated:

"Viburnum is just starting to turn."

"Witch hazel is a common shrub here."

"That's a striped maple; grows to medium size. Notice the wide yellow leaves."

PEST HOUSE • BOND HILL RESERVOIR

As we walked along the Old Salem Path which in earlier times had connected Gloucester's Stage Fork Park to Salem, Ted stopped and told us of the exploits and chicanery that had taken place here during its developing years.

"About the time of the Revolutionary War, the Gloucester Pest House was built along this road to isolate people with smallpox. Sulfur was burned to fumigate travelers and kill any germs they might be carrying into the area, especially from other countries," he explained. "But the men who ran these operations were not above doing a little illegal moonlighting on the side.

"The story goes that they got word one morning that Custom inspectors were on their way to Gloucester Harbor from Salem to raid a shipment of contraband that had just been smuggled into port.   When the officials reached the pest house, they were informed of a serious health problem in Salem, which necessitated their fumigation before being permitted to pass the checkpoint—a delay which allowed time for the contraband to be hidden.   When all was put into hiding, the unsuspecting inspectors were then cleared through to Gloucester, unaware of the trick that had been played on them."

It was the type of story Ted likes to tell—about simple locals outsmarting self-important G-men.

We continued along the park's main trail which wandered through the forest and emerged onto a paved section of Old Salem Road. Instead of exiting the park, however, we bore left past an ancient gnarled red maple commanding an expansive view of its surroundings from a triangular knoll. From here, we walked up to Bond Hill Reservoir, passing along the way a roadside stand of cattails.

The only indication that the large, grassy meadow atop a steep incline was concealing 10 million gallons of water beneath its surface were several pipes protruding from the ground.   These vents allow air in and out of the massive basin below. From this elevated point, the panoramic view of the city of Gloucester is magnificent, from City Hall to Our Lady of Good Voyage Church, a famous coastal landmark, to the shores of Eastern Point and the outer harbor.

The descent from the reservoir's hilltop was somewhat easier than our climb up.   Reaching bottom, we followed the circular service road back to Ravenswood. From the large maple we had passed on our way in, we retraced our steps back to the park's main entrance, enjoying the glorious autumn colors along the way. Oak leaves do not undergo the colorful transformation that other broad-leafed trees experience; they simply change to leathery brown, many clinging to branches throughout the winter.   Leaves of the pretty gray beech turn a luminous burnt orange in the fall and also remain during the wintertime. Both finally get pushed off by new spring growth.

Ravenswood is beautiful every season of the year.   When we walked here again in February, it was a magical winter wonderland. The heavy snowfall that accompanied the bone-chilling Alberta Clipper, which came at us from the west in late January, blanketed the ground. Every turn along the pathways brought winter scenes of woodland beauty as sunlight filtered through hemlock boughs laden with mantels of snow, which also draped boulders and carpeted the forest floor. And everywhere there was shadowed stillness, the only motion an occasional snow shower from an overhead branch, melted by the warmth of the sun.

Ravenswood is an ideal spot for cross-country skiers, with breath-taking scenery and wide trails that dip and turn through the clean, unspoiled forest primeval—a beautiful winter landscape that challenges the body and enriches the soul.

8

1. RAVENSWOOD

1. Park Superintendent's Residence
2. Rocking Stone
3. Mountain Laurel
4. Magnolia Swamp
5. Site of Pest House
6. Site of Hermit's Cabin
7. Site of Stillington Hall
8. Abandoned Quarry
9. Long Hill Overlook
10. Terminal Moraine

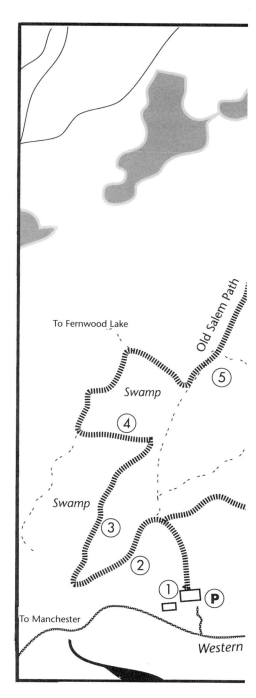

To Fernwood Lake

Old Salem Path

Swamp

Swamp

To Manchester

Western

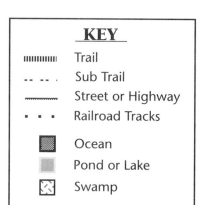

KEY	
ⅢⅢⅢⅢ	Trail
-- -- .	Sub Trail
～～～	Street or Highway
• • •	Railroad Tracks
▓	Ocean
▒	Pond or Lake
⊠	Swamp

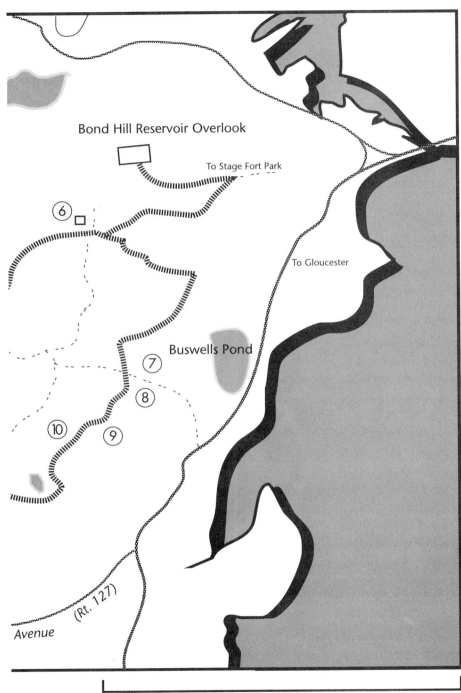

Bond Hill Reservoir Overlook

To Stage Fort Park

To Gloucester

Buswells Pond

⑥
⑦
⑧
⑨
⑩

(Rt. 127)

Avenue

1 Mile

DOGTOWN COMMON

There lie the lonely commons of the dead—
The houseless homes of Dogtown. Still their
    souls
Tenant the bleak doorstones and cellar holes
    Where once their quick loins bred
Strong fishermen who fought with storms at
    the masthead,
And women folk who took their bitter toll
Of death, with only their old dogs to be
    A memory.

From *Dogtown Common*
By Percy MacKaye

"Dogtown" is the colorful name which attached itself to a small community in the heart of Cape Ann set aside for farming in the early 18th century. It was soon discovered, however, that despite the generous land grants by the city fathers for this purpose, farming was not to be part of the town's livelihood in that area. The soil proved much too rocky to plow and cultivate, although with great effort a number of small root cellars (used to store winter vegetables) were carved out of glacial granite deposits to support one-room dwellings for early pioneer families. Only one house in the settlement had two stories, with clapboard construction fastened by wooden pegs. All the others were made of roughly hewn, structural timber.

In sectioning off the area for homesteads, roads were laid out, and common areas earmarked for community activity. Unfortunately, because of the unyielding rocky terrain, poor soil, and brier-filled swamps, the farmers did not remain long despite their strenuous effort to settle the land. Instead, some travelled further south to Joppa on Gloucester's eastern shore, others to areas in Essex and Ipswich where rich dark soil, moistened by surrounding marshes and wetlands, was more tillable.

But Dogtown was not to be abandoned completely; not then. Soon fishermen from the village moved their families into the small houses vacated by the farmers and, since they were away at sea for long periods of time, provided dogs to protect their wives and small children during their absence. It has been said that, because of the large population of canines guarding many of the 175 families then in residence, the area became known as "Dogtown."

Dogtown Trail • Granny Day's Swamp • Adams Pine Trail

Our Sunday morning walk in mid-July began at Dogtown Road Trail, the principal entrance, just off Cherry Street in Gloucester. Lining the wide, open pathway was a sampling of the wilderness beauty before us: Suwannee juniper, red cedar, gray birch, holly, wild choke cherry, and bayberry. The fragrance of blossoming sea roses greeted us as we walked along the gravel roadway leading into Dogtown proper, the stillness broken on this quiet sunny morning by sounds from the rifle range at the nearby Cape Ann Sportsmen's Club.

Blueberries were plentiful. Both high and low bushes were just beginning to ripen. "Berries from low bushes are small and sweet, good for pies," said Ted. Speaking with authority on the qualities of the tasty wild fruit, he continued, "High bushes produce bigger berries, with more water and a good flavor; better in pancakes and muffins."

The main road into the area took us past Common Bars, in earlier times an unforested field used in common by farmers from Riverdale, Lanesville, and Annisquam to fence in grazing livestock. Its name comes from the fact that the common was enclosed by wooden bars. Gently brushing aside the overgrowth, Ted pointed out a cistern which had held the town's water supply—used to water livestock and fight community fires. Next we passed Granny Day's Swamp and continued on to the "DS" rock marking Dogtown Square. Here, we turned left onto Wharf Road for a short distance, passing a sweet-smelling tree he identified as clethra, commonly called sweetpepper.

"It has a spicy fragrance and can be smelled from a long distance when it comes into full bloom next month," he noted.

Soon we were in single file, following a marshy footpath around the other side of Granny Day's Swamp. Throughout our walk, Ted pointed out interesting historic sites—cellar holes, the "arena" where an inebriated seaman lost his life in a bullfight, store and school locations. He also entertained the group with amusing anecdotes and little known facts— from scholarly descriptions of poisonous mushrooms and "galls," a leathery-looking ball made by wasps from the main vein of oak leaves, to humorous remarks about grey reindeer lichen and a red-cloaked species known as a "British soldier."

In the 1700s much of the firewood used in Boston homes came from Dogtown, which accounts for the present open condition of its once–forested woodlands. Records show that in 1706 more than 50 sloops were carrying wood to Boston and Salem markets from several points throughout Cape Ann. In one three-week period, 500 cords were cut and marketed. Most of it came from the Annisquam River section of Dogtown. Lumber and structural timbers soon ushered in the shipbuilding industry. These early thriving businesses, along with farm cows and ground fires, destroyed much of the forest's old growth in this section of Cape Ann.

The Adams Pine Trail runs from the Common Road along Granny Day's Swamp to Dogtown Road. We climbed an incline through a cathedral of tall white pines planted by Charles Adams, pausing to visit the gravesite of the foresighted environmentalist. Our walk through his green woodland memorial was cool and refreshing. It opened onto a field of goldenrod and wild strawberries, more of the natural beauty surrounding this deserted Cape Ann village.

LOOP POND • BRIAR SWAMP • WHALE'S JAW • RACCOON LEDGE

On Labor Day weekend we joined Ted for another walk through Dogtown. However, before we started, a word of clarification was in order, he informed us.

"If one is a purist," he explained, "only that area within the boundaries of Dogtown proper (meaning that defined on the official map published by the Dogtown Advisory Committee) can accurately be described as 'Dogtown.'" Inasmuch as we would be following trails outside the compound, he was reluctant to describe our outing this morning as "another walk through Dogtown." Having been so enlightened, we set out to explore more of Cape Ann's interesting wilderness, no matter its geographical boundaries. Purists we weren't.

This morning there would be no driving to a distant location. We simply walked to the northern end of the mall, took a right at Poole's Lane, walked about 80 feet, *then a sharp left brought us onto the railroad tracks.* I must admit, walking on railroad tracks was a first for me.

"It's all right," Ted assured us, sensing our concern about the danger of walking "live" tracks. "I timed it so we'd be here about 15 minutes before the train" that would soon be coming into the Rockport terminus a few hundred feet away.

About a quarter of a mile down the tracks, he turned onto a footpath to the left that led through a beautiful open meadow of goldenrod, Canadian thistle and staghorn sumac. The path passed a waterworks site housing an old pump station. A government-sponsored WPA project built sometime in the 1930s, it played a major role in meeting Rockport's growing water needs. Today it is being refurbished to meet the town's increasing demands.

We continued to follow as Ted led us down a dirt road to the right, past several modern colonial-style homes nestled among large oaks and bordered by a serpentine stone wall. This network of old stone walls had its beginning during the days of early colonization. As settlers cleared land for farming, large stones were unearthed and piled in clearings which ultimately became property lines and community roadways. Many can still be seen throughout rural New England.

As we trekked behind Ted deeper into dense woodland, the trail soon took us into a stretch of swampy wetlands and past Loop Pond, a four-acre body of brackish water profuse with large white waterlilies. Loop Pond received its name from its location. This area was formerly the loop for trains coming in and out of the Rockport station when a branch of the Eastern Railroad Company was built in 1861 to join Rockport with the Gloucester-Boston line. In the wake of this progress, unfortunately, a number of rare native plants were destroyed, including a variety of wild orchids.

Beyond the pond, as we continued through the swampy section, we noted a number of hardwood trees that didn't seem to mind having wet feet—tupelo, alder, red maple and shrubby willow. Companions to them were cinnamon fern and wild iris, the latter having evidently survived the bulldozers. Two other plants along the roadside drew our curiosity: Japanese knotweed and jewelweed. The former is a decorative garden plant which can only be destroyed when in flower; the latter has yellow blossoms and fat green seedpods which, as Ted demonstrated, burst open at the slightest touch when ripe. Another unusual characteristic of jewelweed is its ability to change color from a vibrant green to silver when placed in water. I wondered about its appearance on rainy days. Despite its chameleon quality, this plant is said to be helpful in treating skin irritations such as poison ivy and nettle rash.

In single file we climbed a gentle rocky slope that took us further into the dense woodlands, Ted clipping the overgrowth and removing "free falls" along the way.

Along the trail, earlier in the year, Ted had painted key trees with color-coded markings to serve as directional guides. Orange slashes over green marked the trail leading into the woodlands; green above orange pointed the way out. Also along the pathway were a few red fox deposits—which evidenced a recent meal of wild choke cherries—left on high rocks to establish the predator's territorial rights. Bright, emerald green hairycap moss, its perky little stars glistening in the morning mist, added to the natural beauty of the forest.

Our route soon brought us along a main artery, Dennison Trail, leading from Dennison Street in Gloucester to Whale's Jaw in the northern section of Dogtown. Whale's Jaw is a large rock formation split by the ancient glacier in such a way that it resembled a gigantic whale, open-mouthed and pointing skyward. Unfortunately, vandals left their calling card. By setting a fire under the lower ledge which formed the jaw and allowing it to burn for quite some time, the jaw broke away, separating from the snout; but, with a little imagination, the overall effect of a huge yawning whale is still quite evident.

Looking at the senseless destruction of the great granite mammal, Ted tried to treat the matter lightly. "Another erratic," he noted, meaning a rock separated from its original formation by glacial force. He then added dryly, "It probably came down from New Hampshire, anyway." But the note of sadness in his voice did not go unnoticed.

Tireless in his efforts to protect the natural resources of this beautiful region settled by his ancestors in the late 1600s, he frequently decries the willful destruction found in many areas of Cape Ann's wilderness.

"The Boy Scouts came out with us not too long ago and marked all the trails with wooden signs at intersections and several points along the route. But vandals came right in back of them and took them all down. They even painted over directional arrows we had on large rocks," he lamented, noting that motorbikes were also a problem.

"We try to strike a balance between environmentalists, bikers, and developers, but it's not always easy to do."

Turning onto the Dorothy Luce Trail, our next stop was along a long, winding boardwalk spanning the saturated bowl of Briar Swamp. Struck by the natural beauty of the plants inhabiting these unspoiled wetlands, we lingered awhile exploring the wild growth close to the wooden pathway. Elliot Rogers, a leading authority on America's regional plant life, estimates that 5,000 varieties of plants can be found throughout Cape Ann, many in swamps like the one we were now enjoying.

Once again Ted called us together to view another interesting specimen of the wilds—the pitcher plant whose long-stemmed flower resembles a large, bronzed pansy. An insectivorous plant, it depends on insects for food as well as for nitrogen, which is very low in swamp soil. Insects, drawn to its sweet-taste, are trapped in the throat of its enfolding leaves, and then digested by the plant's enzyme.

Also along the boardwalk was a patch of waist-high, spiked cotton grass, its white puffy blossoms soft and alluring in the dense swamp. Reeds, holly, shad, bullrush, sedges, partridgeberry, cinnamon fern, and a variety of Indian pike were also identified and admired by the onlookers, some of whom were tourists from cities, exploring the woodlands for the first time. Because of the unusually high amount of rain this summer, vegetation throughout the marshes, as everywhere else on the Cape, was healthy and luxuriant. As we left the boardwalk, a man asked the identity of a high, overhead bush, bright with clusters of red berries. Ted didn't readily recognize it. As a research biologist, he wouldn't be satisfied until he could. Clipping a small leafy twig from one of the lower branches, he put it into his shirt pocket to be studied further. Later, we learned it was a variety of the holly bush commonly called black alder.

The path out of Briar Swamp turned abruptly to the right, running along the bottom of a ridge covered with mountain laurel which had peaked in early-July. It then opened onto a broad gravel path lined with a variety of hardwoods and more low-bush blueberries. As we passed a footpath going off to the left, the purist in Ted remarked, "that goes to the real Dogtown." To the group, however, the direction didn't matter much. Autumn was just beginning to descend upon these deep forested woodlands, brushing the landscape with wide, muted earthtone strokes—a sure sign that New England's spectacular fall foliage would soon crown its many trees and bushes. Nature has a way of balancing the elements so that every season on Cape Ann—spring, summer, fall and winter—has its own special beauty. The walk today in and of itself was invigorating and inspiring, no matter its geological boundary line.

As we continued along the trail near Whale's Jaw, we noticed a difference in ground covering—patches of teaberries, baby blue asters, false lilies-of-the-valley, and something new which I hadn't seen before in our many walks—heather. While this hardy shrubby plant thrives in abundance on the cool, windswept moors of Scotland, it is not usually seen in the wilds of Cape Ann. Needless to say, we were all surprised and delighted at the "find."

"For many years there was only one small patch under an oak tree. We used to keep it trimmed so the heather would get some sun," Ted informed us. He then explained how this pretty little shrub found its way to Cape Ann.

"It was planted about 20 years ago by Rockporter Thomas P. Gibbs, a Scotsman who brought rooted plants back from his native village of Keith in southern Scotland. Most were planted in the garden of his waterfront home on Marmion Way but he brought a few to Dogtown for others to enjoy as well.

"Then a fire burned off the low lying bushes," he continued. "When things began to grow back, heather sprouted up in many places. There's more now than there's ever been," he announced, leading us from one spot to another where delicate pink heather blossoms appeared to be thriving hardily amid other young, shrubby native growth. Many times when a forest is destroyed by fire, a few types of plants find the new conditions more to their liking and grow back more plentifully the second time around. Evidently this was the case with the heather plant from the Scottish highlands.

A short distance further we came to a large glacial deposit known as Raccoon Ledge. This terminal moraine was the nesting place for these masked marauders for many years before the opening of restaurants on Bear Skin Neck which, according to Ted, "lured them east for fast-food service." Across from the ledges, a small vernal pond provides a place of winter hibernation for salamanders, frogs, fairy shrimp, newts and various land turtles. Rounding another bend in the trail, we came upon Indian Rock, sometimes called the "Mystery Rock," which displayed a number of unusual markings some historians feel were made with Indian flint tools.

But Ted has a different theory. "The marks are smooth, which would indicate sharpening of wood, antlers or perhaps swords by the Vikings. That is rather far-fetched. But it was not used for flint."

Leaving others to ponder the origin of the mysterious marks, we set out again upon the trail. Using large rocks as stepping stones, we gingerly crossed over Mill Brook flowing by gravity down to its headlands, eventually spilling into Loop Pond which we had passed earlier. Climbing up a rugged incline, we came to a gravel pit which Ted explained was originally intended to be a retaining pond to feed Mill Brook.

"It didn't happen," he said. "The town is in court with the excavator because of a contract dispute."

Low-bush blueberries, sweetfern and wild asters grew along the trail that soon took us to the top of Squam Hill Road where a painted sign on a huge boulder pointed another way to Dogtown. Walking along the gravel public road, we passed several private residences. A short distance further, we turned into a driveway and walked through what appeared to be a homeowner's backyard. Noting our concern for property rights, Ted explained that the developer had knowingly built this home very close to the town's right-of way. So close, in fact, that a side stairway winding around the corner of the house to the second floor strayed onto town property.

"Unfortunately, we've lost some good rights-of-way due to real estate developers," he informed us. "Sometimes we're able to do something about it, sometimes not. Another problem is the resale of older homes. When property with public trails has been in families for generations, and then is sold to newcomers, they immediately put up a fence and a No Trespassing sign."

He then told the story about a man who bought inherited ancestral property with a right-of-way clause in the deed. The new owner attempted to conceal this fact by landscaping across the path and constructing a decorative granite fence that gave it the appearance of being private. But Rockport's selectmen didn't go along with it. At a public Town Meeting, they advised him that they "were going to bulldoze it down" unless he put up a sign giving public access. The man went home and fumed awhile, but soon realized this was no idle threat and decided to call a halt to the controversy. Walkers today, like generations of nature-lovers before them, travel the historic lane that passes through his property, thanks to the steadfast determination of conscientious town leaders.

Beyond the newly constructed house with the outside staircase, the wide right-of-way, steep and rocky, led into beautiful wooded uplands.

"We could make a very pretty rock garden in this public way," Ted remarked, leading the group up the rigorous trail.

The pathway led to the top of Poole's Hill, the highest point in Rockport at 235 feet. Here the roadway split, the left leading to Hospital Hill above Summit Avenue, the site of the old Rockport Hospital, now demolished. The right rims Briar Swamp, joining the path at the dam we had passed earlier. We turned right and after a short distance, took a left onto a narrow footpath which curved and dipped along a route abundant with false soloman seal. Walking single file through the heavily wooded area, we heard the mournful wail of a train whistle and knew we were nearing the depot at Whistlestop Mall. Soon we were descending the quiet woodlands via a long, winding granite stairway, put in place by railroad men many years ago for safety in wintertime. To the right of the steps was another of the many glacial moraines—accumulations of broken stones found on the surface, along the sides or at the foot of a glacier—seen throughout Cape Ann.

The long descent eventually opened onto Evans Field, the town baseball park whose granite grandstand was another WPA project of the post-depression era. Now over 60 years old, it's still in use and still in fairly good condition. A medium-sized skating rink with swells and banked walls is located at the opposite end of the field. Built by the town fathers to prevent street accidents, the course challenges the most avid teenage skater.

At noon, we emerged from the field at the end of Poole's Lane across from the old anadama bread factory, now occupied by a company called

TADCO which specializes in industrial silk screen products. Rounding the corner and crossing the tracks, we were back at Whistlestop Mall. Another Sunday morning walk with Ted was ended, leaving us relaxed and refreshed from our weekly commune with nature.

TOWN FOREST

We returned to these trails the Sunday before Thanksgiving. It was unseasonably warm for late November, about 55 degrees and drizzling, when we left the mall.

Heading out behind the TADCO building, we took an old road that at one time served as a logging trail for early settlers who made Dogtown their source for firewood. Today it still serves the people of the area, only now it has become a right-of-way for 20th-century nature lovers who hike the labyrinth of trails from Poole's Lane to that historic pioneer village. A private residential driveway, flanked on both sides by colonial lamp posts, climbed a long, winding hill to our right. In earlier times these were gas lamps; today they have been wired for electricity, but they are just as romantic and picturesque as they oversee the winding, hilly drive. Just beyond the driveway was a small spring named for its owner, Esther Johnson, and used by thirsty players and spectators from nearby Evans Field.

The woods in this section of Rockport are currently divided into three parts. The middle nine-acre tract is being preserved by the Essex County Green Belt Association; the other two are privately owned, and one day may be developed into home sites. A few years ago, real estate speculators sought to open up the area by bulldozing further into these woods, hoping to negotiate a trade with the town for land closer to the ballpark. The plan never materialized, however, but it may one day.

Walking up a rocky incline, we came upon an open turn-around area surrounded by pitch pine which, according to Ted, meant "the soil isn't very good here." But as we trekked deeper into the woods, the vegetation changed: low and high-bush blueberries with gorgeous red fall leaves soon gave way to sheep and mountain laurel and gray beech, another indication the space had been wide open fairly recently. A short distance into dense woodlands, we took a sharp left turn, and followed another narrow, leaf-covered trail.

"The paths in this area were developed by settlers sometime during the 1700s," Ted informed us, stopping to brush leaves from a broad flat stone surface.

"You can see where the stone bridges were built for oxen carts to haul their firewood out," he said.

Suddenly, a shot pierced the wooded silence as someone in the back, startled, called out, "Who's that shooting, Ted? Are there hunters in the area?"

"It's coming from the Skeet Range at the Cape Ann Sportsmen's Club," he yelled back. "Hunters won't be back in these woods until December, and only for the first week." The questioner sounded like the spry English gentleman in his sixties who had recently moved to Rockport. Unfamiliar with Massachusetts' hunting laws, he was understandably anxious but Ted, respectful of both hunter and the hunted, is forever cautious. He would never endanger his followers during the hunting seasons—and this was Sunday. No hunting is allowed on the Sabbath in the Bay State.

As we walked through a rather large area of mountain and sheep laurel, he commented that sheep laurel was "not as perky" during cold weather, thus its droopy appearance. Mountain laurel, on the other hand, with its shiny green leaves, seemed to be thriving on these frosty November days. Ted studied the mountain laurel bushes beside the trail, lecturing on their condition.

"I don't see many buds; these get too much shade," he explained as we threaded our way through woods darkened in places by large, towering hemlocks. Pointing out the remnants of a flower blossom, he went on, "These are last year's seeds. If it blooms heavily one year, it will seed the next. It follows an every-other-year cycle."

Beneath beech trees which also dotted the woodlands were patches of "beech drop." A small, woodsy parasite, having no chlorophyll of its own, it sustains life from the roots of the beech. These delicate little brown blossomy plants are everywhere present throughout the forest, sprouting from the roots of mature beech trees.

The flooring under the fallen leaves and pine needles changed to rich, black soil, indicating that we were getting deeper into the 50-acre town forest. Large rocks covered with rock tripe lichen, moss and pine needles continued to line the winding path. As we trekked further and further into its dense, mysterious depths, I wondered if Rockport's tiny town forest in any way resembled the fabled Black Forest of Germany. If sheer beauty is any criteria, I feel sure it does. Again and again we feasted our eyes on scene after gorgeous forest scene. In dark, swampy areas, pitch black watery pools mirrored the rich colors of their surroundings: moss-draped rocks, cinnamon fern and hemlock boughs complemented artfully by coppery reflections of beech and fading oaks. Ted's remark, "With an inch of snow, it's pretty through here" would bring us back this winter.

The rock tripe lichen took many forms and colors in the forested woodland. On one large boulder the woodsy fission (part alga, part fungus) varied considerably—some patches tightly clustered dark green beads, others shiny, smooth lighter, grass-colored leaves, and still others bluish gray and flaky. Lichen is a symbiotic relationship with alga and fungus, as Ted explained on an earlier walk. Alga provides its nutrients, fungus its structure. When lichen forms on places like rocks and decaying logs, it collects and holds scattered soil, then mosses develop, and eventually small plants take over. That's why, on occasion, shrubby plants seem to "grow out of rocks."

Gray beech dominates a section of the forest through which the trail, known simply as the "Town Forest Path," passes. A number of red oak and white birch, along with a few red maples, can also be seen. The red maple found on Cape Ann differs from the popular sugar maple grown in northern New England. A hardy, noble tree, the sugar maple boasts moderately rapid growth and long life. Though a valuable hardwood, it's more likely to be prized for its sap which is used in making maple syrup. Maine, New Hampshire and Vermont, where climates are harsh, are their most comfortable habitat. The leaves of the impressive sugar maple provide dense shade, both green and when they are aflame with brilliant fall colors—which are more orange and yellow than red. The leaves of the red maple are mostly red, with less orange and yellow.

The trail on this day took us alongside a WPA project built sometime in the 1930s to serve as a dam for the town of Gloucester. The purpose of the three-foot stone-and-masonry barrier was to prevent water from Briar Swamp flowing into the Babson Reservoir below. Analytical tests had proven the water to be unusable because of its excessively high iron and manganese content.

On this walk, we paid another visit to Briar Swamp over the long, winding boardwalk that spans the marshes from one end to the other. Built in 1987 by the Dogtown Committee, with the assistance of the Essex County Greenbelt Association, this rustic footbridge provides nature-lovers a close-up view of the many wild plants inhabiting Cape Ann's wetlands. Only a few plants—high-bush blueberry, tufted grass sometimes called "rabbit grass," the pitcher plant, and black alder among them—were readily recognizable today, most having withered and died during recent frosts. A few red cranberries were also spotted along the wooden walkway.

"There were many more before the weather got as dry as it is now," remarked Ted.

Then turning, he pointed to an animal path running through the swamp. Such revelations continually reminded us how very much we'd miss during our weekly explorations if we did not have his sharp eye, keen intellect, and quick wit along to help us understand the many nuances of nature.

Leaving the swamp, we followed the Luce trail to Whale's Jaw, where six young male cyclists brightened the path as they rode toward us out of the mist. When they stopped to ask Ted directions, it gave everyone, walkers and bikers alike, a chance to rest. They rode weekly, we learned, covering a wide range of trails throughout Massachusetts. Dogtown was among their favorites. It was evident from their equipment that they were experienced riders. Colorful helmets and jackets, Spandex cycling shorts, 20-ounce water bottles, and top-of-the line, fenderless bikes with gripping, knobby tires assured their comfort and safety along rugged trails.

A short distance further, we came upon a young couple who also sought directions from our leader. They wanted to view Briar Swamp, so Ted sent them back to Whale's Jaw along the route we had just taken.

As our time together drew to an end, we headed back along Squam Path, a trail we had taken earlier in the year, past the house with the corner stairway built on town property, and up the steep, rocky hillside Ted fancied as a rock garden. Emerging out of the woods into a clearing on Squam Hill Road, we were splattered with heavy raindrops.

Glancing at his watch, Ted apologized. "It's not supposed to do this until 5 past 12," (after our walk) and then added with characteristic humor, "Can't trust anybody."

Like our earlier walk along this trail, we were led down a long flight of granite stairs, placed by trainmen years ago, onto Evans field behind the railroad station at Whistlestop Mall. It was raining rather heavily when we said our goodbyes, but a cozy fireplace and hot, homemade vegetable soup was waiting…

New England was caught in the grip of an old-fashioned winter when we returned to Loop Pond in late January. A bitterly cold Alberta Clipper had passed through Cape Ann a few days earlier before howling out to sea, and we were still in a deepfreeze—a blustery 3 degrees, minus 11 with the wind chill. On this day heavy snowfall was adding to the six inches already on the ground. Only three of us braved the elements to walk with Ted this Sunday and we were richly rewarded for our efforts.

Large, powdery flakes fell softly but steadily against our faces, lacing our heads and shoulders with whiteness as we trekked down Applecart Road toward Loop Pond and the winter trails of Dogtown. Just before the railroad tracks, a small, snow-capped, granite Japanese bridge arching the icy, black waters of a gently flowing stream caught our attention.

Mounds of drifting snow banked the water's edge as it coursed beneath spindly, brown hardwoods and tangled shrubs toward the old pump house.

Because of the thick, white blanket covering the landscape, we couldn't distinguish the trails in some places. But we persevered, following them as best we could. We stayed on the Luce Trail for awhile, turning off at Marker 13 to again tackle the rigorous downhill slope—sans toboggan—that landed us, literally, in a quiet valley of frosted hemlocks. And again we crossed the cold, frigid waters of Wine Brook; today this picturesque valley stream was especially beautiful in its wintry setting.

"This walk is prettier in the winter than any other time of the year," noted Ted.

We followed the snowy depression of a footpath that eventually brought us out behind Babson Museum. Here we took the Tarr Trail, staying in the woods for a short distance before finally emerging at the barrier just below Great Hill where the railroad tracks guided us back to Rockport and Whistlestop Mall.

Throughout the two-hour trek we stopped frequently to savor the magnificent wintry scenes along the route: upturned cups of Queen Anne's lace mounded high with puffs of soft snow, green-and-white polka-dotted pines whispering to each other as we passed, a stand of young beech trees cradled in a ravine, their leaves light and bleached out, and several Japanese yews wandering up a hillside—an uncommon sight in these cold, damp woodlands.

Among the wildlife we saw in Dogtown on that numbing day were two birds—a chickadee and bluejay—and a squirrel or a wild mink, we weren't sure which; he was too far away. The pretty little chickadee is described by bird experts as "the feathered small boy of the woods, always in fine spirits." Like his frequent companions, the nuthatches and kinglets, the chickadee seems to actually enjoy a hard winter snowstorm. In bitterly cold weather he's often seen frolicking from tree to tree, happily singing in a voice filled with tenderness.

The blue jay is quite the opposite. Two other names by which he is known hint at his unsavory character—Corn Thief and Nest Robber. Considered by experts to be one of the handsomest of American birds, he is also the most troublesome. He is a merciless nest robber, eating eggs and killing and devouring small, defenseless birds. "Cannibalistic," "noisy" and "abusive" are some of the terms attributable to this destructive rascal. And it's reported he swears to boot! Stand by and listen as a flock of them mob their arch-enemy, the great horned owl, and you'll see why experts call their antics "variegated vilifications."

It would seem that James Whitcomb Riley sketched this scoundrel accurately in *Knee Deep in June*.

> Mr. Blue Jay, full o' sass,
> In them baseball clothes of his,
> Sportin' round the orchard jes'
> Like he owned the premises.

BABSON RESERVOIR

Many outstanding figures make up Gloucester's colorful past. Among them are Howard Blackburn who was admired as a legendary folk hero by fisherman both here and in the Canadian provinces, and Roger Babson whose generous philanthropic contributions have greatly enhanced the quality of life throughout his native New England.

These two men could not have been more different physically, intellectually, or socially. Yet they stood as equals—giants in the eyes of their peers. Blackburn, born in Liverpool, Nova Scotia, lacked formal education, but he was strong and healthy which helped him survive a tortuous five-day blizzard in a dory off the Newfoundland coast when he was 23. The dory was from the *Grace L. Fears* out of Gloucester, his adopted home, to which he returned after the ordeal. For the next 50 years the sea was his mistress. He made two lone voyages across the Atlantic and became a larger-than-life inspiration to those who made their living from the treacherous high seas.

Babson, on the other hand, was a graduate of MIT. In his early 20s he contracted tuberculosis and turned to securities analysis during his recovery, which caused him to change careers—from engineering to finance. He ultimately achieved great wealth as a Wall Street financier (the Babson Mutual Fund, a highly-rated investment portfolio, is now closed to new investors). Socially conscious, he founded three colleges and established a Bible museum, a scientific center for the study of gravity, and a shelter from atomic bombs. In addition, he gave a reservoir to the City of Gloucester, and donated land for a bird sanctuary and for public nature walks.

Memory of these two historical figures converge on a wooded uplands trail along the southeast tip of Dogtown. Here Blackburn Circle Drive, just off Route 127 in Gloucester, joins the Babson Boulder Trail a short distance from Railcut Hill, Mr. Babson's bird sanctuary. This was the starting point of our walk on a cool, crisp October morning.

A short distance into the woods, the narrow, rocky trail twisted and turned down a long hill. Numerous deposits of glacial rock lined both sides of the path. At the bottom, the railroad tracks of the Rockport to Boston line ran between the eastern shoreline of Babson Reservoir, where a lone red-breasted merganser swam contentedly in the autumn sun, and Alewife Brook which flows from the Annisquam River into Cape Pond.

"The reservoir at one time had been a valley," noted Ted. "Today it plays an important role in meeting Gloucester's water needs."

Crossing the tracks, we followed a dry, mossy footpath going off to the left. A short distance above a gentle incline, we came to the first of many inscriptions carved on some of the larger rocks found throughout Dogtown. Mr. Babson had these carvings done not merely to inspire the passing nature lover, but to provide employment for Finnish stoneworkers during the depression—which he had correctly predicted in his Wall Street newsletter on September 5, 1929.

The inscription on the first rock read *Get a Job*. A short way along the trail, another advises the passerby to *Help Mother*.

"I believe Mr. Babson's messages are telling us to Get a Job and Help Mother," offered someone in the group upon seeing the writings for the first time.

"If you came up the other way," Ted retorted, "they would read, 'Help Mother Get a Job.' I like it better that way."

The next inscription encouraged *Truth*.

We passed many glacial moraines along the trail; in fact, these stone deposits, varying in size from a football to a small house, were everywhere present during our many Cape Ann walks. Knowing a little of the geological history of the area helped us to understand how all these rocks got tossed about so haphazardly when the last glacier tumbled the earth about 12,000 years ago. The glacier deposited many rocks upon which Mr. Babson's Finnish stonecutters could write.

As we emerged into an area of open woodland, cleared by a fairly recent fire, Ted explained the difference between controlled and uncontrolled burning in the wild.

"Controlled burning takes place in early spring before the woods get too dry in order to clean out the underbrush in dense areas. Uncontrolled fires in dry times burn hot and deep, destroying top soil, humus, roots and seeds vital to wildlife survival in the coming winter and regrowth in the spring."

Courage

Mountain laurel, a member of the azalea-rhododendron family, shared the woods with gray beech, hemlock, and red oak. As we continued along the Babson Boulder Trail, the reasoning behind its name became more obvious. There were huge boulders everywhere.

Ideas

Off to our right along an upland stretch of the trail a depression cradled a small vernal pond, "a mating spot for frogs, salamanders and other small wildlife," we were told. The trail then dipped and turned, its surface becoming hardpan, as it threaded its way through pockets of royal fern dressed in various fall shades—from yellow to ivory to brown.

"Blueberries were good this year because the bees pollinated when the weather was warm and sunny," our leader informed us. "Then all that rain we had provided moisture and they didn't dry up in a constantly hot sun."

Passing through a fairly large grove of red cedars, Ted remarked, "shows this was an open area at one time. They like the sun; they die out when other trees grow in and shade them."

Industry

Sweetfern, low-bush blueberries, meadow grass, a tall juniper tree laden with grayish blueberries and cedar clubmoss dotted the winding trail, as did a number of thought-provoking reminders: *Spiritual Power, Study, Be on Time*, and *When work stops, Values decay*.

The vivid autumn colors in Granny Day's Swamp were gorgeous: red and orange high-bush blueberries and swamp maple, scarlet tupelos, yellowing witch hazel and rum cherries—their spectacular foliage highlighted by a light blue sky.

Along the Common Road several white pine stood tall above patches of goldenrod which was just beginning its annual ritual of changing to dark, crusty brown sheaves. Close by, a stand of small red cedars overlooked a clump of red-berried honeysuckle. "Native to China," we were informed.

The trail took us past Common Bars, along the Adams Pine Trail and onto Dogtown Road as we made our way back toward Babson Reservoir. Just before reaching Cherry Street, we took a narrow, leafy footpath to the left, bending under an arched bittersweet vine. It brought us onto a broad, grassy access road which ran from Commons Road to Babson Reservoir.

"This road was built at the time they built O'Maley School," Ted remarked.

Cutting away a large briery blackberry branch from our path as he spoke, he cited an example of unethical business practices and unvarnished greed that often accompany publicly funded projects.

"At the time they were removing gravel from the valley to build the Babson Reservoir, they were building the school. The contractor was paid by the state to remove the gravel from the reservoir, then he was paid again for the same gravel when he sold it back to them for use at the school.

"It wasn't until six years later that the state auditors realized what had happened. By then, the people involved were all gone."

Notwithstanding the unsavory bent of the men who blazed the pathway through this hillside moraine, succeeding generations can be grateful for the peaceful, scenic trail that it is today. Walking this quiet, sylvan lane during the height of the fall season brings into focus all that is truly remarkable about unspoiled forests and woodlands. On this day, it became a pathway through a fairyland of gorgeous fall colors. Its surface in places was gravelly and sandy; in others rocky, hardpan, and mossy— and for long stretches at a time we shuffled through ankle-deep, bright red and yellow leaves under a canopy of the same brilliant autumn splendor.

Ahead the trail bore left along the shore of the reservoir, the water again brought low from constant use by Cape Anners. Along the way we passed over a pretty brook which, unfortunately, remains nameless even though it's considered a major feeder for the reservoir—somewhat like the No Name Storm of October 1991 which was, in fact, a nor'easter of great intensity and destruction, despite its anonymity by the U. S. Weather Bureau.

The rocky, sandy trail around the eastern tip of the reservoir led us back to the railroad tracks beside Alewife Brook. Up, up, up we climbed the narrow, twisting trail to Blackburn Circle Drive. Inches thick with fallen leaves, it was not exactly "the yellow brick road," but certainly there were lots of rocks and lots of yellow leaves. The only difference between our woodland trail and Dorothy's golden path is that here rocks were not laid end to end on a smooth, flat, glowing surface; rather, they jutted unceremoniously onto the rugged, hillside path, boulders of stone amid brilliant maple leaves that made the going rather hazardous in spots. But that's the way it is in unsullied forests in the autumn—and nature-lovers wouldn't have it any other way.

GOOSE COVE RESERVOIR

On a clear, crisp November day, we were joined on our Sunday walk by a very special man, Art Hatfield of Lynnfield, a self-taught botanist who, with his wife, Nellie, led the Cape Ann trail walks for 15 years. A dynamic duo, they were highly respected by both local and state conservation organizations for their tireless efforts in helping to preserve the region's natural resources. Nellie was especially active in the Massachusetts Audubon Society. In recognition of their work, both have had Dogtown nature trails named for them. Art's trail runs roughly one mile between the north end of the Briar Swamp dam southwesterly to the Moraine trail just south of Dogtown Square. Branching off to the north from Art's trail near the Briar Swamp dam, Nellie's trail keeps to higher ground and is more easily travelled. The day before her death in 1986, Nellie joined Art for a last walk along their beloved woodland paths. It was a fitting end for a woman who devoted much of her life to the care and preservation of nature.

Now in his 80s, Art is still keenly interested in Cape Ann's natural resources and was persuaded by a longtime fellow walking enthusiast to join us today. As he emerged from his nephew's car at Whistlestop Mall, he was warmly embraced by everyone in the group. The deep affection between him and Ted was readily apparent.

The service road encircling Goose Cove Reservoir in Dogtown was selected for Art's comfort and pleasure because of its level surface and smooth pavement—and because the foliage was still pretty along its shoreline. Parking at a turn-in on Gee Avenue, we walked behind the barrier and proceeded into the woods. Peppering the blacktop trail were staghorn sumac, pitch pine, and large red cedars now abundant with pur-plish berries. Covering a hillside on our right was a healthy patch of creeping juniper with the same plum-colored fruit. The goldenrod, one of 125 species found in North America—most in the Northeast—had undergone its annual transformation from masses of small yellow flowers with lance-shaped leaves to dark brown tubular clusters of seeds. Bayberries and sweetfern also lined the broad pathway circling the deep, dark waters of the reservoir.

Throughout the walk, Art pointed out plants and trees along the roadside, explaining the characteristics of each. The American horn-beam, also known as the gray or blue beech because of its distinctive blue-gray, muscle-like bark, today was brilliant with golden leaves. Staghorn sumac, he noted, had hairy twigs, brown compact clustered fruit and today its leaves were flaming red. Mountain ash, which to me resembled fern, is not an ash at all but a member of the Hawthorn family. These haws are considered to be a thorn in the botanist's side because they are so difficult to identify. Some authorities set the number in America at 26; others at 150, a telling indication of the difficulty experts encounter in identifying their species.

It was this kindly octogenarian who taught me about one of my favorite wild plants called ground pine clubmoss. I knew it as princess pine when I was a child growing up in Attleboro, where my mother used it in her Christmas wreaths. How interesting to learn that, in the days of the ancient dinosaur, a mighty, towering pine was the forerunner to the tiny lacy sprigs I had lovingly picked for her holiday decorations.

We next came to a gentle rise in the road which afforded a broad view of the area beyond—from the dunes around Gloucester's Wingaersheek Beach to Plum Island, a six-mile beach peninsula off the coast of Newburyport. It was here that I asked my two gentlemen friends to stop to allow me to take their picture, which I did against a backdrop of gleaming waters and beautiful autumn foliage. I gave it to Ted a few days later, knowing how much Art meant to him.

Another point of interest along the scenic service road was a scattered pine grove, which hosted several different conifers. Here both men patiently explained and demonstrated in minute detail the characteristics of three species of pine.

The native pitch pine is tolerant of poor soil, Ted noted, pointing out its needles which grow in groups of three, long and stiff and yellowish green. Round and symmetrical when young, the pitch pine becomes gnarled and craggy as it gets older. Its branches and cones are good for campfires because of their pitch and resin content. The timber of this pine, however, is brittle and gummy and of little economic value.

Moving on to a white pine, Art counted its cluster of five soft blue-green needles. The cones of the white pine are long and narrow with thin rounded scales, its wood light and soft and, unlike the pitch pine, prized for its timber which, unfortunately, was cut indiscriminately for many years. As a result, only a few prime stands of this valuable pine remain although new plantings throughout the northeast are attempting to restore the pine to its natural habitat.

"The red pine has two needles about four to six inches long," Ted added. "Its trunk is straight, reddish gray, lighter in color than the white pine. The cones are about two and one-half inches long and have no barbs on their scales. They ripen the first year and remain on trees all winter."

Comparing the needles of the white and pitch pine, he picked a cluster of each. "See the difference?" he asked, rubbing the slender reed of a white pine between his thumb and forefinger, while holding the stiffer pitch in his other hand.

Art then bruised a small branch of a sweet birch, called black birch or cherry birch, and brought it to me to sniff, "Smells like wintergreen, doesn't it?" he asked.

The twigs of this tree are aromatic and tasty; likewise its sap which is used to make birch beer. Its identity as a "black" birch comes from its dark, black bark which is not papery like other birches. Wood from this tree is used for fine furniture and cabinet work.

To the right, a lane led to Gee Avenue. The foliage was vibrant: flaming staghorn sumac with fat tufts of sour, red, fuzzy berries, green bayberry, a fragrant, yellow-leafed wild crabapple, dried silver rod, delicate pink-tinged lichen, blackberries, hairycap moss and fall dandelions. And another pretty brook. Like the one near Babson's Reservoir, this also did not rate a name although it, too, was a main feed into an important water source.

Passing a path on our right leading to Goose Cove proper, we crossed over the main dam and continued our botanical watch of Cape Ann's beautiful wildflowers: Queen Anne's lace, red clover, sweetfern, and hawkweed, called the Devil's Paintbrush, which in season has tall, yellow, curly stalks. This day almost all these colorful wildflowers had gone to seed.

Along the way, Ted explained that the water in the reservoir is routed under the dam instead of being allowed to flow over it.

"The water drains down a large pipe which keeps it from rising to the level of the dam. It is then filtered through other pipes under the dam and spills out into the wetlands beyond."

On the other side we followed the road as it circled past raspberry vines, juniper and fading fall asters. An embankment on our right sloped down into a valley of high-bush blueberries, bayberries and goldenrod. On the left a tall sassafras tree and a rum cherry stood side-by-side, their colorful orange leaves luminated by the noonday sun. Further along the service road, a climbing bittersweet vine attacked a beechnut, cutting off its circulation as it does to other vegetation. This woody stemmed creeper produces clusters of oval green berries which turn bright, ruby-red in the fall. Because of their attractiveness, they are popular in holiday decorations but are very poisonous.

Growing out of a small, swampy depression on the reservoir side of the road was a healthy stand of cattails which, according to Ted, are of great nutritious value to wildlife. He also noted that the width between their tall—6 to 12 feet—slim reeds allows small amphibians to move freely among the stalks in their shallow water habitat.

Sadly, our walk with Art came to an end. On the way to our cars, we passed a pretty fall scene which begged to be captured on a painter's canvas. A dramatic spray of white birch with twelve slender, graceful trunks fanned out of the ground like long-stemmed flowers in a vase, their foliage brilliant splashes of red, gold, and orange against an azure sky. I thought to myself, this must be nature's way of singing a beautiful love song—one I'm sure Art and Nellie heard often during their many nature walks together.

BASS ROCKS STATION • TARR TRAIL

As I tightened the rawhide laces on my fur-lined boots for an early

January walk with Ted, outside my window large snowflakes increased in intensity and began to blanket the cold, frigid earth. The thermometer registered 15 degrees but, according to a Boston weather forecaster, the wind howling around my deck dropped the actual temperature to 8 below zero. At the mall 12 enthusiastic, woolen bundles were ready to hit the trail, including a reporter who was writing an article on animal tracks. As if smiling encouragement on this bone-chilling morning, a brightly shining sun peeked through the gray sky and beamed down on us—but only for a few moments. It vanished almost as quickly as it appeared, and wasn't seen again for five blustery, storm-filled days.

We drove to the site of the old abandoned Bass Rocks Railroad Station, a short distance north of Babson Museum on Route 127 in Rockport. As we waited for the train to pass before crossing the tracks onto the Dogtown trails, Ted related the history of this small intermediary station along the Nugent Stretch between Rockport and Gloucester.

In the late 1800s and early 1900s, a number of large oceanside hotels were realizing the sweet smell of success as more and more vacationers came to enjoy summer pleasures along Gloucester's seashore. Most of these summertime visitors were wealthy Bostonians, New Yorkers, Washingtonians and Philadelphians who traveled the distance by train. During this same period, commerce in downtown Gloucester and along its inner harbor was also enjoying success, but not the sweet smelling kind. In fact, quite the opposite was true. The foul odors of drying fish and glue, a byproduct of the fishing trade, made travel through these areas quite unpleasant, especially during the heat of summer.

Realizing Gloucester's growing popularity as a vacationer's paradise, city hosts could not allow their rich and famous guests to be greeted at the railroad station by these offending smells of industry. Something had to be done—and it was. A small waystation was built convenient to the hotels and beaches, but away from unpleasant, but lucrative, fishing businesses. It was located inland from the Bass Rocks community, a short distance from the beautiful white-washed sands of Good Harbor Beach, and hotel guests were transported to and from trains by carriage through Nugent Woods. The quaint little depot served the community well during Gloucester's era of grand oceanside hotels and privileged lifestyles.

After the train passed on this snowy January morning, we crossed the tracks and turned onto the Tarr Trail, named for our illustrious leader.

"There are a lot of problems along this trail; that's why they named it after me," he quipped, and then went on to explain how some of the trails were established.

"We usually follow animal tracks because they always seem to know where they're going. But sometimes they lead us where we don't want to go, then we have to make a few detours."

The snowfall lessened as we plowed deeper into the woods. As always, once on the trail, body motion keeps us warm despite low temperatures. Weather conditions always play a major role in Ted's selection of trails, and today's route was intended to protect us from the wind chill that dropped the temperature below the zero mark. When several in the lead took a path to the right onto a wide gravel road, he called them back saying, "It's windy up on that open hill. Let's stay in the woods."

Snow-covered leaves crunched underfoot as we followed Ted into Dogtown, the trail now paralleling the railroad tracks we had just crossed. Mountain laurel and hemlock, in their beautiful rich evergreen, were eye-catching among the tall hardwoods, all now barren except gray beech and a few scrub oaks.

Because of the dominance of beech trees, this section is called Beech Plain. In earlier times, it was known as Beech Pastures. Most cf Cape Ann's rocky terrain once pastured dairy cows, work horses, pigs, sheep and other farm animals. It also was the source of quarrystone and lumber for thriving granite and shipbuilding industries. Over the years, these interests gave way to more pressing needs of the times; left undisturbed, the land was reclaimed by trees. Today, thanks to friends of the environment, the "boundless woodland" that Captain John Smith described when he cruised these shores in 1614 once again covers the Cape Ann landscape and is enjoyed now more than ever by nature lovers of every stripe.

Ted, meanwhile, was right about problems on the trail which bore his name. It began easy enough as a grassy footpath along the base of a rocky hillside terminal moraine. But soon the rocks descended down the hill and across our path, creating challenging obstacles in a number of places.

"We put the path here to discourage dirt bikes," he explained as he led us through the maze of ancient stone.

There were also a number of wet areas, now frozen underfoot, and fallen trees.

"We used to walk *under* this tree," he said, straddling a giant oak that lay across the trail at ground level.

These must be the problems he referred to, we thought, as we made our way around icy waterfills, up steep rocky inclines, and over decaying logs. In some places the trail was indistinct, an orange dotted tree the only indicator that we were going in the right direction. In other places, it was well-travelled and almost leafless, its hardpan base serving as a barrier to help control ground fires.

Continuing on, we came to a wooden post marked "13" where three trails converged—the Tarr, the Dorothy Luce Trail and an unmarked footpath veering off diagonally to the left. We took the latter, staying in the Beech Plain. Soon we passed two interesting rock formations—one pyramid shaped and the other resembling a giant three-legged milk stool—remnants of the mile-wide glacier that rumbled down from Canada to the Carolinas centuries ago.

The trail then took us almost straight down a steep, rocky, leaf-covered ridge, each step requiring extreme care. Grabbing onto nearby tree limbs, as well as each other, and using small rocks and large roots to hold our footing, we inched down the slippery hillside. Safely on solid ground, we continued along the footpath through a dark, damp valley of towering hemlocks. In the still of winter, the forest was beautiful. Ringlets of ice laced the quiet waters of Wine Brook which crossed our path in several places.

We passed through an area that had been badly damaged by fire three or four years previously and was just beginning to grow back. Several dark, charred trunks of white pine bore silent witness to the burning.

As we passed a yellow birch, Ted pointed to its fire-damaged trunk. "Fires open trees to fungus and disease," he explained. "Oaks have thicker bark and can withstand fires better than beech and birch."

A number of nearby beech and oak were marked by woodpecker holes.

"Looking for insects," he noted.

A short distance further, as we passed through a tangled thicket of high-bush blueberries, he said, "We call this the Blueberry Trail."

In the distance, the wail of a train whistle sounded, indicating that we were nearing the railroad tracks. Crouching low, we crawled under three large branches of a fallen oak and continued along the footpath bordered on both sides by low-bush blueberry bushes and sheep laurel. Shortly we emerged into a clearing south of Babson Museum on Route 127.

Walking the tracks back to Whistlestop Mall (by now I was becoming used to this winsome adventure), Ted related the details of a train derailment along this stretch a number of years ago. A faulty section of tracks caused the train to veer off into the woods. Fortunately, no one was hurt. "In fact," he laughed, "some said it was the smoothest part of the ride."

BABSON WATERSHED

A watershed is the ground from which natural water sources, such as springs, streams and lakes, feed into a larger body of water, a reservoir, which has been purified for public consumption. The Babson Watershed includes 1,709 acres surrounding the Babson Reservoir, which is located at the base of a steep hill across the railroad tracks from Blackburn Industrial Park. This expansive watershed includes Alewife and Wine brooks, as well as a number of natural springs and smaller, un-named streams. The reservoir's prime source is its water table, a network of small self-replenishing underwater rivers.

We walked the Babson Watershed trail on a bright, sunny morning in late April, the first time in six months we were blessed with two clear, warm Sundays in a row. However, this beautiful spring weather didn't last. Two days later snow returned to New England, dropping temperatures into the low 30s. Boston recorded just under two inches overnight, and freezing rain and sleet delayed early morning flights at Logan for two hours. The Monadnock Mountain area of New Hampshire, just ten miles from the Massachusetts boundary, received over five inches of the fluffy white stuff. By noon the sun came out, shining brightly over hill and dale, sending the thermometer up to 56, and the surprise storm became a memory. Though unexpected, the late spring snow didn't harm tree buds or new grass; in fact, woodlands and gardens were nourished and rejuvenated by the nitrogen it showered upon them.

We entered the watershed from Route 127, a short distance south of the Babson Museum, walking the Old Rockport Road which terminates at Blackburn Circle. For many years, these woods were rock-strewn fields and pastureland for a number of farms—one a piggery. Beaver Dam Farm, operated by several families during its 200-year history—the Fosters, Mannings, Babsons and Nugents—was one of the largest on the Cape during its existence. Today only the summer kitchen remains on a rise along Nugent Stretch. It is now called the Babson Cooperage Museum.

As we walked past the stone-walled pastures, now forested with oak, maple, tupelo, shad, red cedar and hemlock, we immediately encountered new spring growth. Sprouting up along the roadside were carpets of Canada mayflower, sometimes called wild or false lily-of-the-valley because of its similarity in leaf formation and feathery cluster of white flowers. Deeper in the woods, thick emerald-green moss brightened a pool of pitch-black water. Across the roadway, skunk cabbage grew in basins of mucky soil. Its leaves, coiled into small cones, later would become large, fleshy and leathery. Bruised, they smell like a skunk and the cut stem like a combination of mustard and rotten raw onions. When in bloom, the flowers emit the odor of dead flesh. Why, then, would anyone want to eat this horrible plant?

Naturalists who know about these things say *thoroughly dried* young leaves are quite good reconstituted in soups or stews and *thoroughly dried* rootstocks can be made into a pleasant cocoa-like flour—the key word being *thoroughly dried*. If they are not, the result is a burning and prickling sensation in the throat. The late herbalist Euell Gibbons agrees, noting in his book *Stalking the Health Herbs* that properly prepared, skunk cabbage can be quite tasty—and created several recipes to prove it. In his Skunk-Cabbage Pancake, he mixed wheat flour with crisp root-chips. His old-fashioned Herb-Meat Cabbage Pudding includes dried leaves which he aged six months.

In addition to satisfying the palate of wild-food enthusiasts, this pretty fluted plant serves a number of medicinal purposes. Early New England Indians used powdered dried roots as an astringent to stop bleeding for minor cuts and scratches. It has since become recognized officially as a modern medicinal herb by the *U. S. Pharmacopoeia* and the *U. S. Dispensatory* for its emetic, stimulant, antispasmodic and narcotic properties. The drug is evidently in the fresh plant and dispelled through drying since dried products produce no unpleasant side effects. It also has a built-in heater, we were told by Ted.

"Because of its metabolic rate, it generates its own heat. It's one of the first plants to poke up out of the snow, melting the area around it."

As we rounded a bend, three ladies in the lead signaled for silence: soon we understood why. Perched in the treetop of a towering red maple was the hunched silhouette of what birders in the group thought to be an owl. It was difficult to tell at the moment; his black form sat motionless with his back to us as we crept silently toward him. Eyes glued on the distant tree limb, we approached ever so cautiously, trying not to make a sound lest we disturb his slumber. Suddenly, swift wing beats fanned the air as he took flight through the timber, revealing not a barred or saw-whet owl as expected, but a large dusty brown hawk. Someone thought it was a marsh hawk, "the eye that sees everything," but upon closer study, it was identified as being of the broad-winged species.

Although many firmly believe that all hawks are feathered terrorists, the broad-winged is considered rather harmless, seldom attacking farm animals. Instead, he prefers insects, frogs, meadow mice, chipmunks, red squirrels and occasionally rabbits and moles. Partial to deep woods, he'll remain motionless for hours, seemingly asleep though actually awake, alert to the least movement of his prospective victim—a characteristic with which we fully agree, having watched him closely that Sunday morning on the Old Rockport Road.

Pressing on, Ted pointed out beech and birch buds just coming in.

"Red maples have been in for a couple of weeks," he noted.

We then came upon a large, black plastic pipeline running down an incline from an area that is now Pond Road. Today, because of the development of an industrial park, the clear spring waters that once flowed freely through these woods are no longer usable—the abandoned pipeline a reminder of man's insensitivity to the environment.

Pointing to the brow of a nearby hill, Ted voiced his concern. "By removing stone and gravel in this direction, it will affect the water supply of Babson Reservoir. For industry, you need two things—room and water. If you get rid of the water, you don't gain anything. Unfortunately, many businesses don't realize that."

Further along the trail, a newcomer to the group pulled at a small branch and asked, "What's this coming out, Ted?"

"It's a striped maple," he replied. "The leaves are big when formed, and the bark has white stripes on the trunk."

Actually, the leaves of this tree look like a big goose's foot. One of the smaller maples, it usually grows no more than 25 feet. It begins as a scraggly, tall bush with several stems, then forms into a tree with ruddy brown, rather smooth bark. They were once very prevalent in Western Massachusetts where they're called "moosewood," perhaps because of their abundance during the time moose roamed the area, around 1700. They are also plentiful in Maine but, unlike many of that state's trees, this one has no commercial value. Although its sap has sugar content, the tree seldom grows large enough to allow its trunks to be tapped.

Suddenly, we became aware of the smell of groundfire and were on the lookout for it. Control burning is done in certain areas in the spring, but it seemed a little late for it, Ted thought. Someone pointed deep into the woods beyond a patch of skunk cabbage and shouted excitedly, "There it is."

"Let's see if we can put it out," ordered Ted, racing toward the blue puffs rising over large boulders on a crest above the swamp. We were right behind him as he tramped through the muck, grabbing and trimming a good-sized limb as he ran toward the smoke. Reaching dry ground, we climbed over rocks and around boulders and found the source—about six small groundfires eating away at dry leaves and fallen tree limbs. Work began immediately as some followed Ted's lead and, using rods fashioned from branches, pushed the flames back into the charred ground and covered them with damp leaves unearthed below the surface, quenching the embers. Others extinquished them by stomping their wet boots and shoes. But it was soon discovered the fire was not confined to the immediate vicinity behind the rocks; flames, fanned by a light wind, had spread to several pastures. We worked quickly, moving from one fire to another, then one spot to another, prodding and stamping the flames, which continued to spread. Hurrying over a stone wall where the smoke seemed heavier, a man shouted back to Ted, "It's no use. It goes way back down that hill; we'll never contain it." He was right. The fire was out of control, at least our control. It was then that Ted decided to call for help. Unfortunately, he did not have his two-way radio with him, only his beeper, which meant a quick hike up to the Blackburn offices—hopefully, someone would be there on Sunday.

Ted was not unduly concerned about the fire. "It's a couple of weeks late, but it's a good fire. It won't do too much damage, the ground is still wet," he reasoned. "We won't lose top soil; and with rain, it'll act as a fertilizer for the next generation of growth. There should be enough seeds in the soil to give us a pretty good resurgence."

Fires are a constant threat to nature—birds, animals, plants, trees, soil, streams—everything that makes up the beauty and natural resources of forestation. The conditions Ted described are favorable to the environment, revitalizing the topsoil and in many cases restoring plantlife healthier and more plentiful than before—the heather near Raccoon Ledges being an example. But in other cases, valuable soil is permanently destroyed, the damage irreversible. This is true to a small degree along several sections of the Babson watershed where once healthy vegetation prevented soil erosion, but now the topsoil is gone, the ground bare, exposed to further destruction by severe weather conditions. This destroys the water-retaining capability and adversely affects both the quality and quantity of water going into the reservoir. An instance where uncontrolled burning changed forever the condition of a forest is Mt. Monadnock, mentioned earlier, whose peak today is rock-bare, the result of ancient forest fires.

Locally, two major wildfires darkened much of Rockport in the early 1930s. The first was an early spring blaze which took two days to contain. It began at the Rockport end of Dogtown Common and spread to Lanesville and the South End, scorching more than a thousand acres. The second started at Squam Hill on a windy autumn day and spread rapidly across to Pigeon Hill, leaving five hundred acres blackened in its wake. Today both the Rockport and Gloucester fire departments are well-equipped and well-trained to fight forest fires, gaining access to many areas by fire roads that take them deep into swamps, marshes and upper woodlands.

As we hurried along to report the groundfire again threatening the Rockport end of Dogtown, Ted pointed to a hill on our right. "That's Railcut Hill, designated as a bird sanctuary by Roger Babson. He had a summer cottage up there where he did a lot of his writing."

Budding trees bordered the roadway—white, gray and yellow birch, alder and red maple. As we came up behind the industrial complex, Ted again expressed concern for the quality of water feeding into the reservoir as a result of development. "Water in the back of that manufacturing plant drains into Babson when it gets high. Any chemicals will pollute the water supply."

After reporting the fire to personnel in one of the offices, Ted rejoined the group and we continued on. From the Blackburn Industrial Park, we returned to the woods, crossing the Old Rockport Road, onto the Babson Trail which we had explored on one of our earlier walks. At the bottom of the steep hill beside the reservoir, a young man approached us asking if we'd seen his dog, a small collie named "Friskie." Unfortunately, we hadn't, but took his telephone number in the event we found his canine friend lost in the woods.

"He'll probably beat me home," he said hopefully as he waved goodbye and walked off in another direction.

Along the bank of the reservoir, a large pussy willow bush was just going to seed. We noted hairycap moss, lichen, dried goldenrod and staghorn sumac beside the trail as we climbed a gentle rise. Continuing along the winding footpath, bordered mostly by high and low-bush blueberries, we zig-zagged between and around boulders and erratics, reminders of the glacial force that tumbled the rocks and scored the land thousands of years ago. The woods were brown with last year's fallen leaves. A red-dotted trail to our left marked the way to Dogtown. On a downward slope on the right, a small mountain of rock sprouted tiers of rich, green polypody fern—creating a pretty natural woodland terrarium.

Then we came upon a section where groundfire had destroyed trees and groundcover. Pointing to deep, black holes in several large trunks, Ted lamented, "Fires open them to rot and insects." And poking his shoe into the shallow, dry dirt, he continued, "It's not a very good watershed because of the damage done to the soil by extensive fires. What used to hold water now allows it to run off over the dam and out to sea." Ironically, these bare spots now serve as firebreaks.

At a bend in the trail the word "Rockport" with an arrow pointing upwards appeared on a rock. "I've tried a number of times, but I've never in eight years found a trail to Rockport that way," said Ted knowingly as he led us past the sign and continued along the Babson Trail.

Next we passed what he called "an important lagoon," though we didn't hear any wood frogs yet. In a few more days, a week at the most, he predicted.

Several times along the trail, Ted drew our attention to a delicate blue butterfly—a spring azure—which seemed to be following us, adding to the beauty of spring. Arthropod scholars call butterflies "the frail children of the air," a fitting term for these fragile, winged insects.

The spring azure is a member of the Blue species, one of three tribes belonging to the family of Gossomer wings—the other two being Hairstreaks and Coppers. Their characteristics include small, slender bodies, thin wings, and threadlike antennae. It's a beautiful little butterfly, earning it the fanciful description of "a floating violet." The markings vary among the species, but as a whole the upper surface is blue, the lower ash-gray dotted with dark brown and the wings are without tails.

"Usually the mourning cloak comes out a week before the azure blues, but I haven't seen any yet," our nature-loving trailmaster informed us.

The mourning cloak—so named because of its funereal, nearly black membranous wings and creamy white borders—is considered to be the crowning glory of any serious British butterfly collector. Which is surprising, considering the fact that this exquisite specimen was first observed in Surrey, England. What happened to the species over time remains a mystery, but today it's very prevalent in America and extremely rare—almost extinct—in England. In fact, only one or two specimens a year have been observed by British naturalists since 1819.

The change from a slow-moving, slug-like caterpillar to a dainty, spritely butterfly is probably one of the most fascinating phenomena in the world of living creatures. (As fascinating, I believe, as the little pink shrimp which changes its sex several times in its short lifetime—all by him/herself!) The life cycle of the butterfly is a complete physical transformation as opposed to progressive stages of growth, such as a baby grasshopper developing into an adult grasshopper.

First a butterfly lays an egg upon a leaf. A caterpillar hatches from the egg as a tiny creature with soft skin covering its body, firmer tissue protecting its head. Its first meal is the empty egg shell. Next it tries the green leaf; future meals also come from the leaf as it grows. After several days, it's ready to "burst at the seams," it's eaten so much. Nature comforts it by providing a new skin under the first one, which splits open in a straight line down its back. Wiggling free, it finds itself in a brand new skin, soft and pliant like its first. It rests for a bit while this new skin hardens, then it's back to the green leaf buffet for more nourishment. Again its girth expands and again nature provides another new suit. Four in all. About ten days after the last change, which naturalists refer to as a "moult," it's ready to undergo a remarkable transformation—radical surgery, so to speak—in which all its caterpillar organs become the very different organs of a beautiful butterfly.

It brings about this transfiguration by securing itself against a surface, first entangling its hind legs and then hanging downward. Then it gradually shrinks upward until the final skin splits open along the middle of its back. In a very short period of time, it evolves from a caterpillar to a chrysalis or pupa (cocoon) then to a butterfly. Naturalists theorize that, because the chrysalis skin shows many characteristics of the future butterfly, this evolutionary process really began in the larva, that is, in the caterpillar stage of development. In any event, it's a fascinating series of changes, which result in the procreation of day-flying insects that are almost ethereal in their delicacy and beauty.

As the spring azure danced around us, we set upon a broad, grassy footpath coming in from Dogtown Square which would take us back to Rockport. On our way we passed the Luce Trail, part of the network of trails that wander through Dogtown and its environs. Despite a valley full of glacier stones we noticed in passing, the woods were taking on the sparkle of spring—bright green clubmoss perked up the landscape, the polished green leaves of sheep laurel lost their droopiness and now turned upwards toward the sun, and bushes and trees of all shapes and sizes wore rose-colored crowns of bursting buds.

As on previous walks along this route, we climbed under the three-pronged trunk of a huge oak, then emerged from the woods into a clearing by the railroad tracks parallel to Nugent Stretch.

"Is it time for a train, Ted?" someone asked, voicing the concern of others.

Taking out his schedule, he checked his watch. "It leaves Rockport at 12:15. We have plenty of time," he assured us, turning left onto the tracks.

But we needn't have worried as we left them almost immediately and followed a footpath through open woods where we climbed over a large gray beech before hooking up with a wide grassy trail.

"This was probably used for taking out firewood," Ted told us, referring to early settlers.

Passing a pretty tree swamp, we noticed fiddleheads coming in. On the left were the flowing waters of Alewife Brook.

"This becomes Mosquito Alley in hot weather," Ted said, reminding us of hurried, swatting walks through the area last summer.

The road then rounded a bend and brought us under a canopy of spreading apple trees and tangled grapevines mixed with bittersweet, remnants of the old Babson Farm.

In a clearing beside the trail, two capped pipes poke out of the ground. Although the land on which they stand belongs to Rockport, the pipes are owned by the City of Gloucester, which was given permission to conduct watershed tests in the area for the Babson Reservoir.

As we passed through a grove of staghorn sumac, we heard the whistle of the Rockport-to-Boston train. We didn't have to consult our watches to know the time—12:15, exactly. Crossing Route 127 to our cars, someone said, "Not bad, considering the time we lost fighting the fire, then detouring to report it."

But then, Ted always managed to gets us back in plenty of time for Sunday lunch.

2A. DOGTOWN
BRIAR SWAMP

1. Loop Pond
2. Raccoon Ledges
3. Dam
4. Briar Swamp Boardwalk
5. Whale's Jaw
6. Evan's Baseball Field

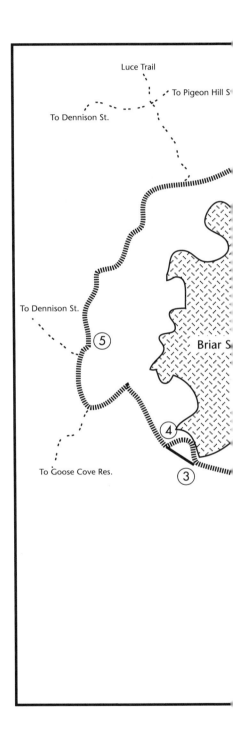

Luce Trail

To Pigeon Hill S

To Dennison St.

To Dennison St.

⑤

Briar S

④

To Goose Cove Res.

③

KEY

ⅲⅲⅲⅲ	Trail
.. .. .	Sub Trail
‒‒‒‒	Street or Highway
. . .	Railroad Tracks
▨	Ocean
▨	Pond or Lake
▨	Swamp

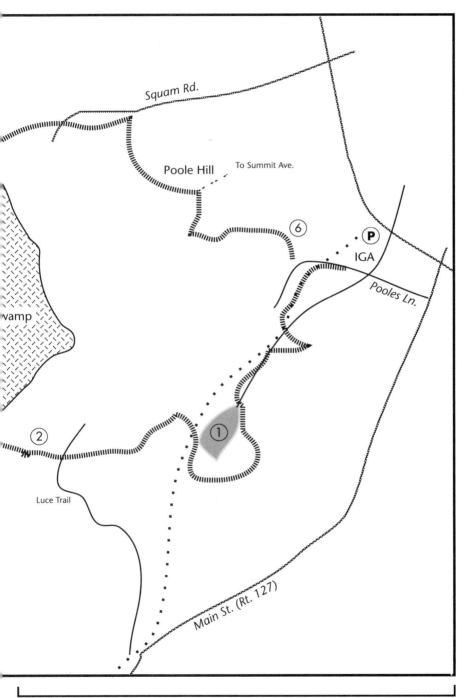

Squam Rd.

Poole Hill   To Summit Ave.

⑥

Ⓟ

IGA

Pooles Ln.

vamp

②

Luce Trail

①

Main St. (Rt. 127)

1 Mile

44

2B. DOGTOWN
LOOP POND

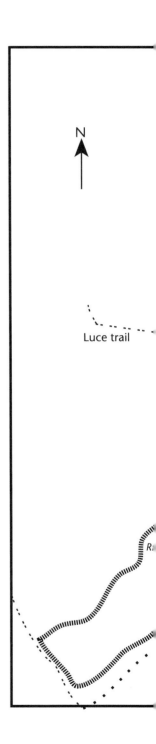

Luce trail

KEY

▬▬▬ Trail
-- -- Sub Trail
─── Street or Highway
• • • Railroad Tracks
■ Ocean
■ Pond or Lake
⊠ Swamp

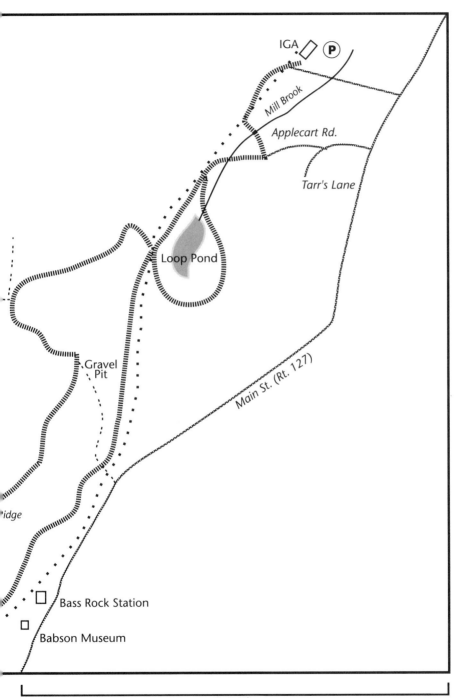

IGA

P

Mill Brook

Applecart Rd.

Tarr's Lane

Loop Pond

Gravel
Pit

Main St. (Rt. 127)

idge

Bass Rock Station

Babson Museum

1 Mile

2C. DOGTOWN
TOWN FOREST

1. TADCO
2. Town Forest
3. Whale's Jaw

Briar Swamp

3

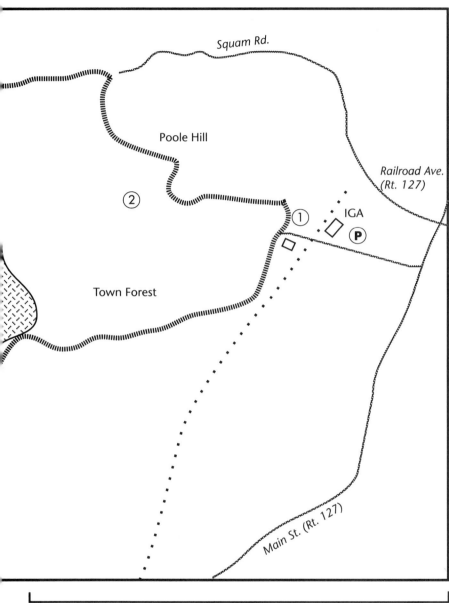

Squam Rd.

Poole Hill

Railroad Ave.
(Rt. 127)

②

① IGA

Ⓟ

Town Forest

Main St. (Rt. 127)

1 Mile

2D. Dogtown
BABSON WATERSHED

1. Abandoned Pipe
2. Old Mill Site
3. Vernal Pool
4. Meadow
5. Babson Cooperage Museum

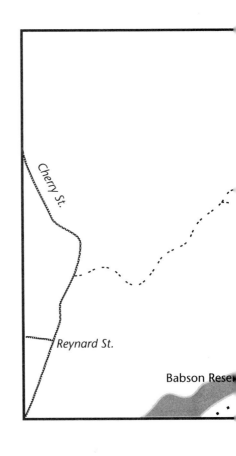

Cherry St.

Reynard St.

Babson Rese

KEY

⦙⦙⦙⦙⦙⦙⦙⦙⦙	Trail
-- -- .	Sub Trail
⌇⌇⌇⌇	Street or Highway
▪ ▪ ▪	Railroad Tracks
▦	Ocean
▨	Pond or Lake
▨	Swamp

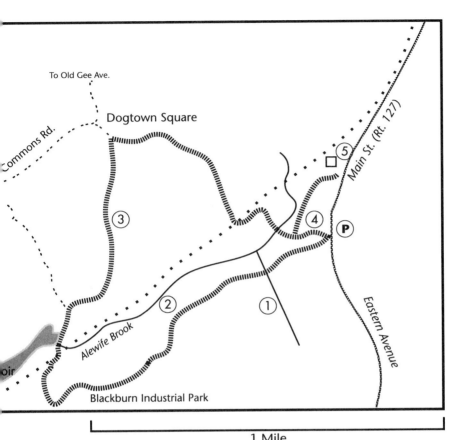

To Old Gee Ave.

Commons Rd.

Dogtown Square

③

② Alewife Brook

④

⑤

Ⓟ

Main St. (Rt. 127)

Eastern Avenue

①

oir

Blackburn Industrial Park

1 Mile

2E. DOGTOWN
BABSON RESERVOIR

1. Inscriptions begin
2. To Rockport
3. Dogtown Square
4. Common Bars
5. Bull Pasture
6. Gravel Pit

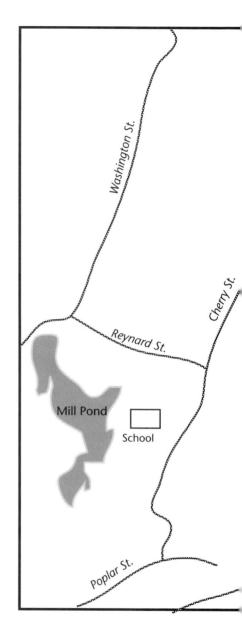

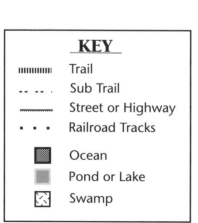

KEY

ⅢⅢⅢ	Trail
-- -- ·	Sub Trail
〰〰	Street or Highway
· · ·	Railroad Tracks
▨	Ocean
▨	Pond or Lake
▨	Swamp

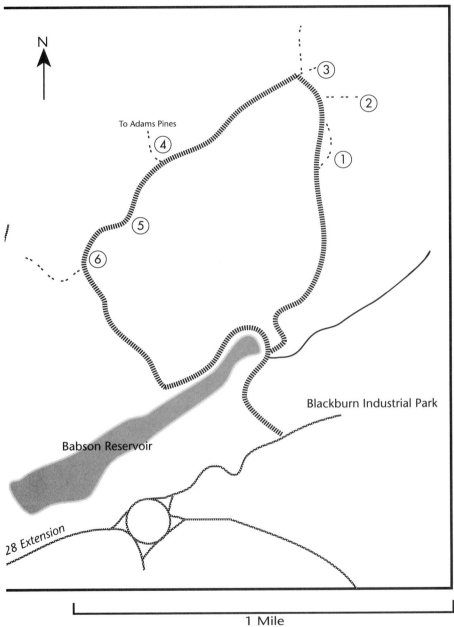

N

To Adams Pines

③

②

④

①

⑤

⑥

Blackburn Industrial Park

Babson Reservoir

28 Extension

1 Mile

2F. DOGTOWN
GOOSE COVE RESERVOIR

1. Overlook
2. Adams Pines
3. Granny Day's Swamp

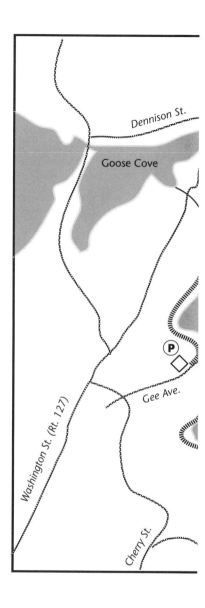

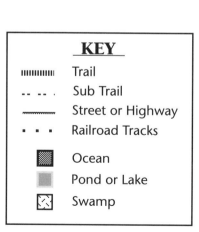

KEY

ⅢⅢⅢⅢ	Trail
-- -- ·	Sub Trail
⌒⌒⌒	Street or Highway
· · ·	Railroad Tracks
▓	Ocean
▒	Pond or Lake
▨	Swamp

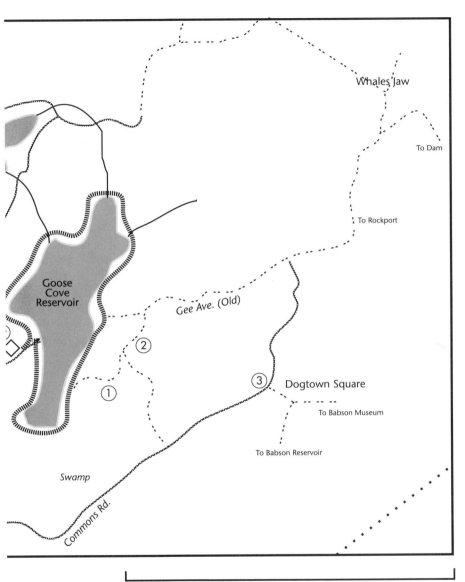

Whales Jaw

To Dam

To Rockport

Goose
Cove
Reservoir

Gee Ave. (Old)

② ③ Dogtown Square

① To Babson Museum

To Babson Reservoir

Swamp

Commons Rd.

1 Mile

Cape Ann Quarry Walk

Granite Pier • Keystone Bridge

The destination for our Sunday morning walk in late July was Rockport's abandoned granite quarries across Granite Street from Granite Pier. It's difficult to imagine that, from 1800 until around 1930, our beautiful, picturesque "city by the sea" was the granite capital of the world! But a leisurely walk around the sky-high rims of her numerous quarries brings into focus this bustling period in Rockport's past.

The starting point for our scenic two-hour trek was an idyllic spot beneath Keystone Bridge, a beautifully arched Romanesque structure located at the Rockport-Pigeon Cove town line. Built in 1872 (the recorded time from planning to completion was 18 months—11 weeks to build the bridge alone!), it's supported only by solid arched granite. There is no binder. Held together by the keystone wedged into the top of the arch, it's a fine example of how bridges were constructed in earlier times. The bridge is a magnificent testimony to Yankee ingenuity and craftsmanship—those "Yankees" being Finnish, Swedish and Irish immigrants.

Our view from the ground of the towering gray stone span above was breathtaking. Walking the wide, sun-splashed roadbed leading into the quarries, we noted a huge black pipe trailing along the ground beside us, which Ted said provided gravity-fed water to the town's main pump station at Cape Pond.

"It leads from Flat Ledge Quarry into Carlson's Reservoir, and then is treated and pumped into the water supply," he explained. "In the spring we're OK, but when the water's low, we have a problem." A problem, I might add, he has pursued diligently with state and federal authorities for a very long time.

Rockport Quarries

At a bend in the grassy trail—once a roadbed for a steam locomotive—we veered off to the right onto a narrow footpath overlooking Flat Ledge Quarry, the pit closest to the bridge. We climbed higher and higher over small rocks and around huge boulders. Hardwoods and pine trees mottled the dense woodlands. Finally we emerged into an open look-out area offering a sweeping view of land and sea.

From our vantage point on a rocky ledge high above the village, we gazed down into the deep, green waters of Flat Ledge Quarry, gleaming brightly in the morning sun. Beyond its rim was the wide expanse of the Atlantic Ocean, a flotilla of sailboats dotting its placid blue horizon. Off to our right was Rockport, the little city by the sea, known and loved by tourists throughout the world for its rugged coastline, magnificent period homes and gardens, its historic fishing village and friendly local residents. We stopped for a few minutes to catch our breath and quietly drink in the beauty below—at peace with ourselves and the world around us.

Then we were back on the narrow footpath which took us from one quarry to another, at times winding gently through dark forested groves of stately hemlocks, but also drawing us perilously close to the edge of the quarries' steep granite cliffs.

Continuing on we were again taken back to that long-ago time when the granite industry played a vital role in the making of our tiny seaside village. Along the path were remnants of its bygone era—iron posts, anchors, cables and pieces of derricks. These were used during the height of the quarrystone's glory days to hoist massive slabs—gray, green, blue, and rust—out of the deep, yawning pits. Also left behind were piles of grout, discarded granite which didn't split right because of irregular quartz, and rubblestone—all traces of a thriving, bustling enterprise now laid to rest.

Walking the rims of these great open pits, one senses the aura of this historical period. Hidden beneath the squalor of penniless immigrants, railroad ties, steam engines, and rocky terrain is a timeframe of business development known as "America's early industrialization." A time of industrial growth, to be sure, but more than that, it was a time of dynamic entrepreneurship—a time of long days and hard work, when tyrants ruled industry, but also a time when justice found its reward in the simple joys of human endeavor. For it was during this time—the making of America—that big trees from little acorns grew, and economic development emerged from the mind and spirit of harsh times and sedentary accomplishment.

Many historical structures of the early 1800s through the 1930s owe their architectural beauty and enduring qualities to quarrystone carved out of the bowels of Cape Ann pits. In Massachusetts, the number is endless: St. Peters Episcopal Church and the City Jail at Salem, the Bunker Hill Monument and Custom House in Boston, the Myles Standish Monument at Duxbury (a 14-foot statute mounted atop a 70-foot monument) and 28 bridges along Route 128 (all still in use). Other buildings throughout the country built with stone hoisted out of these pits include the Masonic Temple in Philadelphia, the Seaboard National Bank in New York City, the Mellon National Bank Building in Pittsburgh, the Federal Reserve Bank in New Orleans, the Winters National Bank in Dayton, Ohio and the Scott County Savings Bank in Davenport, Iowa. Paving stones from Cape Ann quarries were sent to Berlin, Liverpool, London, Paris, Vienna and Havana, in addition to major cities throughout the United States.

Amid the remnants of this long-ago enterprising industry, today's nature lover will find a peaceful, inspiring walk along its abandoned sites. To our left as we approached a trail leading to the ledge of Potato Pit Quarry, Ted pointed out "a very good lady's-slipper trail," and a little further on, we came upon a tranquil, shaded lily pond (called a "little motion," a quarryman's term for a small surface operation, usually a two-man quarry).

Throughout the walk, he pointed out a variety of vegetation: white oak, beech, honeysuckle, sweetfern, witch hazel, and hemlock where it was moist. Here, as in Dogtown, because these woods provided firewood for early settlers before the use of coal, not much old growth is evident today. But one thing that is plentiful is sweetpepper—lots of it.

"It's just about ready to blossom," Ted informed us on that warm summer day, "and when it does, if you're anywhere near here, you'll know it. Its spicy aroma can be smelled for miles. In early times on foggy days, sailors always knew when they were coming into Cape Ann because they could smell it from way offshore."

As we emerged from the quarries and crossed Granite Street to the parking lot at Granite Pier, our genial trailmaster drew our attention to the harbor of refuge at Pigeon Cove which in earlier times had seen much coastal ship traffic. With spirited community pride, he regaled his ecology-minded flock with an amusing parting story.

About 15 years ago, officials from an oil company came to Rockport intent on rebuilding the harbor's breakwater so supertankers could unload and distribute oil to the region. Their plans included laying pipelines along Route 128 to transport oil from ocean tankers to refineries which they planned to build throughout New England. But the enlightened civic leaders of Rockport would have none of it. Remaining steadfast to their principles of Yankee stewardship, they rejected the proposal out of hand, threatening to buy their own submarine and "blow the tankers out of the water," thus squelching the grandiose plans of the mighty oil barons.

On New Year's weekend, we returned to the quarries for another walk around this interesting historic site. The temperature had dipped to the teens overnight, but climbed up to 22 by 10 o'clock when we met Ted at the mall. Three stormy weekends—including a record-breaking nor'easter officially categorized as the Blizzard of '92—had cancelled most of our December walks. Since I had spent Christmas in Atlanta with my family, my weeks away from the trails numbered four and I was anxious to get back into the woods—and after the holidays, back into shape.

Typical New England weather greeted the brand new year. Boston temperatures (with wind chill factor) ranged from 8 below zero to 62 above during the first full week of 1993. On this day, though blustery cold, the sun shone brightly over Cape Ann.

What was it Ted said last July about getting down to "12 nuts in the dead of winter?" Today, next to the coldest day of the season, 19 heavily-clad walking enthusiasts signed his yellow lined roster, including six-year old Kathleen from Natick who, with her mother and grandmother, made up three generations of nature-lovers trailing behind him on the first Sunday of the new year.

Because most of the low-lying areas would be damp Ted felt, he headed for the "high and dry" trails skirting the quarries. Parking our cars at Granite Pier, we again walked under the beautiful granite arch spanning Keystone Bridge and followed the roadbed into the skeletal upland woods. In their winter starkness, the spindly trees now permitted a broad view of the rocky terrain. On our left, we came upon a long flowing white waterfall frozen in space as it cascaded down the side of a granite gorge. Likewise, the waters of Flat Ledge Quarry coming up on our right were frigid green on this clear, cold winter morning.

Climbing a narrow, leaf-strewn footpath over rocks and boulders to the overlook high above the yawning pit, we experienced the only worrisome mishap encountered during the six months I had been exploring Cape Ann's wilderness with Ted. The incident involved his loyal canine, "Springer."

In the woods just above Flat Ledge Quarry, a great deal of blasting had taken place during its busy stone-cutting days. As a result, in addition to scattered glacial deposits, the landscape along these trails includes large blocks of abandoned granite, as well as discarded rubblestone and grout. Some of the blasted stone is stacked into neat piles as high as a one-story building—other pieces were left on hillsides, in swamps and wherever else they happened to land when the dust had settled. The watchword in walking these trails anytime of the year is caution—but especially when thick layers of leaves blanket the ground, concealing dangerous depressions and rocky crevices. Which is what caused Springer's dilemma.

As we made our way up the incline to a lookout high above Flat Ledge Quarry, we had to climb over several medium-sized rocks blocking a winding curve in the trail. By carefully jumping from one to another, we managed the obstacle course quite well. Suddenly, an alarmed voice called out.

"Ted, Springer is in trouble."

In following closely behind us over the rocks, Springer attempted to leap across what appeared to be a small trench onto a rock and missed. He slid hindfeet first into a hole between two rocks—and continued sliding down seven feet below ground, landing in a rocky hillside tunnel.

"His head was the last part to disappear," a witness reported to Ted who came back to investigate.

Lying on his stomach and leaning into the pit as far as he could, Ted struggled to reach the barking Springer, but it was no use—the chasm was too deep. Springer continued to bark his displeasure as Ted raised himself and tried a different tactic. This time he'd go in feet first as Springer had. Fortunately, the hole was large enough for him to descend. Carefully lowering himself into the blackness, he, too, disappeared between the rocks.

By now everyone was on the scene, concerned that a serious incident was in the making. We could hear Ted talking to Springer under the boulders. Several men dropped to their knees to peer into the hole. They could see the top of his blue wool hat as the rescue attempt continued.

"How far down are they?" someone wondered.

"Is Ted all right?" another asked.

"Do we need to go for help?" queried a third.

Anxious moments passed. The group on the hillside fanned out to look for an exit in the rockpile from which Springer might escape. To the right, they found none, nor did those searching around to the left.

Finally "I got him" came Ted's muffled voice from deep within the hollow.

Amid happy applause, several pairs of arms reached into the darkness for the furry speckled bundle he held up to them. Once freed, Springer greeted his rescuers with happy brown eyes and wagging tail, then patiently waited while Ted, emerging from the pit, checked him for injuries. There were none, fortunately, and to the delight of everyone, he hightailed it up the hill. As an animal-lover, I was deeply touched as I watched Springer's adoring eyes on Ted's face as they walked side-by-side up to the overlook.

"That's what happens when I break my own rules," Ted apologized, referring to his pet restriction on our Sunday-morning outings. Dogs instinctively chase wild animals, causing delay and disruption—two things Ted prefers to avoid during the limited time we have together. Springer comes along only when weather conditions limit attendance or threaten cancellation. If no one shows up, they walk alone. Today, however, the weather did not discourage attendance, and his nature-loving flock all share his affection for the friendly, floppy-eared spaniel.

The frosty winter scenes along the quarry trails contrasted dramatically with those of last summer. During our July visit, wildflowers bloomed profusely throughout the woods, frogs croaked in little motions and songbirds serenaded us from limbs of leafy bushes and shade trees—and far below on the distant horizon, white sails cruised the blue summer sea.

Today, only a thick brown carpet of leaves covered the ground beneath denuded hardwoods, colored in spots by native evergreens—pine clubmoss, mountain laurel and hemlocks. The little black ponds were silent this morning. Swirls of ice laced the water's edge where noisy frogs and wiggling salamanders, now in hibernation, had splashed last summer. And songbirds no doubt serenaded others exploring trails in warmer climes. The dull gray swells of the mighty Atlantic carried no sailboats or luxury crafts. Only a few weathered seagulls flew low along the deserted shore.

Along the trail, Kathleen stopped to pick teaberries.

"Is it alright to eat these?" she asked Ted.

He approved her tasty find and then, picking up a gall, gave her a brief lesson in biology.

Further on, he drew us together in a small open area. "This is my favorite wildflower patch," he said. "In the summer, there are lady's-slipper along both sides here, absolutely beautiful, also bunchberries, partridgeberries and Indian cucumber."

The walk continued around the rim of Butman Pit, a one-time favorite skinny-dipping spot known as "Butt Pit" by young boys who swam in its cool green waters.

A short distance up the trail, a small stream of clear water flowed across our path then widened and splashed down the embankment into the quarry. Some of the water had frozen into the hillside, forming sheets of foamy white ice under the waterflow. Like Ted's lady's-slipper spot of last summer, this winter scene, too, was absolutely beautiful.

"Do you like whitewater canoeing, Dog?" he asked Springer who waded into the stream perilously close to the edge of the slippery rocks, "because you're going to be the canoe if you fall over that bank." Fortunately, he didn't.

Continuing on, we followed the trail leading out of the woods, emerging at the barrier on Quarry Road above Keystone Bridge. This Sunday's walk, so invigorating in the brisk, clear air, left us pleasantly refreshed—and ready to greet the challenges of the New Year with anticipation and renewed strength.

Easter is a special occasion on Cape Ann. It begins with ecumenical sunrise services at a number of beautiful spots overlooking the Atlantic Ocean—at the Headlands, on top of Pigeon Hill, at the end of Bearskin Neck, on the sands of Good Harbor and the dunes of Wingaersheek beaches, and along Dog Bar Breakwater at Eastern Point—to list but a few. The early morning worshippers are then invited to a community pancake breakfast at the Baptist Church on Rockport's Common.

The dawn of this Easter morning was not the brilliant array of dazzling sunshine which Christians everywhere envision on this holiest of holy days. Instead, a gray shroud of drizzle, rain and fog blanketed both land and sea. However, the dreary weather did not dampen the spirits of many who joined the celebrations taking place all up and down the New England Coast.. After sunrise services at the Headlands and breakfast with the Baptists, followed by a traditional service with the Episcopalians, Ted met us at the mall for another walk around the quarries.

We had walked these trails in the summer and again in early winter, and both times enjoyed the challenge of rigorous climbs and the beauty of the uplands which provide splendid views of the ocean, as well as the quarries themselves. During our summer visit, the pits' waterfill gleamed bright green in the blazing sun and later, on that cold, cloudy New Year's weekend, it was almost depressing in its colorless gray. Since then storm after storm brought bone-chilling wintry days and heavy snowfall, layering the basins with ice, then painting them winter-white. Today the temperature crept up only to the low 40s and a few icy patches still clung to the smooth, mirror-like surfaces.

Early into the walk, we again passed the small waterfall spilling gently over a rocky ledge and flowing down the sides of a steep wall of granite, which prompted a quip from Ted about it being "Rockport's answer to Angel Falls." (The highest waterfall in the world, Angel Falls is located in the Guiana Highlands in southeast Venezuela. Its waterspout drops 3,212 feet and its base is 500 feet wide.)

Following the footpath we had taken earlier around Flat Ledge

Quarry, we carefully climbed over "Springer's Folly," the seven-foot crevice that had swallowed our friendly mascot last January. Revisiting its small, jagged-edged opening, Ted expressed surprise that he had been able to maneuver himself into it to retrieve the hapless spaniel.

Although there were still a few patches of snow here and there, we looked for signs of new spring growth along the path, but all we found were a few winterberries—a carry-over from last year.

"The cold weather is holding everything back," Ted informed us. "Among the first to bloom are wood anemones. But it's too soon; the snow just melted." It's not surprising that this pretty little wildflower, a member of the buttercup family, is cup-shaped. It blooms in a variety of colors—yellowish, white, purple, violet and red.

"Wildflowers are all so weather dependent," Ted said, "which is why they come in so late after a long, cold winter, like we've just had. The lady's-slipper, bunchberries, partridgeberries, bluets, violets, Indian cucumbers, and wild oats will all be coming along when the weather warms up."

In New England, it's impossible to draw up a calendar of woodland spring within a week, or even two. After a few warm days, the red-osier dogwoods begin to blush, pussy willows pop a few scales and meadowlarks and mourning doves silhouette the azure sky. Crocuses, daffodils and tulips push their heads above ground, tender and delicate, but oh, so eager to greet the new spring. After that, almost anything can happen—warm, sunny days, or another winter blizzard. This year, 1993, the "Storm of the Century" arrived in late March, just short of a week before the official first day of spring. For that reason, gardeners have learned to be cautious and patient. The rule of thumb 'round these parts is don't put any young plants in the ground until Memorial Day and it seems to be a wise rule to follow.

Later in our woodlands walk, we looked for signs of marine life in the shallow, crystal clear edges of Big Parker Quarry. "It's too early for pollywogs," Ted said, then, leaning closer, "The bullfrogs are probably in those leaves. They'll be coming out, too, when the weather warms up. Someone at church told me they heard peepers (tiny frogs) last night."

Walking around the rim of the quarry, we followed the trail a short distance to Steel Derrick Pit. Here we stopped to rest for a few moments, gazing across the smooth, dark water and enjoying the peaceful scene. On the northeast side, fingers of lingering snow ran down the walls which, because of drillhole lines, looked checkered in places. Suddenly Ted called our attention to something he'd never noticed before—not in the 20 years he had been walking this rim.

"Look at the design left by the quarrymen when they cut pieces from that side," he said, pointing to the northern wall of the pit. Carved into the massive gray granite ledges was a huge, dark octagonal design framing a round, buff-colored circle.

"It looks like a camera lens!" he exclaimed, noticeably surprised as he studied the form from the distance.

"Look again, there's a man in the lens," someone pointed out. "He's on his side, but it's definitely the figure of a man."

With eyes focused on the opposite wall, one by one each person in the group discovered the image and then, gasping in delightful surprise, added many others. Large and small, male and female, they represented different cultures—mostly Egyptian or Tibetan ancients in clerical garb—but also several royals, wearing ornate crowns, capes and other finery. Lengthwise, it looked like a huge totem pole—a royal gallery. The huge horizontal mosaic of forms lining the quarry wall was perfect in every detail, although obviously the figures developed by happenstance over a period of time through the removal of stone of various shapes, sizes and colors. The overall effect created by the finely marked borings and the natural color formation of the quarrystone was startling. Dark, slate-gray granite formed the components of the camera, rust shades (caused by iron in the granite) colored the faces, grays and greens their clothing, and a light buff shade provided the background for all the images. It was a spectacular display, one that I'm sure will become a focal point of quarry walks in the future.

The woods were wet from the overnight rain and drizzle. We continued along the path, skirting Butman and Carlson quarries. Floating in the dark, still depths of Carlson (recorded to be 120 feet) was a small flock of herring gulls. They, along with the new cliffside homes being built in the vicinity, threaten the quality of this water reserve and in time measures will have to be taken to keep the supply purified for consumer use.

As we walked the quarry's upper ridge, a gently flowing stream crossed our path, washing over the ragged, rocky ledges and cascading down into the pit.

"That's the only stream that goes into a quarry," Ted remarked. As we watched the clear, cool water splash over the wet rocks and wash down into the reservoir, we recalled New Year's weekend when the woods were white with snow and the spillway laced with ice—and Springer almost rode the falls as a whitewater canoe.

A short distance further and our quarry walk ended as we emerged out of the woods onto the slope of Doctor's Run, a wide street circling the Quarry Cove community of luxury oceanview homes. Traces of lingering snow slithered down embankments in places shaded from the sun, remnants of the "storm of the century." Turning left, we headed down the hill where busy Granite Street (Route 127) follows the shoreline along the back of the Cape. However, safety-conscious Ted thought better of challenging the heavily-travelled highway and instead led us up a steep wooded hillside behind the Ocean Ledge townhouses. After a rigorous climb, we enjoyed a pleasant, leisurely stroll along Bayridge Lane which wound its way down to Keystone Bridge—and our cars parked at Granite Pier.

Unfortunately, we didn't find any budding wildflowers or see (or hear) songbirds or scampering wild animals on our quarry walk Easter Sunday. But later during lunch with a friend at Tom Shea's (their squaw bread is delicious!) overlooking the tidal waters of Essex Bay, I was entertained by an aquatic ballet, featuring a family of common loons, two large harbor seals and a flock of herring gulls. Surely spring was on its way.

3. QUARRY WALK

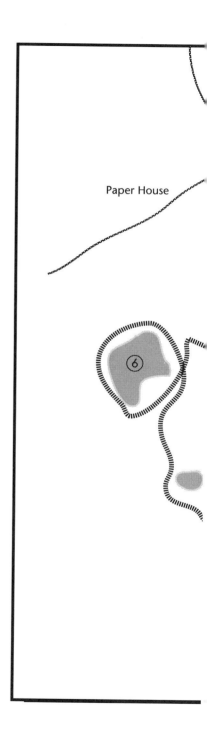

Paper House

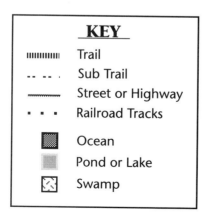

KEY

‖‖‖‖‖‖	Trail
-- -- -	Sub Trail
⎯⎯⎯	Street or Highway
• • •	Railroad Tracks
▓	Ocean
▒	Pond or Lake
⊠	Swamp

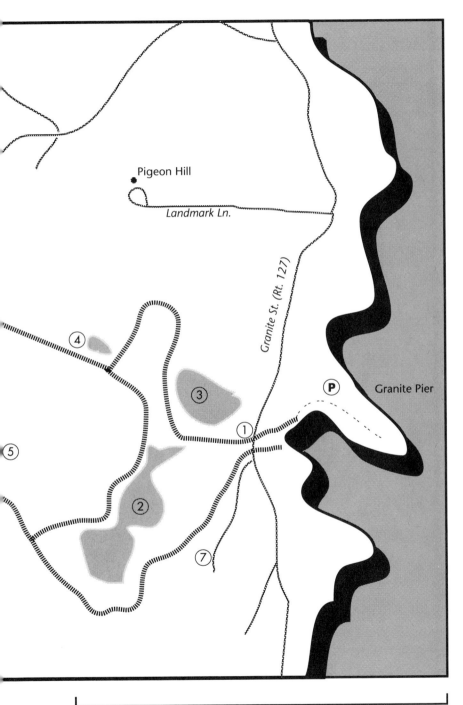

Pigeon Hill

Landmark Ln.

Granite St. (Rt. 127)

④

③

①

⑤

②

⑦

P Granite Pier

1/2 Mile

Halibut Point State Park
and Reservation

The Atlantic Path

The Atlantic Path hugs Cape Ann's jagged coastline from the Ralph Waldo Emerson Inn in Pigeon Cove to the Halibut Point Reservation at its northernmost tip. Twelve and one-half acres of the 52-acre, state-owned park face the ocean. The terrain throughout this beautiful seaside wilderness is varied: twiggy brush uplands, rocky headlands, forested woodlands and open, rock-strewn meadows of dense, low shrubby growth. In recent years, after long and persistent effort by Rockport residents, the state purchased the abandoned Babson Farm Quarry and added it to the reservation site, which is owned by the Trustees of Reservations.

The main entrance to the park/reservation is across from the Halibut Point parking lot on Gott Avenue in Rockport, just off Granite Street, two and one-half miles north of the village. However, our approach to this scenic overlook on a golden summer morning took us along the beautiful shoreline Atlantic Path. Parking at the tool factory in Pigeon Cove, we began at the breakwater and walked up the lane to the Ralph Waldo Emerson Inn. Across the street, a sign posted at the path's entrance reads:

> This path crosses private property.
> It has been used by the people of
> Rockport for more than fifty years.
> You are welcome to use it.
> Try not to abuse it.
>
> Pedestrians only   Cross at own risk.

Like much of coastal Cape Ann, this stretch sustained extensive damage to both private property and the rocky shoreline during the greatly under-rated nor-easter which local residents refer to simply as the "No Name Storm." It arrived unexpectedly the day before Halloween '91, and decided to stay around for a few days, its rain-filled winds, furious and persistent, battering everything in its path. Like another great seasonal storm in October 1841, it was disastrous for those who lived along the shoreline.

On the day before our walk in early August, Ted led vounteers and a crew of prison trustees who helped clean up the path and restore the reservation. We greatly appreciated their work as we made our way effortlessly along the enchanted oceanside trail.

The walk began along a grassy footpath bordered by banks of sweet-smelling sea roses which thrive along New England's coastline, from the dunes of Cape Cod to the rugged shores of Maine. A wider path soon opened up, allowing the group of nature lovers to observe and enjoy the quiet surroundings. Because of the greater-than-normal rainfall this summer, vegetation was lush green. Grapevine, greenbrier, Virginia creeper, bracken fern, and pitch pine covered the landscape before a bend in the trail took us over flat rocky ledges and down closer to the water's edge. Soft breezes wafting in from the ocean brought a lingering, pungent smell of salty air as gentle waves swirled over and around the rocks and blue-green alga below.

ANDREWS POINT • TARR'S BYPASS

Attractive oceanfront homes, with wrap-around decks and carefully tended lawns and gardens, dotted the shores of Andrews Point. As we passed a house close to the trail, a family enjoying a seaside brunch waved gaily from their deck. "Are you going to take them to the 'Tarr Bypass?'" a male voice called out.

Laughing his response, Ted answered, "Yes, as a matter of fact, I am." He explained that the caller was a friend who had helped clean the pathway for today's walk. During the clearing, it was necessary for Ted to re-route the trail slightly because of the obstruction of large rocks and debris from the No Name Storm. His good-humored fellow workers saw his maneuver as a new point of interest along the trail—and promptly dubbed it the "Tarr Bypass."

A major point of interest along the Atlantic Path is the gravesites of the literary genius William Rose Benet and his wife, Marjorie Flack, a writer and illustrator. Their ashes have been placed beneath a granite boulder in a natural wooded setting overlooking the ocean. Benet, a world-renowned anthologist, scholar, teacher, poet, editor and writer, was a member of an intensely literary family. Among brother Stephen Vincent's work were *The Devil and Mr. Webster*, and *John Brown's Body*, both of which became popular movies. Sister Laura wrote several fine biographies of artistic greats she admired—*Enchanting Jenny Lind*, *The Boy Shelley*, and *The Mystery of Emily Dickinson*. Her book *When William Rose, Stephen Vincent and I were Young* is a delightful memoir of their childhood years. The family resided in Pigeon Cove and were part of the creative literary community that produced other famous writers of the early 20th century, such as Ross Lockridge, author of *Raintree County*, and Thomas Heggan, who penned *Mr. Roberts*. All of these classics were written on Cape Ann which even then, as now, provided an atmosphere of beauty, harmony, and relaxation that allowed human thought to flourish into great expressions of classic literature and art.

CHAPIN'S GULLY • HOOP POLE COVE

A short distance further along the Atlantic Path is "Chapin's Gully," a dramatic natural ampitheatre where, in earlier times, crowds of local residents and summer visitors gathered to hear Sunday sermons by the Reverend Edwin H. Chapin, a noted theologian from New York City whose summer home later became the seaside retreat of William Benet and his wife.

Further still is Hoop Pole Cove, appropriately named by crafty early settlers who caught fish with what must surely be the forerunner to the lobster trap and fishnet in use today. First they cut and trimmed small trees and soaked them in salt water until they were pliable. The softened wood was then shaped into hoops and covered with netting, providing easy maneuverability for scooping up fresh seafood for the family table.

A special treat along the way was a side trip to a large, privately-owned sassafras grove, thanks to arrangements by our thoughtful guide. Having been on the sun-drenched trail for almost an hour, we welcomed the respite which allowed us to rest awhile in the cool shade. While most sassafras trees are scrawny and short with green twigs, the trees in this grove are tall, with many branches and full-bodied leaves. Of interest concerning the sassafras tree, Ted pointed out, are the three distinct shapes of its leaves—one resembling a child's mitten, another a spear, and the third a trident.

HALIBUT POINT STATE PARK AND RESERVATION

Leaving the refreshing shade of the grove, we returned to the path which would take us to Halibut Point. Again, we enjoyed another cool interlude crossing a boardwalk over a marshland. Lining the walkway on both sides were masses of large, waist-high royal fern and fiddleheads.

Finally, we emerged from the woodland onto an open grassy roadbed below Phillips Avenue. A lane to the right posted a sign pointing the way to the park. We journeyed forth on the wide, well-traveled path past a tiny fresh-water pond (we could hear the frogs), steeplebrush, wild-flowers, scrub oak, aspen, and more royal fern.

The vegetation throughout the open uplands of the reservation is a dramatic change from that found along the oceanside Atlantic Path, which winds in and out of verdant shaded woodland. Here great vistas of low shrubby growth line the terrain as far as the eye can see from several points within the park. Growing in the sandy, dry soil of the upland ledges are low-bush blueberry, huckleberry, sweetfern, bayberry, and bluestem grass. Further evidence of the fury of the No Name Storm is seen throughout the park in patches of soil that had been peeled back from rocks like an orange, exposing the roots of low-lying plants.

Meeting up with other visitors to Halibut Point that day, we marveled at the breathtaking panoramic views observed from several overlooks. The main overlook is an immense hill of discarded grout. From this peak, the view is a broad vista of land, sky and sea. Off to the left, ten important New England sites dot the eastern coastline from Massachusetts to southern Maine: Hog Island, Crane's Beach, Castle Hill, the Mouth of the Ipswich River, Sandy Point State Reservation, Parker River National Refuge (Plum Island), the Mouth of the Merrimack River (Newburyport), Seabrook Nuclear Power Plant (Salisbury Beach), the Isles of Shoals (New Hampshire-Maine), and Mt. Agamenticus (Maine).

BABSON FARM QUARRY

After spending some time enjoying this magnificent view, we fol-lowed a wide footpath leading to the park's entrance on Gott Avenue, passing on our way a small quarry on the left and a "little motion" on the right. For a few moments the walk was shaded by arching, black locust trees, but soon emerged into the sunlight and a circular walkway enclos-ing a colorful garden. A short turn to the right led us to the overlook at Babson Farm Quarry, from which we had a spectacular view of quarry, ledges, uplands and sea. So spectacular, in fact, the site appeared on the state's list of special places in October 1986 because of its beauty and unique qualities.

As we looked across the quarry's expansive rim, nothing marred our appreciation of God's handiwork. Deep in its basin is the same soothing green water seen glimmering in the summer sunlight in quarries throughout Cape Ann, still and tranquil. Surrounding the great pit are massive walls of granite, remnants of ancient glacial tides. And scattered across the upland terrain are many native plants and shrubs which today basked contentedly in the noonday sun. All of which played against a backdrop of the mighty Atlantic Ocean—framing a perfect portrait of nature at work in our time and in our place.

Winter lingered on. On Palm Sunday, the ground was covered with a light overnight dusting of snow and temperatures hovered in the low 30s. Slowly melting, sooty snowbanks still rimmed Whistlestop Mall when we gathered to plan our Sunday walk. Because cold rains had drenched New England during the past few days, Ted felt the uplands at Halibut Point would be drier than other places on the Cape. Piling into cars, we headed north on Granite Street toward Folly Cove, the little sea inlet just north of the park's overlook.

"The Silva property (directly across from the entrance) is being acquired by the state as an addition to the park," Ted informed us, as we walked from the parking lot. Included in the purchase is a large, white 1880 Victorian country house set on an acre and a half of land, Mrs. Silva's family homestead since 1930. The imposing nine-room structure was originally erected near the Babson Farm Quarry and moved to its present location in the early 1900's. Its closest neighbor is the weathered, gambrel-roofed Gott farmhouse, built in 1702.

Our approach to Halibut Point this time was to the right of this picturesque landmark along Gott Avenue, which soon became a winding dirt lane leading past two other aging private homes. The first, a turn-of-the century, colonial-style farmhouse, was painted barn red. On the gate a sign displayed a big red heart and implored passersby: "No Dogs...Please, I love my cats." Stretched out lazily on the front porch were two beautiful, large tabbies.

During a late-afternoon visit with the lady-of-the-house, a pleasant life-long Rockport resident, she explained the reason behind her tender plea.

"I really like dogs, and always had one," she told me in a friendly voice. "But now I only have cats—six of them."

Glancing at one of the tabbies that eyed us from a distance, she continued, "Many times park visitors allow their dogs to run free and they chase my cats. Their fights cause injuries," she said, adding sadly, "I lost one and I don't want it to happen again."

"To live on Cape Ann is to live with the birds," wrote Herbert A. Kenny in *Cape Ann: Cape America.* Truer words were never spoken. During all seasons of the year, the Cape plays host to a myriad of feathery flocks. The natural conditions found here—seasonal climates, woodlands and forests (both deciduous and conifer), wildflowers and shrubs, sandy beaches, salt marshes, rivers, swamps, open fields and meadows, rocks and dunes—all contribute to a quality of life that enables birds and plants to thrive abundantly. The woodlands, shoreline, offshore islands and village communities are alive with the flutter of wings and musical notes of songbirds most of the year.

In addition to spring showers, April brings the purple martin, golden-crowned kinglet, and the blue-gray gnatcatcher. And with May flowers come marsh wrens, bank swallows (burrowing small holes into river banks and gravel pits), vireos, sparrows and Baltimore orioles (nesting mostly in elms and other shade trees). Throughout the spring and summer months, the great majority of birds we see are males in their breeding plumage, among which are thrushes, solitaires and bluebirds, a family of fine singers.

A number of hardy game birds winter on Cape Ann, including Canada geese, mallards, and merganzers. Sparrows, starlings, meadowlarks, cardinals and robins also stay year-round, hibernating in the thickets at Ravenswood. And who could miss the American goldfinch, described by a birder friend as an "adorable little thing, whose olive green feathers turn bright yellow in the spring."

On this chilly April morning, we saw two different species, both tolerant of New England's severe weather—the slate-colored junco and the little tree sparrow. These jaunty snowbirds often travel together from their Arctic breeding grounds, winging into southern Canada and the United States with the first hard chills of autumn. Their feeding habits are similar—both forage for seeds in brown weeds poking up through the snow and swarm to dooryards and feeders for handouts. The feeding notes of the tree sparrow are soft and sound like tiny bells. As spring nears, his notes become sweeter, and increase in volume. The male junco, like the cardinal we saw on an earlier walk, is a family man, singing sweetly from a treetop perch during his mate's incubation, and later helping her with domestic chores, providing food and tending their young.

Many birds are monogamous and mate for life—Canada geese, starlings and mute swans, for instance. The depth of devotion the latter feels for his mate became painfully clear several years ago near the millpond in Riverdale. A pair of these elegant Old World aquatic birds enjoyed a pleasant afternoon swim in the pond one fine day, their beautiful S-curved necks portraying their elegance and grace. After their dip, they took flight above the water toward Essex Bay. Tragically, the female flew into a wire, suffered a broken wing, and was later destroyed. Her grieving mate refused to leave the area where the incident occurred. For six months he mourned his loss, remaining near the millpond where they spent their last afternoon together. Then one day—who knows what was in his aching heart?—he joined a passing flock and flew away, hopefully, regaining strength to overcome the sadness of having lost his lady-love.

During the swan's period of grief, neighbors around the millpond became aware of the tragedy and reported it to authorities. The response from the Audubon Society was immediate. Today large orange beach-balls hang from electric wires near the Riverdale pond and around other areas where the swans are known to visit—a cautionary measure to lead them out of harm's way.

The lane past the tabbies' house soon led us to a downhill slope into the reservation, along a trail made difficult by ruts and erosion from the latest rains. Run-off water flowed freely along its path. Tangled, gray, barren branches and twigs of shad, sumac and wild cherry bordered the spillway, lending an air of bleakness and desolation. The dismal mood seemed to permeate the entire park this raw April morning. In their dormant, wintry condition, the low-lying shrubs—mostly poison ivy, catbrier and bayberry—were leafless and spindly, and looked like a tangled mass of gray-white hair. And this graying head was balding a bit, its bushy, unkempt crown laid bare in spots by large, flat rocks across the upland terrain.

"Ralph Waldo Emerson wrote poetry from one of those rocks," Ted remarked, gazing across the shrubby landscape toward the jagged shore, today being sprayed by the crashing surf. How enriching, I thought, to walk on soil that fertilized the creative minds of literary giants like Emerson, many of whom waxed eloquently from spots such as this along the North Shore—among them T.S. Eliot, Rudyard Kipling, John Greenleaf Whittier, Henry David Thoreau, Henry Wadsworth Longfellow, and William Rose Benet (buried a short distance away).

On our way to the overlook, we studied the trees and shrubs along the path—the light bark of an aspen grove, protected from the northwest winds by a pile of discarded grout; red cedars and junipers (not so lucky) tinged orange from salt and windburn and bent inward by powerful gale-force ocean storms; sea roses, viburnum and budding pussy willows whose silky white catskins would soon bring pleasure to many walking these wooded trails. On the chilling, wind-swept summit overlooking the sea, we strained our eyes to follow the thin, bluish-gray shoreline creeping up to Maine. In the distance, the hump of Mt. Agamenticus rose out of the sea, at times disappearing into the morning haze and re-appearing when it cleared.

"Halibut Point is made up of sheets of granite which step down from a bluff to tidal pools below," explained Ted as our eyes searched the land and seascape. "Rockport granite is the hardest in the world," he noted, "It was used to build Boston's drydocks, the largest in America, because of its strength and durability, and has been used to pave cities in many foreign countries."

Then, as we trod along a winding road around Babson Farm Quarry, he pointed out several new points of interest we had not seen on last summer's walk: wide, flat rocks, imprinted with highly polished glacial striations, a poled birdhouse intended to draw nesting bluebirds, and in a large, open field, several granite bollards—more remnants of the active quarrystone business. These large granite posts were cut by hand and set in the ground or placed along piers to secure ships to docks and wharfs. Most of the ships that tied their lines to these rock-solid bollards carried other products of Cape Ann's granite industry on their decks.

Also prominently displayed in the clearing was a lone granite statue, carved during a summertime "Art in the Park" exhibition several years earlier. Titled simply "Old Man Carrying a Satchel" by its sculptor, Ron Rudniki of New Bedford, others attach more significance to this stone-faced recluse. The staff at the park refer to him as "Sir Halibut." But most visitors, including our leader, see him as an ancient Viking.

"I call him the Spirit of Halibut Point," joked Ted, referring, of course, to the Spirit of 1776, the famous artistic rendering of New England patriots marching to freedom during the American Revolution.

PARK HEADQUARTERS

A short distance seaward from the stoic old man of stone, the road joined the main drive to the park's headquarters, formerly a military observation post. Built in 1942 by the U. S. Army Corps of Engineers to defend Boston, it was one of 20 such stations designed to look like modest New England summer cottages. Another dozen were constructed with steel or concrete observation towers, also disguised in various ways to conceal their military purpose. Here at Halibut Point, the station's tower was mounted by a small steeple, intending to give it the appearance of a church from a distant submarine periscope. Further down the coast, another tower sprouted a make-believe windmill. Occupying these attractive "seaside vacation cottages" were 20 well-trained soldiers, wartime guests of their uncle—Sam, that is. Others bivouacked in tents nearby.

These camouflaged stations dotted the Massachusetts coastline from Plymouth Bay to Portsmouth, New Hampshire, a distance of 60 miles. They were actually fire control towers, not Coast Guard stations; there were no guns here. The slits in the observation pits allowed sentries to coordinate charts with military coastal defenses and line up targets at sea if necessary. In such an event, this defense would have come from Battery Murphy at Nahant (Masssachusetts), Odiorne Point Station at Rye (New Hampshire) and the huge cannons manned by the Portsmouth Naval Station. Fortunately, America's mainland remained secure; nary a gun was fired—except for test purposes.

"The Silva house will be used as a major education facility when the park takes it over," Ted informed us, as we approached the small compound. In the meantime, the old furnace room on the floor of the "cottage" was being converted into The Walter E. Johnson Exhibit Room.

Mr. Johnson, then 90-years old, was the park's self-taught granite historian. He didn't work in the quarries, but attended the laborers and stonecutters as a "tool boy," carrying tools from blacksmiths' shops when they were needed at the sites. His father was a foreman in one of the quarries. It was during America's Bicentennial Celebration (in 1976) that his interest in Cape Ann's quarry industry piqued when he was asked to speak on the subject for the first time. People became so fascinated by his lectures that they pressed him for further information which he provided after thoroughly researching historical records. It wasn't long before he became an expert on Cape Ann granite and everything involved in its development into world trade. In 1981 the state purchased Halibut Point (in time, acquiring Babson Farm Quarry) and the learned Mr. Johnson became the park's resident granite historian. A program soon followed, in which he gave lectures, presented guided tours, and narrated a video on the subject.

A dedication ceremony was held two weeks after our visit which opened the Johnson Exhibit and acknowledged the contribution he made to preserving the heritage of Cape Ann granite. Among interesting artifacts on display is a Union Badge worn by Mrs. Silva's father, Carlo Balestraci, during military service in the Civil War. Included also are blacksmith tools from the antique collection of Ray Parsons, owner of Parson's Iron Works—among them forging and hammer tongs, swages (a device for shaping metal), and a top fuller (a hammer used for making grooves and spreading iron). Also exhibited are stone cutters, a large tin dinner pail, and oxen shoes (worn by those strong, over-burdened beasts before the advent of the steam locomotive).

Others who have played important roles at Halibut Point are Russell "Ozzie" Norris and George Anderson. At the base of a small, budding osier dogwood, a bronze plaque describes Norris as having been a "Bird lover, Friend of Nature, and Member of the Halibut Point Association." A short distance away, an apple tree commemorates George Anderson, a park tour guide who devoted many years of service to the Essex County Greenbelt Association. Spring visitors to all three memorials would soon enjoy the beauty and fragrance of lilacs and roses which, along with Japanese yews and a golden euonymus, lend picturesque charm to this historic "cottage by the sea."

4. HALIBUT POINT

1. Cape Ann Tool Company
2. The Atlantic Path
3. Halibut Point Overlook
4. Babson Quarry
5. Main Entrance to Park
P Park at Tool Company or
  Halibut Point Parking Lot

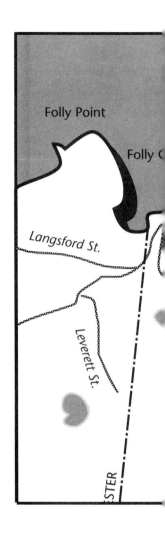

KEY	
ⅲⅲⅲⅲⅲ	Trail
-- -- ⋅	Sub Trail
‒‒‒‒	Street or Highway
∙ ∙ ∙	Railroad Tracks
▦	Ocean
▧	Pond or Lake
▨	Swamp

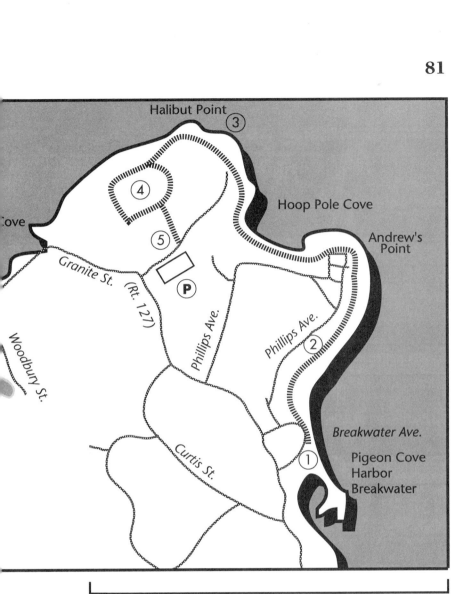

Halibut Point ③

Hoop Pole Cove

Andrew's Point

④

⑤

.ove

Granite St. (Rt. 127)

Ⓟ

Phillips Ave.

Phillips Ave.

②

Woodbury St.

Breakwater Ave.

Curtis St.

①

Pigeon Cove Harbor Breakwater

1 Mile

Long Beach and Environs

On a warm, summer morning our weekly exploration with Ted covered a variety of terrain, starting with a gingerly caper atop a small seaside mountain of cobbles, then a brisk stroll along two white sandy beaches. Next we stretched our legs on a rugged upland climb which descended into a valley of soggy, brackish wetlands.

The beaches we visited were Cape Hedge and Long (in Rockport) and Good Harbor (in Gloucester). The woodlands climb took us through the old Joppa section of Gloucester then across a two-acre tract abutting Thatcher Road and the saltmarsh behind Long Beach which, Ted happily informed us, had recently been donated to the town of Rockport for conservation land. Conservation land—*especially Rockport conservation land*—always makes Ted happy.

We began our walk at Cape Hedge Beach. There are two ways to approach this lovely sandy shoreline. Coming from Rockport, one is at the end of South Street which forks to the left from Thatcher Road at Turk's Head Inn, a modern version of an earlier seaside hotel that once occupied this spot. Turk's Head is another interesting name with a colorful past, taking us back to colonial folk hero Captain John Smith, who is said to have slain three turks while in the service of the Emperor of Austria. The name originally was given to the three islands off Rockport's coast—Thachers, Milk and Straitsmouth—which Captain Smith called the Three Turks' Heads when he sailed into Cape Ann (which he named Tragabigzanda in honor of a Turkish lady). The Cape, the islands, and the town itself all took on more permanent identities later.

Another approach to Cape Hedge Beach is via the parking area at the end of Seaview Street, three streets south of the inn off Thatcher Road. Both areas require a Rockport resident parking sticker in the summer. For those not having one, early birds will find parking along surrounding streets (except where posted), as well as further south at Good Harbor Beach (for a fee).

At Cape Hedge Beach we climbed the wooden walkway up onto a flattened path atop a huge mound of cobblestones (some up to 12 inches in diameter) which serves as a breakwater between the ocean and the parking area. Cobbles from this shoreline, washed and smoothed by centuries of crashing waves from the Atlantic Ocean, in earlier times were placed aboard whaling ships out of Nantucket for ballast, and later used in paving streets.

As we made our way along the ridge of loose stones, Ted pointed out the brackish wetlands on our right beyond the parking lot; to our left, softly undulating waves rolled onto the white sandy shore of Cape Hedge Beach. It was a day bright with sunshine, clear and still.

After a walk of about 100 feet, the pebbly mound descended to sea level, forming an embankment to the edge of Saratoga Creek, a small tidal inlet separating Cape Hedge and Long beaches. A wooden footbridge took us across. We walked briskly along Long Beach, which followed the curve of the sea. As we walked, Ted related some interesting bits of information about the long-time summer resort.

The number of modest oceanfront summer cottages lining the mile-long boardwalk above the seawall totals 150. Many of these vacation homes have been in "old-line" New England families for generations, providing summertime pleasure to active children, busy parents and loving grandparents.

Like many other communities along the Massachusetts shoreline, the land fronting Long Beach is owned by the town—in this case, Rockport—and leased to homeowners on a renewal basis. The lease carries with it a number of building codes and land-use restrictions; it also carries an assessment of property taxes.

The cottages are attractive and tidy, all having wide, front porches facing the sea. The plots of land on which they stand average 60 feet wide and about 80 deep. While most are typical New England "shoreline shingles," some are painted various colors, brightening the crescent-shaped beachfront. Names such as "Sandpiper," "Twin Lights" (an obvious reference to two blinking lighthouses on nearby Thachers Island) "Breakers," and "Driftwood Cottage" lend personality to these oceanside hideaways. Pretty flowers heighten the color scheme along the shore from the bridge at Sarasota Creek to the Gloucester line—red geraniums, white shasta daisies, golden marigolds, green hostas, and pink sea roses were in bloom the day we passed by.

No two homes are exactly alike: architectural designs may appear similar, especially those built for families on adjoining properties, but every house has its own unique character. One in particular is interesting. Painted battleship gray, its rounded front is boat-shaped; nautical decorations—anchors, buoys, a ship's lantern—complete the maritime theme. Because of such creative influences, it's pleasant to walk the length of the boardwalk viewing each one. Carefully tended lawns and flowers evidence their owners' joy at living here. But these manicured lawns may soon become a victim of today's ecological concerns.

Because of the constant threat of erosion along the shoreline, Rockport enforces a state ordinance restricting new lawns on beachfront property. Native Cape Ann grasses—salt, meadow, spike, switch, thatch (cord) and wooly sedge (wool grass)—hold their various types of sandy and rocky soil in place naturally. Left undisturbed, these grasses provide far more protection from erosion along the shoreline than their domestic cousins. Because the latter are grown in imported, aerated soil, possess shorter, weaker root systems, and are kept mowed to one or two inches, they offer little or no protection against erosion. When Rockport was settled, Thacher Island boasted 80 acres. Today only 52 acres remain— even this rock-solid barrier is no match for the ocean's fury during hurricanes and nor'easters which batter Cape Ann's coastline with frequency.

The cottages along Long Beach were ravaged by gale-force winds and 30-foot waves during the No Name Storm. All those lining the beach sustained damage, some more than others, depending on the age and condition of the structure. Most have now been repaired or rebuilt.

Located midpoint along the boardwalk is the former Chicataubut Inn, a venerable old New England hotel recently converted to condos. Chicataubut is an Indian word meaning *warm* or *happy home*, and the name could not have been more appropriate for the charming seaside inn which welcomed guests to Cape Ann for more than 80 years.

Leaving the shoreline, we walked south along Rockport Road to Briar Neck, a rocky bluff separating Long Beach and Good Harbor Beach. Taking a left onto Palfrey Road, we came to Salt Island Road, its numerous dips and twists meandering through an attractive community of pretty oceanview homes and gardens. The number and variety of pine trees along the route are noticeable—hemlock, pitch pine, red cedars and juniper. The intersection at Cliff Road and Salt Island Road is a good point from which to view tiny Salt Island, which is within walking distance from shore at low tide. This small island of rock is a lovely picnic spot, but timing the tides is important.

From the top of a steep hill just above the Good Harbor Inn, we looked down on dunes, ocean, beach, and marshes. At the bottom, a path alongside the inn led to the beach, crowded this morning with swimmers enjoying the summer surf. In the distance, the Bass Rocks community reached high into the wooded uplands where several shingled cottages peeked through the trees. The rugged coastline remained in view until a rocky promontory blocked its winding course to Brace Cove and Eastern Point.

We walked the length of Good Harbor Beach—originally named No Good Harbor by early fisherman who found it troublesome to navigate. Near its southern tip, we were treated to the artistry of master sandcastle builder, Justin Gordon, in rehearsal for the annual Sandcastle Day competition held in late August at nearby Crane's Beach. Located in Ipswich, this four-mile barrier beach, a long finger of sandy land, beach, dunes and salt marsh, is one of the most beautiful spots on the Atlantic Coast. Under the protection of the Trustees of Reservations, it has retained its natural shoreline environment—no hot dog stands here; even the necessary houses are hidden away in the woods, far from the view of bathers.

Widely known as the "fairytale castle builder," Gordon is considered a professional sandcastler and snow sculptor, competing successfully in many such events throughout the United States and Canada. His award-winning works are the delight of young and old. Like everyone else along the beachfront that day, we stopped to watch his amazing talent with sand as he put the finishing touches on an elaborate architectural wonder of towers, turrets, winding stairs, and drawbridge.

As he dribbled watery mud onto a cone-shaped tree to form the landscaping, someone asked, "Do you have a building permit for a structure that large?"

A grandmotherly-type in a floral bathing suit beamed happily, "Last year, he was here on my birthday and built a beautiful castle. I considered it a special birthday present to me."

Leaving others to enjoy his masterpiece before the rhythms of the planet washed it away, we pressed on across the dunes to the parking lot. We followed Ted across busy Thatcher Road, carefully walking the roadside to Witham Street which took us into the old Joppa section of Gloucester. After about a half-mile, Ted turned right between a clearing of white birch trees and a gray shingled bungalow. This is an unpaved county way leading past a larger, white frame house and into the upper woodlands behind Cape Pond. A number of beehives lined an old fieldstone fence in an overgrown meadow to our right; on our left, the rock-strewn hillside reached high into the trees.

Rich, green bracken fern lined the dirt roadway beneath large white pines and hemlocks, offering a cool respite after our seaside walk in the blazing sun. Along the trail, Ted pointed out several wildflowers to first-time visitors: Indian cucumber, false solomon seal, a hobble bush and clintonia—a delicate bell-like yellow flower.

A short distance into the woods, he pointed to a connecting trail to the left. "That's the Old Rockport Road coming in from South Woods," he said. A little further, we approached a fork in the trail. "Left goes to Cape Pond, right comes out behind the old furniture factory on Thatcher

Road." We turned right, continuing along the county road in an easterly direction, soon emerging behind the furniture plant, which is now a machine shop.

Crossing Thatcher Road, we followed Ted through Rockport's newly-acquired conservation land which opened onto an expansive bog—about 150 acres—of sedges, grasses and other water-loving plants fed by the brackish waters of Saratoga Creek. As we skirted the edge, we kept our eyes open for raccoons and foxes known to hunt marshes for muskrats that rely on grasses for food and their mound-like houses. We didn't see any as we pressed forward amid shrieks and giggles (and some grumbling) when feet sunk deep into mucky spots—a reason, I might add, for comfortable, old footwear on these outings. Emerging onto a private road behind the crescent of Long Beach cottages, we retraced our steps back to the footbridge and the parking lot at Cape Hedge Beach.

5. LONG BEACH
& ENVIRONS

1. Salt Marsh
2. Summer Cottages
3. Brair Neck
4. Old County Road

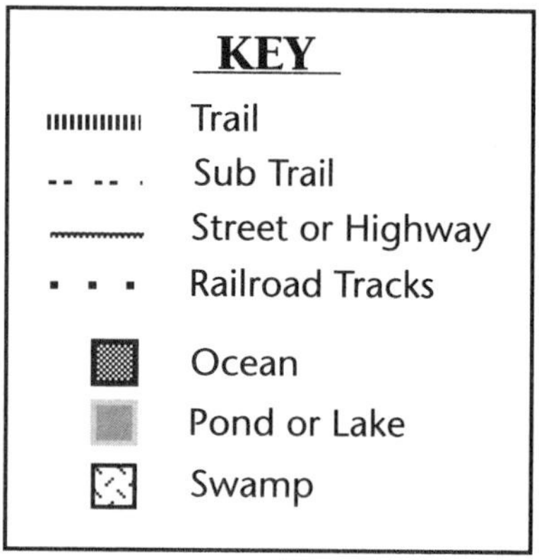

Main St.

Eastern Ave.

_W/_

Thatcher

	KEY
ꟷꟷꟷ	Trail
-- -- .	Sub Trail
‐‐‐‐	Street or Highway
▪ ▪ ▪	Railroad Tracks
▓	Ocean
▓	Pond or Lake
⊠	Swamp

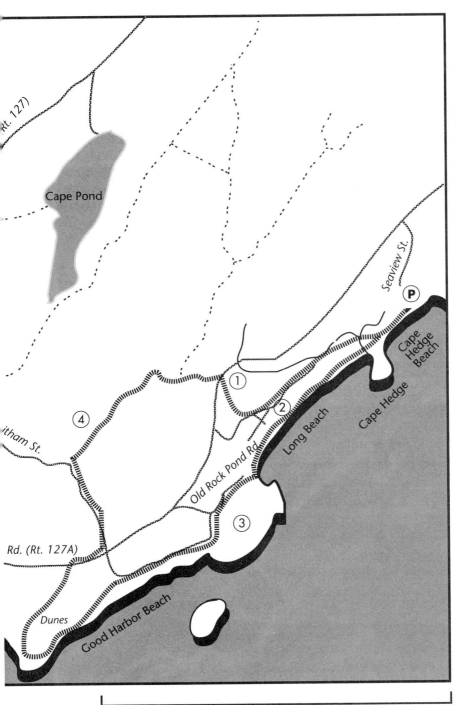

Cape Pond

Seaview St.

P

Cape Hedge Beach

Cape Hedge

Long Beach

①

②

③

④

Old Rock Pond Rd.

itham St.

Rd. (Rt. 127A)

Dunes

Good Harbor Beach

Rt. 127)

1 Mile

STONEY COVE • PRESSON RESERVATION

Stoney Cove is a small inlet/marsh to the right of Route 128 north, just before the Andrew Piatt Bridge in Gloucester. The 53-acre reservation, consisting of Hodgdon Hill, Presson's saltfarm and Susan's Point, follows the bend of Little River which joins the Annisquam on its run to the sea from inland Gloucester. The cove's colonial history (dating back to 1694) and ecosystem (forest, pasture, marshes, channel and clam flats) combine to make it one the most valued properties protected by the Essex County Greenbelt Association.

Historically, Stoney Cove had its beginning on a major water traffic route which saw wood, lumber and salt hay floated and poled down the Annisquam River to a thriving market in Boston. In the 1800s, barges passed by at high tide loaded with granite from quarries off Concord Street headed for market, both foreign and domestic. Ecologically, Stoney Cove, adjoined by Susan's Point, is an ideal spot to study the successional stages of life in a forest. Marshland is slowly filling in and turning to upland. A young pine grove is a quarter of the way through its maturation process (which takes 100 years). Old pastures, having given way to ground and red juniper and gray beech in the open sunlight, are now seeing these shade-intolerant trees overcome by hickory, oak and maple.

We explored the Stoney Cove Reservation in early August. To reach it from Whistlestop Mall, we drove to Gloucester and took Route 128 south to Concord Street (Exit 13). Since we were a sizable group, we parked our cars at the roadside pull-off at the bottom of the exit ramp. From there we walked west on Concord, past the Wingaersheek Motel (on the right) and entered the woods behind the West Gloucester fire station next to the Amvet Post. However, this "back-door approach" to the cove was necessitated by the size of our auto caravan and is only recommended for large groups. Limited parking is available at the stone pier on the reservation site. To reach the pier, take Route 128 north and look for the break in the steel barrier at the Greenbelt sign, located three-tenths of a mile past the Concord Street exit. The Stoney Cove trail is along the margin of the saltmarsh to the right of the pier.

In back of the fire station, Ted led us onto the top of a long flat rock which descended into an open forest of towering white pines. The floor was covered with knee-high sassafras and sarsaparilla saplings, which we plowed through in the direction of the river.

Among the wildflowers we passed was an unusual plant most of us had never seen before—an Indian pipe, also called the corpse-plant. A member of the wintergreen family, the plant is swollen at the base, where it attaches itself to its host plant. It has a white scale-like stem and a single pipe-shaped flower. After Ted pointed out the first one, we looked around and found several more along the pathway.

Passing through the pine grove, we came to a section of hardwoods which continued to a fresh-water marsh on our left. Since Ted had not been along these trails for a year or so, the underbrush had grown up considerably, which kept him busy with his clippers.

"Dead-falls and vines take over awfully fast," he said as we walked under a wide-leaf butternut entangled by a wild grapevine.

The path took us along the southeastern edge of the Presson farm, waist-high with lush-green cinnamon fern. Mosquitoes accompanied us along the route. Climbing over a stone wall, we emerged into a clearing with the saltmarsh in the distance to our right.

"Why don't we do some cross-country?" Ted asked, leaving the path and heading through the trees toward Susan's Point.

Following closely behind, we struck out across the woods—over rocks and fallen trees, through ferns and under pine branches, over another stone wall and through briers and poison ivy. As we pushed aside low-hanging branches, Ted joked, "Think positive, they'll brush the mosquitoes off."

Climbing over another stone wall, we reached a crescent of saltmarsh along the edge of the Presson farmland and Susan's Point. Since there had been no appreciable rain during the previous week, the marshes were relatively dry. Sea lavender, also called marsh-rosemary, and seaside goldenrod added color and interest to the grassy plain.

On the western edge of the point, Ted turned back into the woods, blazing another cross-country trail, which brought us to the shoreline of Little River. The view at the water's edge was typical of a summer weekend. Sailboats and other small pleasure craft filled the waterway. To the south, distant houses dotted Gloucester's tiered hillside. Ted pointed out several landmarks: Camp Annisquam across the channel, the marina at Rust Island, and Nichol's Candy House beyond the granite pier.

We walked the rocky shore, enjoying the view. Then it was time to press on.

"Back into the woods and the mosquitoes," moaned the young grandson of a summer resident from New York.

"You don't want them to die of starvation, do you?" chided Ted.

The footpath continued to follow the curve of Little River around the point, past lichen-covered erratics and through a clearing. Straight ahead, across the highway, were the auto dealerships on Route 128. As we passed a huge red oak, Ted drew our attention to its pointed leaves. Other trees were tupelo, red maple and white pine.

Then we crossed a larger marsh. This time Ted cautioned us to "watch the sink holes." Along the way, he stopped and picked up the dry shell of a large horseshoe crab, which he described as an "ancient living fossil. It's been around for a long time," he said. "During summer migration, the female comes up with a long trail of males behind her."

He pointed out its light-sensitive eyes at the beginning of its skull, then went on to explain the importance of this crustacean to medical research. "The blood of these crabs is blue and copper-based. Among its applications is its use to test for Hansen's disease (leprosy). That's why we've got to be careful about preserving areas such as these."

Another natural resource in these marshes is glasswort, a woody, jointed herb of the goosefoot family, used in pickling and in making silica crystals for scouring devices. As we walked along the southwest arm of Little River, Ted pointed to evidence of other wildlife among the marshes: a pitted embankment inhabited by periwinkles, ridge mussels and crabs. But not all of nature's creatures were grounded in muck and mire. A small band of hog sphinx moths followed us along the forest edges, river margins and across the marshes. Marshes like these are their natural habitat throughout the eastern half of the United States. Their powerful wings, colorfully patterned in brown and orange, beat so rapidly that some resemble humming birds or large bees.

The walk across this section of marshland brought us to Stoney Cove, an upland next to Route 128 south of the granite pier. From the parking area at the pier, we turned left onto a narrow, rocky trail leading into the woods behind the Greenbelt sign. The path took us to a small open park overlooking Little River and the expanse of marshes on both sides of the highway. In the quiet of tall, white pines, a log seat invites rest and contemplation, a memorial to Bruce Anderson 1956-1977. Stoney Cove is one of several parcels of land donated to the Essex County Greenbelt Association by the young man's parents who summered on Cape Ann for many years.

From the park, we followed an upper path behind homes lining Concord Street, which ultimately led to the fire station and our starting point.

6. STONEY COVE
PRESSON RESERVATION

1. Nichols Candy House
2. Bruce Anderson Memorial Park
3. East Gloucester Fire Station

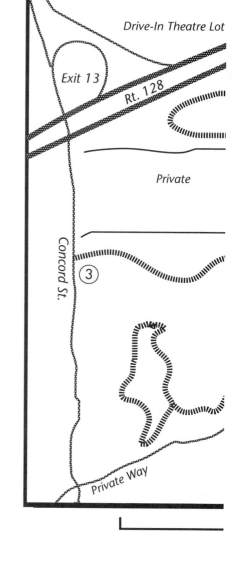

KEY

‖‖‖‖‖‖‖	Trail
-- -- -	Sub Trail
⌐⌐⌐⌐	Street or Highway
• • •	Railroad Tracks
▓	Ocean
▓	Pond or Lake
◪	Swamp

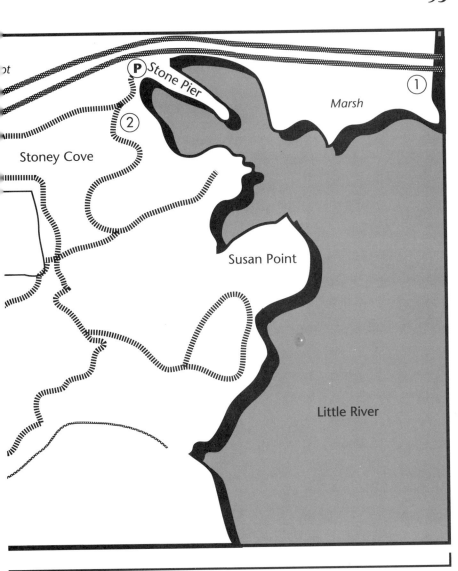

ot

P Stone Pier

①

Marsh

②

Stoney Cove

Susan Point

Little River

1/2 Mile

Red Rocks

Route 128, the "gateway to Cape Ann," slices through an extensive area of granite ledge outcrop one-half mile south of Route 133 in West Gloucester. East of the highway, Mount Ann rises 270 feet above sea level. On the west side, Red Rocks, a popular rock-climbing spot, is slightly less at 240 feet. Ted's fondest hope is to one day see a pedestrian footbridge spanning the highway to connect these two scenic overlooks, which are Gloucester's highest points.

We explored Red Rocks on a warm summer day in late August, leaving Mount Ann for another time. From Whistlestop Mall, we drove south on Route 127, then took Route 128 to Route 133 (Exit 14). Several footpaths adjacent to the North Shore Mini Storage warehouses, located across from the exit ramp, lead to the site. Hikers are welcome to use these paths and are asked to respect the privacy of warehouse tenants by avoiding the storage areas. The main trail-head to Red Rocks is at Forest Lane, exactly nine-tenths of a mile west of the Route 133 exit ramp, which was our point of entry. This road is owned by the City of Gloucester, which imposes restrictions on its use because of its access to a watershed and dam at Haskell Pond, a main water source.

Turning left onto Forest Lane, we passed Skater's Pond (formerly Tysver's Pond), a public recreation area used mostly during the winter for skating. The lane is paved for a short distance. On the other side of a barrier, it becomes a dirt service road into the forested upland. Limited parking is available along the paved roadside.

Our first point of interest on this morning's walk was an abandoned pump house and meadow. Forest Lane bears to the left of the pump house and up an incline to the dam at Haskell Pond. The pond can be seen along a strip of Route 128 south and is especially pretty in the fall. Today its shoreline was teeming with water beetles, known locally as "stink bugs" and "whirl-a-gig bugs."

We followed the service road along the curves of the shoreline. A short distance beyond the dam, we turned onto a wide footpath to begin the climb up the hilly terrain. Morning sunlight filtered through the peace and quiet of towering hemlock and witch hazel. The trail split shortly, the right continuing on to Route 128, the left winding slightly northeast toward Red Rocks. The path, brown with leaves and pine needles, cut through patches of birch, mountain laurel and lichen-covered rocky humps, some sprouting small pitch pine, others bracken fern. It then led us through a dark, piney dell of waist-high cinnamon fern.

"Watch the footing," Ted called after he slid from a slippery rock hidden in the dense greenery.

Climbing over a large fallen oak, he blazed a trail up a steep hillside. Stepping sideways, we inched up after him, plowing through low blueberry bushes, finally emerging onto several medium-sized erratics left by the glacier.

"Apparently, it didn't have room for them in my garden," he joked, referring to the laborious task Cape Anners experience in removing rocks from their property.

Today, a young film producer named Chris Molinski joined us to videotape the walk for a travelogue on "Hidden Treasures of Cape Ann." With Chris was his mother and brother, Adam. It was obvious the family enjoyed their work; they handled their equipment with care and efficiency, while capturing dramatic scenes of woodland beauty.

The trail continued into the uplands, past a number of large granite outcroppings. As their size and number increased, Ted explored the area, seeking a suitable way around them. Seeing a deep cleft between two ledges, he stopped.

"It'll be difficult to climb down one side and up the other," he said. "They're pretty steep."

Turning, he set upon another undefined path, skirting a 15-foot drop into a valley. As I hurried to keep up, my foot sank into a deep hole. Fortunately, it was dry. Ted's sense of direction, always on target, brought us onto the main trail to Red Rocks.

"This must be beautiful in the winter," he remarked, noting the cathedral of hemlocks, dramatic rock formations and colonies of polypody fern. "I'll make a winter trail through here." Taking a red ribbon from his pocket, he fastened it to a nearby tree. "That will be my next project."

We approached Red Rocks from the north-northwest, along a cool, damp trail that dipped and curved around its base. We followed Ted to the right where the path joined another coming in from the Forest Lane service road. The climb to the top was not difficult; the rocks were smooth and the soil, what little there was, sandy and pine-covered. Stretching and, at times jumping, from one ledge to another, we were able to reach the top with minimal effort. Brier patches, low-bush blueberries, sweetfern and pitch pine grew out of crevices in cliffs and on top of the granite outcrops. Our curiosity was piqued by shallow, saucer-size holes on the top ledges, which Ted explained was a natural phenomenon, caused by centuries of erosion.

The unobstructed views of Cape Ann from the summit are spectacular. Looking north over the Essex marshes and hills, we gazed down upon Hog Island, the Essex River, and Wingaersheek and Crane's beaches. Lanesville, Bayview and Annisquam lay to the east. Other distant scenes included the water towers at Pigeon Hill and Rockport, Blackburn Circle, Good Harbor Beach, West Gloucester and Magnolia. And across the snake-like ravine that is Route 128, Mount Ann rises from the south. Because of heavy growth around this overlook, Red Rocks offers better views.

Unfortunately, Mount Ann is not accessible to the public at this time (which might be a reason for the overgrowth). When it was purchased by the Trustees of Reservations and made into an 87-acre park, the original roadway into the area was across from Red Rocks' 27-acre site, directly off Route 128. For safety reasons, this entrance was closed several years ago, blocking Mount Ann's only public access. Since the main purpose of this conservation trust is to make land available for everyone's enjoyment, access is a problem that begs resolution. Ted's idea of a pedestrian walkway across the highway to connect these important overlooks has merit and, hopefully, one day will come to pass.

Although our walks each week take us to many spots of woodland and ocean beauty, we do not often get an opportunity to view the entire sweep of Cape Ann from such a high elevation so we were in no hurry to leave. With the ocean on three sides, we walked from rock to rock, looking far into the distance at sites and landmarks familiar to some, unknown to others, but enjoyed by all. I was glad Chris Molinski was along to capture on film the scenes we saw that golden summer morning.

On our return trip, Ted detoured from the trail for a quick excursion to the main scaling area of Red Rocks. Its impressive stone face, at a 90-degree angle to the ground and about 45 feet high, attracts climbers from all over New England. Because of its distinct cracks, they enjoy a long, adventuresome climb, right up to the top. We stood at the base and looked up at the shear cliff reaching skyward. Quartz in the granite glistened in the sunlight.

Returning to the path, we continued in a northwesterly direction to the gas-line right-of-way, a wide rocky roadway running from the North Shore Mini-Storage property through to Forest Lane. Here we turned left, circling a pretty swamp of burr-reeds, water-plantains and arrowheads. A short distance up the road, Ted pointed out a patch of unusual looking mushrooms, burnt-orange with patterns resembling tree rings.

On higher ground, we stopped to pick large, juicy blackberries which were abundant along the route. Then it was downhill to the coolness of towering hemlocks lining Forest Lane, where a right turn brought us back to the barrier and our cars.

7. Red rocks

1. North Shore Mini Warehouses
2. Climb Area
3. Red Rocks Overlook

KEY

ⅢⅢⅢⅢ	Trail
-- -- -	Sub Trail
———	Street or Highway
• • •	Railroad Tracks
▨	Ocean
▩	Pond or Lake
▨	Swamp

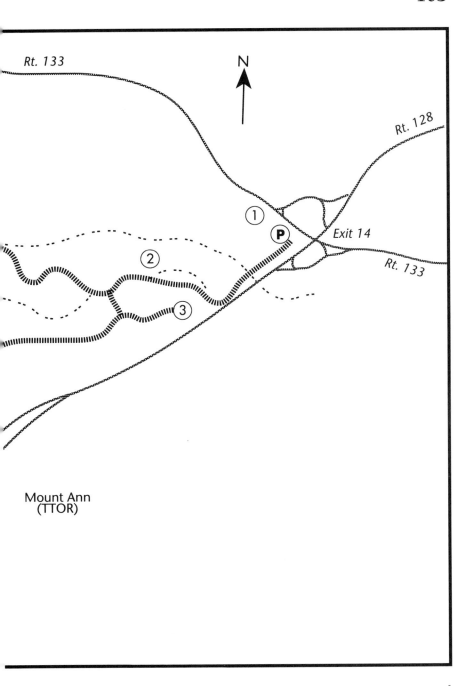

Rt. 133

N

Rt. 128

① ② ③ **P**

Exit 14

Rt. 133

Mount Ann
(TTOR)

1 Mile

Eastern Point

We arrived at our rendezvous spot on a cool sunny morning in mid-September to learn that Ted would not be with us. He was attending a political breakfast and had asked a woman in the group, a long-time walking enthusiast, to lead the walk in his absence. A brief discussion led to the decision to walk the shoreline of East Gloucester which offered a collage of historic sites, scenic views and interesting trails: Niles Beach overlooking Gloucester Harbor; Eastern Point's beautiful mansions; the Coast Guard Lighthouse and Dog Bar Breakwater; Mother Ann, a natural rock formation resembling a reclining woman; and Brace Cove, a romantic sea inlet noted for its encircling arms (of land). This area of Cape Ann, like many others along its rocky coastline, captures the rich flavor of New England's intriguing past.

Rocky Neck • Niles Beach

From Rockport, we took Route 127 south to the 128 interchange in Gloucester. Here we bore left onto Route 128 which ended at the next traffic light (Exit 9). Continuing straight onto East Main Street, we followed the shoreline of the inner harbor to Eastern Point Road, passing Knudson Square on our left and the Rocky Neck Art Colony on our right. Looking across Wonson Cove, it's possible to snatch glimpses of the turrets topping Hammond Castle beyond Mussel Point toward Magnolia. Rounding a sharp curve onto Eastern Point Boulevard, we pulled into a parking spot at Niles Beach where the Boston skyline could be seen on the distant horizon—38 miles south by car. Rockport, incidentally, juts 12 miles further into the Atlantic than the city of Boston.

Our walk began at the entrance gates of the exclusive Eastern Point community in Gloucester. Foot and motor traffic are permitted along this private shoreline drive to allow access to the Dog Bar Breakwater at the end of the point, a popular fishing spot.

Tourist-like, we admired the elegant homes along the scenic drive, many of which bore names such as "Sunset Rock," "Overlook," "Belmar,"

"Three Waters," "Stoneacre" and "Beauport." A short distance inside the gates is the former residence of the late Clarence Birdseye, the entrepreneurial giant responsible for many of the fresh frozen foods enjoyed on dinner tables throughout America today. The red-brick, white-columned Georgian estate is no longer in the Birdseye family, but remains privately owned. However, further along the drive, secluded behind a high wall, the home of another distinguished early resident takes on quite a different stature.

BEAUPORT MUSEUM

Beauport (the Sleeper-McCann House) on Gloucester Harbor, is considered one of the most fascinating houses in America by the late Samuel Chamberlain, a pre-eminent photographer of beautiful homes. Deeded to the Society for the Preservation of New England Antiquities as a museum, it started out in 1907 as a modest three-room Queen Ann cottage overlooking the harbor. By 1934, it had evolved into a magical maze of 40 enchanting rooms spanning many phases of American life, from the austere kitchen of a pioneer cabin to the opulence of a Georgian Chippendale drawing room. After a visit, one overwhelmed interior designer described it as an "architectural domino game." In his book *Cape Ann: Cape America*, author Herbert A. Kenney, literary editor of the Boston Globe, has choicer words: "an eclectic pudding of a piece."

Furnishings in the 40-room labyrinth range from the simple to the extravagant: iron kettles used by the Pilgrims to chairs of the type of Jerome Bonaparte, from a tripod candlestand for reading the Scripture to Lord Byron's sleigh bed from Newstead Abbey, from bellows and buckets and bowls to Waterford chandeliers, Jacobean cabinets, and Chinese wallpaper.

This extraordinary house with its elaborately furnished rooms offers a rare glimpse into the artistic mind and opulent lifestyle of its famous owner, Henry Sleeper. A bachelor, Sleeper lived at Beauport—French for *pretty harbor*—with his widowed mother until his death in 1934. It makes one wonder if, having read Oliver Wendell Holmes' *Chambered Nautilus*, he took literally the writer's eloquent words, "Build thee more stately mansions, O my soul."

Other homes along the shoreline are not as ostentatious, but almost all hide behind attractive fences. Some are low and unpretentious—neat, white pickets, ivy-covered fieldstones, rustic split-railing. Others are tall and impenetrable—high red brick, gray granite, black wrought iron, and weathered stockade. In some instances, huge boulders, dense rows of cedars and tall privet hedge serve to protect homeowners' privacy.

Landscape designers made practical use of the many rocks and boulders left in the wake of the glacier, using them as natural focal points for beautiful flower gardens. Azaleas, hostas, chrythanthumums, geraniums, impatiens, and petunias splashed a rainbow of colors amid the rocks the day we visited the area.

"There's the last rose of summer," remarked our guide-for-the day, pointing to an unusually large pink sea rose along a stockade fence.

Further down the road, we passed a swampy marsh of bullrushes and cattails, their sheaves and cylindrical heads forming a hedge in the shallow roadside waters. This land is the northern boundary of a marshy wildlife sanctuary maintained by the Massachusetts Audubon Society. It is here that the beautiful monarch butterflies spend a night during their migratory flight from Canada to Mexico, usually about the first of October.

The butterflies come by the thousands and nestle in the trees overnight, then leave early the following morning after being warmed by the sun. Their long flight inland takes them to a mountain valley in Mexico where they are joined by another migrating flock from Pacific Grove in the western part of the Monterey Penninsula. The California monarchs are denser in population and remain longer on the west coast before beginning their flight to Mexico. In fact, their stop-over, which lasts for a few days, allows the community of Monterey enough time to celebrate with a Butterfly Festival. Unfortunately, lumbermen in Mexico are cutting down the forests where these beautiful butterflies spend their winters. Whatever position one takes on environmental issues, there's merit in saving trees to preserve wildlife. In the case of the monarch butterfly, it is doomed to extinction if cutting continues.

The monarch is the most familiar of the species to inhabit our area. Its colors are orange-brown with black borders and veins, its spots mostly white. This day-flying insect is protected from birds by its bad-tasting body fluids.

When the butterflies arrive at Eastern Point, they blanket the trees with wings spread wide, creating a scene of unimaginable beauty in the sunlight. To view this local migratory extravaganza, it's necessary to rise at daybreak and take up a position near the lighthouse at the tip of the point, facing into the trees (behind the cattails) about 6:30 or 7 o'clock. It might take two or three days, or a week of waiting but it's worth it. I promised myself I'd be at the viewing stand early every fall morning during their migration period to witness their glorious departing flight.

Around the curve from the sanctuary, the road ends at the Coast Guard Lighthouse, where public parking is permitted for sightseeing and fishing during daylight hours.

COAST GUARD LIGHTHOUSE • DOG BAR BREAKWATER

We picked our way carefully over the rocks to the Dog Bar Breakwater which extends a half mile into the waters of Gloucester's outer harbor. The massive superstructure consists of two dry walls of heavy split stone mounted on an underwater substructure 31 feet wide. Its interior is filled with rubblestone. Heavy granite slabs cap the ten-foot-wide top course. Eleven years in the making—from 1894 to 1905— it has proven invaluable in protecting Gloucester's busy harbor during violent storms.

It was on the shores of Gloucester's inner harbor that the first schooner was built by shipwright Captain Andrew Robinson in 1713. As his sleek new vessel, masted and rigged for launching, slid smoothly into the water, a spectator exclaimed admiringly, "Oh, how she scoons." Robinson liked the term and decided to coin it for his new vessel. "A scooner let her be," he pronounced enthusiastically. In later years, an "h" was added to the spelling.

It was a special day in every way. The sun shone brightly on the glistening sea. Salt spray and the smell of seaweed tinged our nostrils, as plump gray and white seagulls circled overhead. Cormorants, too, joined the flight. These black shore birds are not as graceful as seagulls because of flight restrictions—a shorter wingspan and oil deficiency. While other species retain natural oils on their feathers, causing moisture runoff "like water off a duck's back," cormorants do not have this built-in water repellant. In order to prevent becoming waterlogged, they spread their wings out wide and limit their flights to shorter duration than other large birds. They can often be seen with wings fully extended drying themselves in the sun. But they are compensated by being powerful swimmers and possessing excellent underwater vision.

Sport fishing had been very good during the past several weeks along the New England Coast and in inland waters. A young Cape Anner hauled in a 52-pound striped bass from the Ipswich River the previous week. A few days later his brother thought he would try his luck and caught a 50-pounder in the same waters. Along the breakwater several men and women were tossing their lines into the gentle surf, also hoping to hook "the big one."

But there were other fish in the sea for a young lad named Quinton who came over this morning from Lawrence, about an hour's drive away. He was happy bringing in a few small ones.

"I catch quite a few flounder, skate, and blue fish," he told me as he baited his hook, adding, "When the blues are in, they scare the other fish away because they're so vicious. But I'm getting lots of crabs, too, which my family likes."

At the end of the breakwater was a small computerized station, doll-house in size. Like Coast Guard watches all along the Atlantic coast-line—whitewashed towers and houses with red shingled roofs—this little gem had its own character and personality. A tiny white steeple atop its miniature gabled roof housed a rotating beacon to caution sailors out of harm's way. This small, quaint, structure is vital to maritime travelers who sail these treacherous waters during the fury of a blustery nor'easter, in the darkness of a moonless night, or through the silent gray lines of a morning fog.

As we walked back to the shore along the wide stone ramp, we saw further evidence of the strength of the infamous No Name Storm. Several huge slabs of granite used to line the breakwater walls, some weighing as much as 12 to 13 tons, had been tossed aside by the force of the turbulent sea. But the breakwater held during the height of that dis-aster and, hopefully, will continue to do so, having been designed to withstand the endless rhythm of the ocean's tides and the violence of its many storms. One proud Gloucester old-timer who walks Dog Bar often put it succinctly: "It was built to last forever."

It was in these waters during the years 1817, 1818, and 1819 that Gloucester Harbor laid claim to its own "Lock Ness monster." The sea serpent was seen numerous times by men and women along the shore, sailors from passing ships and navigational experts using spyglasses. Records show that its appearance in these waters went back as early as 1638 when it was spotted "coiled like a cable on a rock." Fearing the monster would attack if not killed instantly, Indians prevented colonists from shooting it.

As to sightings in the 1800s, one witness considered quite reliable was Reverend Cheever Felch, a passenger in a longboat from the *USS Independence*. He, along with a crew on a government ship surveying the harbor, saw the serpent at fairly close range. Reporting the incident to a Boston newspaper at the time, the pastor wrote:

"The animal was then between 30 and 40 yards distance from us. He soon sunk, but not so deep but we could trace his course. He rose again within 20 yards distance of us, and lay some time on the water. He then turned, and steered for Ten Pound Island (a short distance offshore from Gloucester Harbor); we pulled after him, but finding he was not pleased with the noise of our oars, they were laid in, and the boat sculled. We again approached very near him. From my knowledge of aquatic animals, and habits of intimacy with marine appearances, I could not be deceived. We had a good view of him for half an hour. His color is a dark brown, with white under the throat. His size we could not accurately ascertain, but his head is about three feet in circumference, flat and much smaller than his body. We did not see his tail; but from the end of his head to the farthest protuberance was not far from 100 feet. I speak with a degree of certainty, from being much accustomed to measure and estimate distances and length. I counted fourteen bunches on his back, the first one say, ten or twelve feet from his head and the others about seven feet apart. They decreased in size toward the tail. His motion was sometimes very rapid, and at other times he lay nearly still."

The Reverend's story, as compelling as it is, does not seem to have shed further light on the subject—at least not in terms of present-day aquatic monsters. People still are intrigued at the possibility of seeing ancient sea serpents thrashing about in waters off their shores—and they're still looking for answers. If those Indians had not thwarted the plans of the English colonists who went after the one sunning himself on the rock, perhaps we'd be a little more enlightened about such things today.

MOTHER ANN

We didn't see any monsters in the Gloucester waters that day, but there was something unusual in the rocks just left of the Coast Guard Station. In fact, it is considered one of the most interesting natural rock formations on the Cape Ann shoreline. Nestled among the rocky outcrop overlooking the Atlantic Ocean is the figure of a reclining woman. Maritime travelers have named her "Mother Ann" because, for centuries, she's kept watch over them as they sail past her on their way down to the Bay of Massachusetts. Area fishermen also know her as the "Woman of the Sea."

To the left of Mother Ann is Brace Rock, a small island of stone rising from the water a few hundred feet offshore. Here, too, the rocks have company. A myriad of seagulls of different species have claimed this as their nesting place. Here, as on Thachers Island, they lay their eggs out in the open, and the eggs are often preyed upon by other sea birds. We watched as the gulls circled overhead looking for a spot to land, their wings dipping gracefully as they glided onto the massive rock. Below us waves rolled gently around blackened, jagged rock formations, swirling salty seaweed in their midst, but stones closer to shore were smooth and clean from centuries of tidal washings by the sea.

BRACE COVE

We retraced our steps back along the Eastern Point shore road, past Fort Hill Avenue to the next street on the right where a sign points to the Catholic Retreat House. Unfortunately, the street name is not posted; but it is Toronto Avenue, located opposite an oceanfront residence with a large boulder at the curb marked "Green Alley."

After turning right, we continued to a fork, then turned right again at a roadsign pointing to Niles Pond Road and the Catholic Retreat House. After a short distance, this road split. We stayed on the Retreat House road, passing the main entrance, to the service road. Niles Pond continued along on our left. At a sharp right bend, the road became private. On our left lay Brace Cove, a beautiful inlet whose encircling arms form a graceful bowl of regal blue sea. To our right, shorebirds circled Brace Rock a short distance offshore.

We climbed over large granite blocks to walk along a high, grassy mound separating the brackish waters of Niles Pond from the cove. Goldenrod, loosestrife and phragmites covered the embankment by the pond; on the seaward side, tufts of seagrass lined the shore. The barrier ends at a private beach at Brace Cove. From here, we followed a gravel path through thickets of alder, sweetfern, and sea roses. Bending under low-lying branches of wild choke cherries, we finally emerged onto a turn-around on St. Louis Avenue. Turning right, we walked past Bemo Ledge and continued along the shore road and footpaths to Eastern Point Boulevard (East) which brought us to Farrington Road. From here, we turned left where a one-mile roadside walk took us past an historic Gloucester landmark—a grassy meadow which, in earlier times, was a field where fishermen brought their seines to dry. Seines are large nets with sinkers on one edge and floats on the other that hang vertically in the water and are used to gather fish in large quanties.

Farrington Road returned us to the entrance gates at Eastern Point and Niles Beach. A word of caution: this road is well traveled and there are no sidewalks. Please be careful.

8. Eastern Point

1. Audubon Nature Preserve
2. Coast Guard Station
3. Mother Ann Rocks
4. Tidal Pools
5. Seine Field

P Park at Niles Beach
or Dog Bar Breakwater

Glouc
Light
Dog Bar

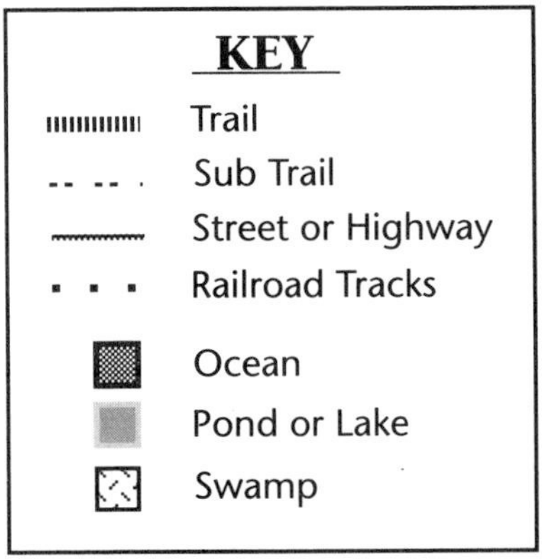

KEY
Trail
Sub Trail
Street or Highway
Railroad Tracks
Ocean
Pond or Lake
Swamp

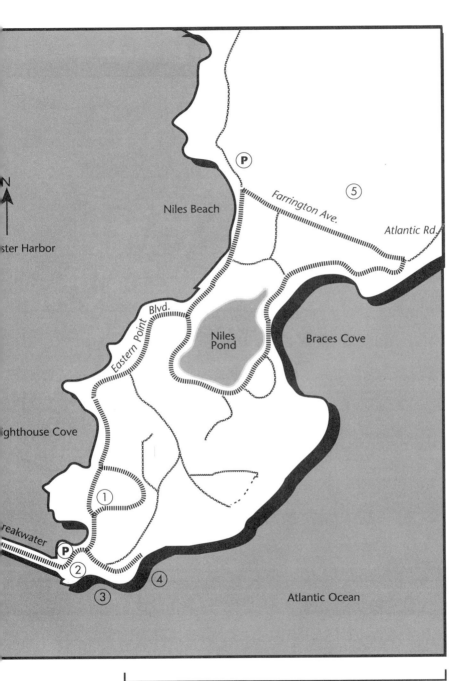

Along the Ocean Road

Today, 48 hours short of the autumnal equinox, reminds us that winter can't be far behind. Ted has decided we'll view the early fall foliage along the coast, leaving the deep woodlands for another few weeks when magnificent fall splendor adorns Cape Ann. Today's walk will take us along Penzance Road, to Loblolly Cove, Emerson Point and Paradise Rock, the latter being the shortest distance from which to view Thachers Island, a mile off Rockport's mainland.

Penzance Road

From Whistlestop Mall, we drove south on South Street, bearing left at Turk's Head Inn and continuing toward Cape Hedge Beach where the street dead ends at the sea wall. Penzance Road is to the left just before the sea wall. This area of Rockport is known as Land's End.

Parking on Penzance Road, we set out to explore the fall wildflowers and rocky terrain along the shoreline. Extensive repair work had been done to the shore roads during the past year to remove the huge rocks and boulders left by the No Name Storm. On this pleasant, sunny September morn, we plodded along a temporary lane of crushed gravel built to serve area residents until a more permanent roadway could be put into place. This stretch of Penzance Road separates the briny brown waters of Henry Pond and the ocean.

Cogswell Farm Landing • Milk Island

The first stop on today's walk was Cogswell Farm Landing, a rocky overlook along Penzance about a half mile north of the sea wall. Originally a large sprawling farm, the property has been sold as home-sites offering panoramic views of the Atlantic Ocean. However, the town of Rockport retained the landing, which provides a good spot for fishing, mostly blues and stripers.

Pointing to Milk Island, a small rocky stretch in the waters to our left, Ted explained the origin of its name.

"There used to be a sandbar between these rocks and the island, and cows from Cogswell Farm were taken out there to graze at low tide, then brought back when the tide lowered again."

For many years Milk Island was a bird sanctuary where herring gulls, night herons, cormorants and black-back gulls nested.

"Now the only thing there are black-back gulls and cormorants," Ted said. "They drove out the other gulls which then took over Thachers Island and the black-backs and cormorants stayed on Milk Island."

LOBLOLLY COVE • EMERSON POINT • THACHERS ISLAND

Along the roadside, wild asters, baby-blue and white, and dried goldenrod and loosestrife showed signs of autumn. The road ended at Loblolly Cove which, like Penzance Road and Tregony Bow, received its name from a village in southern England. Gardeners often come to this picturesque inlet for seaweed. Called "sea manure" by early settlers, it has been used by generations of Cape Anners to enrich their gardens for spring and fall plantings.

A nearby boulder bore the name of a girl who had lost her life scuba diving in the waters off the cove. There are no restrictions on the activities of divers along the shorelines, and authorities never know when or where they enter the water unless there is a tragedy of some kind.

To the right of the landing is a turn-around and a path leading to higher ground. We climbed the rocky slope through knee-high shrubby growth, finally reaching the high flat rocks atop Emerson Point. From here the view is stupendous. A mile out from Loblolly Cove is Thachers Island with its famous twin lights, called "Annie's Eyes" by many trusting seafarers who have been guided away from its treacherous rocks.

Thachers Island—spelled without the "t" in the middle—is named in honor of Reverend Anthony Thacher who, having recently arrived from England, set out with another minister, John Avery, to accept positions in Marblehead. The date was August 11, 1635. Sailing in a pinnace—a small sloop of that era—from Ipswich, the party of 23 was caught in a violent hurricane off the tiny island a mile from Rockport's shore. The site of the disaster was Crackwood's Ledge, a submerged reef about 300 feet from the island. Everyone, except Thacher and his wife, was drowned. Miraculously, they survived, after being tossed onto the treacherous rocks surrounding the island. Throughout the night, they were battered by high winds and crashing waves. Badly bruised and exhausted, they held on until help arrived the following day. Thacher's four children and Avery's six were among those lost to the fury of the Great Storm, as it was known.

Later, when he had recovered sufficiently, Thacher penned his heartbreak to his brother in London.

"...Now came to my remembrance the time and manner, how and when, I last saw and left my children and friends. One was severed from me sitting on the rock at my feet, the other three in the pinnace, my little babe (Ah, poor Peter!) sitting in his sister Edith's arms, who to the uttermost of her power sheltered him from the waters, my poor William standing close unto them, all three of them looking ruefully on me on the rock, their very countenances calling unto me to help them, whom I could neither go unto neither could they come at me, neither would the merciless waves afford me space or time to use any means at all either to help them or myself. Oh I yet see their cheeks, poor silent lambs pleading pity and help at my hands . . ."

The heartache of that humble, sensitive man rings down through the ages. How can anyone reading his letter—even after 360 years—not cry with him at the memory of his tragic loss?

At one time, during the early days of maritime travel, there were 45 lighthouses along the European and North American Atlantic coasts but the twin sentinels at Thachers Island, from the beginning in 1773, were considered among the most important. The others are at Eddystone Rocks in the English Channel in SW England, and Cape Hatteras off the North Carolina Coast. "Annie's eyes" are the first lights seen by ships enroute from England to the Massachusetts Bay, and the last when leaving Boston for England, Maine and the Canadian provinces.

In her book *Thachers Island*, Eleanor Parsons reveals many interesting facts about the long and often controversial history of this 52-acre rock. Today it's a historic landmark, listed on the National Register of Historic Places. The light in the south tower remains a navagational aid, now computerized and operated by the Coast Guard from a main network in Boston. The north tower light, maintained privately by the Cape Ann Lighthouse Association, is known locally as Ned's Light, in honor of Ned Cameron, long-time activist in preserving Thachers Island.

Margaret Thatcher (she has retained the "t" in the spelling of her name), former Prime Minister of England, is somehow connected to the family of Anthony Thacher. In keeping with Cape Anners' avid interest in local history, a group hosted a reunion of the Thacher/Thatcher family about five years ago. Over fifty family members traveled to Rockport to attend a picnic on the island. (Mrs. Thatcher was not among them.)

Scanning the broad, blue limitless sea from Emerson Point, we were able to follow the coastline for many miles both north and south, gaining a different perspective of Milk Island, Loblolly Cove and Pebble Beach. Then it was time to leave this beauty spot. Once again taking the lead, Ted headed for the trail that would return us along Penzance Road, describing the wild plants we passed along the way: bayberry, fall asters, small choke cherry trees, seaside goldenrod (a salt-tolerant variation of that found closer inland) juniper, raspberry, jewelweed, sea roses, rum cherry, and maple-leaved viburnum. Poison ivy, its shiny green leaves already donning brilliant fall colors of flaming red, burnt orange, bright yellow and deep purple, wandered along beside us. Pretty to look at, but menacing to the touch.

Our route took us past a long stretch of bullrushes growing in freshwater wetlands beside the road. We also passed black alder (which is actually a holly bush with red berries), loosestife, and ground nut vine tangled with bittersweet climbing high into the trees. Just before we turned right from Penzance Road onto the private section of Eden Road, Ted pointed to a spot where staghorn sumacs crowded each other down to the shore.

"President Taft's favorite dining spot used to be there," he said, nodding toward the woods where the once-famous Haskell's Seafood Restaurant occupied the corner of Penzance Road. "He had a home in Beverly and came to Rockport often for seafood dinners."

As we continued on, we were greeted by others enjoying a late summer walk along the ocean road: a young couple, the mother obviously very proud of the beautiful, smiling baby she pushed in a visored pram, the father leashed to a playful brown-and-white springer spaniel, and summer residents whom Ted hadn't seen for a number of years. New England's unpredictable weather had favored us with a morning bright with sunshine, mild temperature, and a gentle ocean breeze. It was a perfect day for a walk. And for them and us, Cape Ann was the perfect place to be.

FLAT ROCK POINT (PARADISE ROCK)

A half mile down Eden Road—past Rocky Shores and Eden Pines inns—we came to a posted right-of-way pointing the "Way to Flat Rock Point," another rocky promontory maintained by the town of Rockport as a small public park. Several medium-sized staghorn sumac shaded two stone posts at the entrance to the point. As the name implies, the rocks on Flat Rock are flat and smooth, with many broad ledges forming platforms and wide steps down to the sea. Also known as "Paradise

Rock," this, too, is an excellent spot for picnicking, overlooking Thachers and Straightsmouth islands and Loblolly Cove. The problem here is parking; there is none in the immediate vicinity. However, parking can be found along several inland streets not far away.

After viewing the tranquil morning seascape from this high rocky plateau, we once again returned to Eden Road. Wild asters, goldenrod and loosestrife continued to line the roadway, joined in spots by a bright yellow flower called "butter and eggs." At the next curve, the road changed from private to public, but ownership doesn't seem to be an issue here; both foot and auto traffic pass freely along its entire length with no restrictions—and it has the appearance of a public street all along the route.

But that was not true at our next turn. Taking what seemed to be a private unpaved driveway on the left, a short distance from the curve, Ted noted the hesitency on the part of several in the group. "It's all right," he assured us. "It's a public way, you'll see."

"You learn a lot on these walks," remarked a long-time villager. "I didn't know there was a street back here."

The "street back here" was a narrow winding country lane which took us through a rocky meadow of bayberry, up a steep hill and around a sharp curve past several homes overlooking the ocean. From this higher elevation, we gazed down upon a panoramic view of Thachers Island. Descending the hill around another curve, someone joked about the "low-maintenance road" we were traveling, referring to the fact that it was "paved" with large, flat, ancient stone, eliminating forever the problem of "pot holes." A clever engineer had the good sense to plan the roadway along the path of the level, whitewashed moraine, providing a rock-solid granite lane through the neighborhood. A public road it was, indeed. A very fine public road at that.

The hill snaked down around another sharp curve, at the bottom of which were two picture-perfect New England gardens. A small weathered Cape Cod cottage sat alone at the edge of the woodlands, its front dooryard overflowing with a profusion of cosmos—brilliant pink, white and magenta—mixed with blue bachelor buttons and orange poppies. Walled in by large boulders, it quietly reflected both harmony and simplicity.

Across the street, the scene was even more harmonious. The lower part of an "S" curve angled sharply to form an elbow bend where the rocky lane met a dirt road at the bottom of the hill. A carefully-tended U-shaped garden tiered down the slope of the hill, abundant with colorful flowers and vegetables. Flaming red begonias with shiny green leaves lined the front tier, followed by golden chrysanthemums with double flowered heads. Bringing up the rear was a healthy stand of sturdy corn-stalks heavy with yield, their golden tassels glistening in the bright sun. A narrow band of granite wound around its base, ribbon-like, giving the garden a final touch of tidiness and tender, loving care.

The dirt lane at the bottom of the hill brought us back to Eden Road where we retraced our steps to Penzance. Along the way, Ted pointed toward a tower poking through the distant trees, saying it was one of two military observation posts built on Cape Ann to scan the coast for German U-boats during World War II.

"Men in those towers kept watch through high-powered binoculars. If they sighted anything, the cannons at Fort Dearborn in Portsmouth (New Hampshire) were ready for action."

The cannons to which he referred reminded me of the movie "The Guns of Navarone." The site of this mammoth coastal defense artillery, housed in cavernous concrete bulkheads, is now a public park along the bank of the Piscataqua River. Once, when the cannons were test fired, the air concussion from the huge guns blew out all the windows of the Wentworth Hotel a short distance across the river—all 350 of them!

And how often were they fired to ward off the attacking U-boats along the Massachusetts coastline? someone asked.

"Never fired a gun," was Ted's solemn reply, adding quickly, "But a local story made the rounds during the war that a German submarine did surface once or twice, approaching lobstermen at sea. Not to harm them, but to buy their lobsters. They paid in cash using American money. So the story goes," he finished with a wide grin.

His next story was even more entertaining. As we passed a beautiful-ly landscaped oceanfront home, he identified it as the former residence of the mother of a well-known Boston trial attorney who shall remain nameless. This flamboyant counselor is as much at ease piloting his pri-vate jet and helicopter as he is defending many of his infamous *causes celebre*. One day, after visiting his mother in Rockport, he took off from the helicopter pad on her side lawn, but ascended only a few hundred feet into the air when engine trouble brought him crashing into a ravine covered with briers and poison ivy.

"He started yelling for help," laughed Ted. "When people saw he wasn't hurt, they weren't about to go into the briers and poison ivy to get him out. They yelled back, 'You can get yourself out of everything else, get yourself of this!'"

Since none of the neighbors were willing to come to his aid, he judi-ciously radioed the Coast Guard for help. Eventually a second helicoptor pulled him out of his predicament. Because the solicitor is widely known for his massive ego and extravagant lifestyle, the group enjoyed hearing the story about his embarrassing caper in the poison ivy patch, thus ending our morning outing on a jovial note.

Following six weeks of severe winter weather, I joined the group for another walk along the shore roads. The calendar indicated the waning days of March, but Old Man Winter still held a firm grip on New England. About a foot of snow remained on the ground and streets, and driveways were lined with black peppered embankments, the exquisite beauty of freshly fallen snow now hidden beneath layers of grimy residue from road traffic. Intermittent, sunny days had brought about a gradual melting, causing slush, icy puddles, and some flooding in the low-lying moors and swamplands.

We parked our cars at the end of South Street, beside an abandoned site that had once been the summer home of Judge J.E. Cotter, a prominent figure in the Lizzie Borden murder case. The large, shingled beach house with wrap-around porch and second floor deck had commanding views of Cape Hedge and Long beaches, Thachers Island and the ocean beyond. It later became the Cape Hedge Inn, then the Sandpiper Inn before it was destroyed by fire. Today only the foundation remains on the rocky cliffside.

We set out along Penzance Road, following the shore roads we had taken last summer. Fog hung heavily over the coastline as we made our way past Henry's Pond still wearing a frosty white blanket of snow above a thick layer of ice. Roadside shrubs and wildflowers which had separated the pond's brackish waters from the ocean's tides last summer were gone now, washed away by the violent storms that had pounded Cape Ann during the winter. Today, stones and pebbles covered both sides of the road, and the salty pool was pushed further inland by the ocean.

Rockport had awakened this morning to temperatures in the mid-30s and a gray shroud of heavy fog. As we started out for the shore road, I gazed along the coastline and was reminded of a walk I had taken several years earlier off the English coast of the North Sea. Although it was June, like today a cold sea breeze accompanied an oppressively thick fog, creating a chilly, damp climate so "typically English." So similar were today's conditions to those of my walk on the other side of the sea—jagged, rocky cliffs, cozy cottages dotting the bluffs, a cold breeze coming off the ocean, and the thick gray lines of fog—that I fully appreciated, then especially, why early settlers named this spot "New" England after their coastal homeland.

Climbing over a 3-foot ashy snowbank, we pushed open the gate to Cogswell Landing, where last summer we had stood in the morning sunshine and viewed the long line of cottages in miniature along crescent-shaped Long Beach. But this was another day and weather conditions foiled our plan to visit the landing. The trail was impassable; a large, deep icy puddle spread across our path into the woods, causing us to make a quick retreat back to Penzance Road. We continued on to Loblolly Cove and Emerson Point, past banks of heavily sooted snow lining both sides of the street.

Ted drew our attention to a stand of red-osier dogwoods, grown for their red stems in the wintertime. Nothing is prettier than this little dogwood with its horizontal limbs reaching skyward at their tips, forming a delicate lace pattern, especially when there is snow on the ground. During the winter, the stems are dull red but in late March their color begins to quicken like pulsing blood as red as that in human veins. It's a pretty little tree that lends beauty to the landscape in all seasons.

Old Penzance Road (a short wayside off Penzance Road) was muddy, its potholes filled with icy, murky water as we retraced our summer walk to Loblolly Cove. The embankment above the small inlet had eroded about ten feet due to the severity of the winter storms. While we were there, the tide was out, allowing us to walk along the cove's old sandy landing cleared of rocks by fishermen of an earlier time. The hovering fog added mystery and intrigue to the stillness that surrounded us.

"This is what happens when the ocean starts acting up," Ted said as we came upon a large pile of tangled lobster traps that had washed up onto the shore. A confusion of wood, nets, ropes and buoys again evidenced the turmoil wrought by stormy seas.

"Once the seas start heaving and churning, they toss the traps onto each other and gather others on the way into shore. The end result is what you see there, a tangled web of broken traps washed ashore by the storm."

"Look at the seals!" someone shouted, pointing toward the misty sea. Just beyond a row of seaweed, barely visible in the haze but close enough to be seen, were three seals cavorting in the water.

"Most of them go north during the summer," Ted informed us, "but we see quite a few in these waters during cold weather."

Returning to Penzance Road, we continued on to Eden Road, riddled with potholes by the harsh winter weather. Our walk today took us past familiar spots—a huge black willow and small summer cottages on the left, wiry greenbrier, juniper and low-bush blueberry bushes climbing a bluff a little further along the road, and on the seaward side, a rocky ledge tumbling down to the water's edge.

"Those rocks along the shore are blackened by the iron and manganese in them, and by the algae which swirls around them," Ted explained. "They're extremely slippery when wet," he cautioned.

The Atlantic Ocean, which had so beguiled us from this spot on a warm summer morning was now hidden behind a thick, damp curtain of silver mist. Poor visibility prevented a view of Thachers Island, but the mournful blast of a foghorn came eerily out of the silent grayness.

"How far is that ship out at sea?" Ted was asked.

"It's not a ship," he replied. "A laser beam sounds the foghorn on Thachers Island."

He then explained that all navigational warnings and markers maintained by the Coast Guard have special characteristics that distinguish them from each other. Mariners use these navigational aids for dead reckoning (line-of-sight) navigation and to avoid hazards such as rocks, shoals, islands and sandbars. They are to the seaman what road signs are to the motorist, guiding them safely through troubled waters.

At Thachers Island, the South Tower beacon flashes red every five seconds and the foghorn blasts twice at 60-second intervals during bad weather. A strobe light aimed out to sea activates a light sensor when fog sets in; the light reflects off the dense moisture back to the sensor which sounds the horn in the tower's equipment room. The sequence of warning is a 3-second blast, followed by 3 seconds of silence, then another 3-second blast, followed by 51 seconds of silence. The North Tower has a constant yellow beacon but no foghorn.

Other navigational aids along the Rockport-Gloucester coastline include a flashing green buoy with a loud, clanging bell at Dry Salvages, a flashing green beacon and horn on Straitsmouth Island, and another bell buoy slightly to its north where an engine is reportedly submerged 275 feet on Flat Ground. Seaward from Thachers Island are two more buoys—one green which is lighted, and the other red and equipped with a high-pitched whistle. A Daybeacon (a black cylindrical cage on an iron spindle) warns vessels away from Londoner Rock, and a red buoy tends watch at Salt Island Ledge. Eastern Point is just as diligent in protecting seacraft, with a flashing white light, radio beacon and foghorn at the Coast Guard Lighthouse, located at the entrance to Gloucester's outer harbor, and several whistle and horn buoys in nearby waters.

Seafarers today can take great comfort in the latest state-of-the-art safety measures borne of modern oceanographic technology. From shore, we often hear the blare of foghorns and sometimes see a bobbing buoy or two—and can only hope that all goes well with the many commercial fishing boats and pleasure craft that sail the rugged, time-worn Atlantic seaboard.

Returning to our walk, we found the barren trees bordering Eden Road to be mostly viburnum and black willows, one of the latter having been blown down and cut about six feet from its base. But hope springs eternal as seen by the profusion of healthy branches sprouting skyward from its prostrate trunk. Juniper also lined the roadway and surrounded large flat rocks on the hillside above the shoreline. In several places Ted pointed out the lighter wood of the American Beauty tree, today its feet wet and chilled in a pool of icy water. Close by, a large skeletal wild choke cherry looked just as weathered and forlorn, surrounded by lingering drifts of snow. Further on we came upon a slowly melting snowbank that had formed itself into the shape of a camel's head.

As we turned onto Irvana Road, two flashes of red winged across our path. The cardinal, said by experts to typify everything that is elegant and chivalric, is indeed a fine specimen of bird character. In the spring, cheerful, active and industrious, the male especially is noticed for the affection he bestows upon his mate and offspring. He's often observed leading his family to favored food and singing to them from high in the tallest tree while they are down by the brook in the valley. These pretty "redbirds" with their brilliant coats and lilting serenades bring much pleasure to birdwatchers.

We continued to make our way along the unpaved lane past a rock-strewn meadow of low–bush blueberry bushes and up to a high ridge overlooking the Atlantic.

"It's a beautiful view from here on a clear day," Ted remarked. Remembering our walk last summer when we gazed down from this spot above Eden Road across a calm, shiny blue sea to the twin lighthouses on Thachers Island, most agreed. But weather conditions today brought their own haunting beauty, I thought. Surrounded by vaporous clouds, we were part of the misty mystique that permeated both land and sea. My eyes strained to make out the ghostly outlines of the shingled cottages I knew were hidden in the opaque stillness.

After a few moments, we continued on, passing a tupelo grove as we wound our way over the "maintenance-free" roadway we had travelled earlier. Tumbled into place by the ancient glacier, its rock-solid base was pot-hole resistant—which no doubt pleased the budget-conscious Selectman Tarr.

Returning to Eden Road, we climbed up the long paved driveway to the Rocky Shores Inn, cresting high on a bluff overlooking the sea. Large banks of snow lined the drive which wound around back of the inn, under a portico and exited onto Oaks Lane, today slushy and muddy in the damp, early spring thaw. Following Ted down the narrow, windy country lane, we came upon a pretty snow-capped pasture next to a tree swamp. Our slushing evidently disturbed two beautiful mallards which, in turn, startled us as they exploded out of the swamp into the air when we neared their watery nest. We stopped for a few moments to watch their graceful flight which took them southward toward Cape Hedge Beach.

This hardy waterfowl remains in the North during the winter, seeking food and open fresh water wherever it can. Wise, handsome and strong, both wild and domestic, this ancient gamebird has furnished mankind with an enormous amount of food—flesh and eggs—for thousands of years. China, the most populated country in the world, has savored its gamey taste for centuries, giving the world one of its finest culinary delicacies—the Peking Duck.

From Oaks Lane we turned left onto South Street and walked the road's edge back to our cars. The woods along this stretch were somber in their shroud of winter dress—icy wetlands, scattered patches of snow, and a rising fog throughout. Abruptly a clearing in the trees revealed another peaceful pasture, this one framed in fieldstone and frosted white.

Following our walk that Sunday, we were invited to brunch at the home of a congenial British couple—he from the Wimbledon area of southern London, she from Newry in County Down, Ireland—who joined the group last summer. Their elegant hilltop townhouse and delicious fireside buffet—topped off with a scrumptious English trifle—was a fitting finale to our chilly, foggy "typically English" walk by the sea.

126

9. ALONG THE OCEAN ROAD

1. Sea Wall
2. Seaview Street Parking
3. Cape Hedge Beach
4. First Atlantic Cable Landing
5. Pebble Beach
6. Site of Judge Cotter's Beach House
7. Site of Old Haskell Restauraunt
P Sticker Parking at the Sea Wall
   and at the bottom of Seaview St.

KEY

ⅲⅲⅲⅲⅲ	Trail
-- --.	Sub Trail
⌁⌁⌁⌁	Street or Highway
• • •	Railroad Tracks
▓	Ocean
▒	Pond or Lake
⊠	Swamp

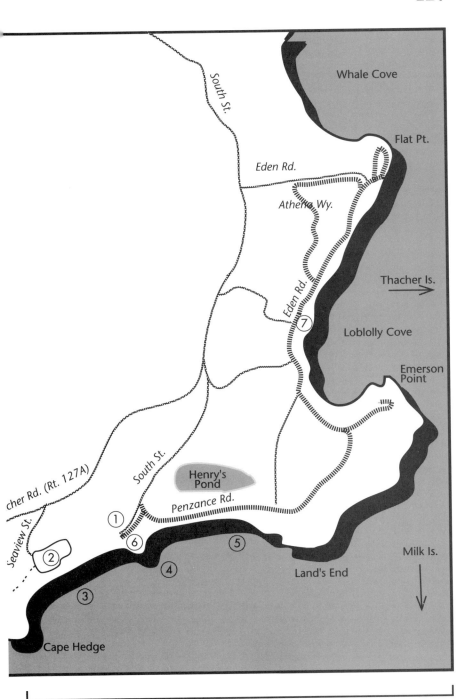

South St.

Whale Cove

Flat Pt.

Eden Rd.

Athена Wy.

Eden Rd.

Thacher Is.

Loblolly Cove

7

Emerson Point

cher Rd. (Rt. 127A)

South St.

Henry's Pond

Penzance Rd.

1

6

2

5

Milk Is.

Seaview St.

4

Land's End

3

Cape Hedge

1 Mile

THE OLD RAILROAD TRAIL
PIGEON COVE

PIGEON COVE VILLAGE

Saturday it had rained again, but the first Sunday in autumn dawned warm and sunny despite its "mackerel skies." According to an old New England weather proverb,

> Mackerel skies and mare's tails
> make tall ships carry low sails.

Meaning that when cloud formations have the appearance of fish scales and long flowing mare's tails, it usually indicates the approach of moisture in the middle to upper atmosphere. Put simply: more rain was on the way. Knowing this, we wanted to make the most of the morning sunshine. Since we were all anxious to view the early fall foliage, Ted decided the upper woodlands of Pigeon Cove along the old railroad route would be a good place to explore since its broad path would be relatively dry after yesterday's rain.

To reach our destination, we simply took a left at the mall's entrance and continued north on Granite Street (Route 127) to the tiny village of Pigeon Cove, then another left onto Curtis Street brought us to our starting point at Pine Pit. This stretch of Route 127 is very scenic, offering many splendid heightened views of the ocean, as well as interesting places along the way. The building next to the Keystone Bridge, formerly the office of the Rockport Granite Company, now a private residence, as well as two large homes close by, are fine examples of the beautiful granite structures built throughout New England in the 1800s using Rockport granite. Indeed, many buildings throughout the country owe their structural integrity, beauty and enduring quality to the various strains of colored granite from Cape Ann quarries.

The romance and charm of New England village life is typified by the picturesque homes, inns and churches lining Granite Street from Summit Street in Rockport to the Pigeon Cove Post Office. Houses are mostly of the Colonial and Federal periods with a few imposing Victorians and Greek Revivals, some finished in weathered shingles, others of white clapboard construction. Roses climbed a white picket fence to drink in the morning sun as Old Glory waved from a flagpole on a front lawn the morning we drove past. Golden mums, red geraniums, orange marigolds and pink and white hollyhocks added harmony and beauty to the road-side scene.

Two lovely, old Cape Ann churches—one Lutheran and the other Swedish Congregational—have also been made into private homes. The latter is now a handsome gray townhouse, its clear glass-arched windows attractively trimmed in white and turquoise, its steeple of ample size to be made into a small room above the narthex. A checker-patterned granite wall colored rust and buff lines the front sidewalk, its tasteful effect pleasing to the eye. Down the street the Lutheran Church is now a large chocolate-brown residence. Its bright red entranceway looks out onto a green privet hedge and stone picket fence, also of multicolored granite.

Granite Street passes quietly along the tree-shaded lawns and gardens of the Yankee Clipper Inn, a beautiful seaside hotel consisting of three imposing, period homes. The main inn, formerly an elegant oceanfront mansion, is on the shoreline, as is the Quarderdeck, a lovely New England lodge. Across the street, on the upper slope of Pigeon Hill, the old Bullfinch House, a classic 1840 Greek Revival, commands a panoramic view of the Atlantic Ocean.

In addition to its gracious historic homes, beautiful ocean views and sprawling grounds and gardens, the Yankee Clipper is also known for its excellent food. Candlelight dining by the sea in a closed-in glass veranda facing Rockport's picturesque harbor is another inviting feature—one of many which keep guests returning year after year for summertime plea-sure.

The distance from the mall to the center of Pigeon Cove is exactly one and one-half miles. But before going on to our walk, let's stop for a moment in the heart of the North Village where several buildings link the past and present. A short distance north of the post office, the road curves and widens to greet Curtis Street approaching from the west, and Edgemere Road from the east. The small village green at Edgemere cor-ner is the peaceful setting for the town clock, a monument to a fishing captain lost at sea. A simple plaque on a beautifully crafted polished granite shaft from the Johnson-Persson Quarry reads:

Presented to the people of Pigeon Cove
1967
in memory of
Captain Daniel S. Tarr
By
Ella B. Tarr

Across the street at a lazy right angle, Story Library occupies the mid-Victorian homestead of Abigail Story, Ted's great-grandmother who founded the Village Improvement Society. Beginning inauspiciously in the 1870s as a cooperative lending library by area summer folks, and progressing gradually throughout the next 100 years, this enduring institution eventually became a branch of the Rockport Public Library in the 1970s.

Another attractive granite wall follows the curve of Granite Street onto Curtis, enclosing the Pigeon Cove Veterans Memorial, an honor roll of men and women who served in the armed forces. An American Legion post nearby bearing a star and a small American flag tells us that this is Leon W. Kantala Square, named for one of the 12 Rockporters who made the supreme sacrifice during World War II.

Also in the dramatic tree-lined enclosure, a sign penned in Old English script describes a historic village landmark:

Old Castle
Museum
~ 1715 ~
Sandy Bay
Historical Society
and
Museum

In 1853 the Wheeler house, which stood on a rise overlooking the ocean, became known as the "Old Castle," sheltering several generations of Pigeon Cove families before being deeded to the Sandy Bay Historical Society as an antiquity. Built by Jethro Wheeler about 1715, this old weathered saltbox is typical of many dwellings dotting the New England landscape during the early days of colonization. Like most houses of that period, it is of simple design, its front door centered and balanced by two windows on both sides. The interior of the Old Castle Museum can be viewed during July and August when it is open to the public.

A directional sign nearby points the way to another interesting Cape Ann landmark, The Paper House. Because of its uniqueness, this local attraction is also worth a side visit. After it was featured on John

Cameron Swasey's national television show, many tourists found their way to upper Pigeon Hill Street to view this unusual structure. What they saw was a house and its furnishings made completely of outdated newspapers.

Mr. Elis F. Stenman began his project in 1922, working solely with Boston newspapers. Intended merely as an experiment to see what could be done with newspapers without destroying the print, the end result both astonished and pleased its humble "inventor."

With the help of his family, Stenman assembled the walls (just over six feet in height) of layered newspaper, which was then pasted and folded for rigidity and strength. When finished they totaled 215 thicknesses. Approximately 100,000 copies of newspapers, which soon reached beyond the presses of Boston, have been used in the construction of the house and all its furnishings.

Like Beauport at Eastern Point in Gloucester, here, too, we see creativity and a designer's eye for detail. For the paper furniture, Stenman fashioned newspapers into rolls of various shapes and sizes. A group of tables, chairs, lamps and a settee are made in an octagonal motif. The Christian Science Monitor supplied the material for a desk. A cot contains newspapers saved since World War I, while nearby a radio cabinet made in 1928 brings us news of Herbert Hoover's presidential campaign. Of aeronautical interest is the writing desk made exclusively of the stories about Charles Lindberg's history-making flight across the Atlantic, and a grandfather's clock made of newspapers from the capital cities of the then 48 states.

Pigeon Cove has a long and rich history in terms of famous people and important events, both of which shaped the development of this small New England coastal community.

A little further north on Granite Street, set back from the street, is an old saltbox-style house built in 1692 by two caring brothers from Salem as a hiding place for their mother who was accused of witchcraft during that infamous period in New England history.

Now let's return to our Sunday walk. At the town clock we turned left from Granite Street onto Curtis Street. Passing Pigeon Hill Street, we continued straight for a half mile to an unpaved town road leading into conservation land running alongside Pine Pit which, unfortunately, is not marked at the street entrance. To help pinpoint its location, look for the word SLOW painted on the narrow winding road; the entrance to Pine Pit is on the left a few feet before the warning. A short distance into the woods the road forks, the right leading to a parking area and Pine Pit, the left into the wooded uplands. A sign posted at the fork reads:

Town of Rockport
Conservation Commission
Commonwealth of Massachusetts

Pine Pit, another of Cape Ann's many abandoned quarries, gets its name from the surrounding green pines mirrored in its depths. In addition to pitch pine, red oak, black cherry, birch, tupelo and red maple are also prevalent, today casting gorgeous earthtone reflections in the dark waters. To the right of the pit, bordering the northern edge of the parking lot, are beautiful unspoiled wetlands, dense with tall stands of phragmites, a bullrush look-alike. Unfortunately, these phragmites have no nutrient value and pose a danger to the environment because they are crowding out and replacing bullrushes and cattails which do provide valuable nutrients for small marine life.

Leaving the parking area, we began our walk along a wide dirt road leading into the conservation area. This broad pathway had been the roadbed of a busy railroad winding its way around Cape Ann's great yawning quarries and little side motions during the height of the granite industry. Rough-cut pieces of granite were hauled from pits onto open railroad cars and pulled by steam engine locomotives down to the pier behind the tool factory where it was off loaded and put onto sloops, schooners and lighters for market. These locomotives transported quarrystone from 1879 until the last days of 1930 when the sites were closed as a result of the Wall Street crash. The tracks carrying these heavy burdens remained in place for another 12 years, then were taken up and used for scrap metal during the war.

Today this once-treacherous railroad route has evolved down to a broad, grassy lane meandering through the deep, still woodlands. All that remains of those hectic days of sweltering heat, billowing steam engines and pressing deadlines are piles of cast-off grout. Of the thousands of tons of granite taken from deep within the bowels of these huge stone wells, only 20 per cent ever found its way to market. The rest was destroyed because of irregular quartz in the grain or unsuitable color formation.

The town of Rockport acquired this tract of abandoned land about ten years ago, having refused a similar offer 20 years earlier. Unfortunately, lack of foresight on the part of those then serving as city planners has proven very costly, considering the escalation in real estate prices over the past two decades.

Ted is understandably worried about the future of these beautiful woodlands. As we passed a knoll of low-bush blueberries, he pointed beyond it to property recently purchased for condominium development.

"This strip of land is bordered by two larger sections which are privately owned," he explained. "Rockport has a special interest in keeping the middle section as conservation land because if all three parcels were owned by one interest, this whole area would soon be lost to development and there wouldn't be a thing we could do about it."

An abundance of luxuriant growth dotted the mossy, winding path. Wild lilies-of-the-valley and royal fern grew in healthy patches alongside discarded grout and glacial stone, bearing silent witness to the fact that, having withstood years of ecological disruption, this rich woodland soil was once again thriving and producing nicely in its natural environment.

These forested woodlands abut Woodbury Lane in Gloucester. Walking along a ridge in this area, we looked down upon one of the most enchanting scenes of rural life I've ever encountered. Carved out of a large broad basin was a small family farm, but this was not a farm in the usual sense of the word. Every detail of its spanking new buildings and worn landscape was carefully designed, creating a storybook bucolic setting. A cozy rustic farmhouse and matching barn, nestled deep in a picturesque hollow, were enclosed by neatly tiered fieldstone walls, which also partitioned off a cleared pasture. Stony Brook, which flows from Johnson Quarry in Rockport to Folly Cove, washed down the hillside and through the property, passing under a miniature stone bridge. The idyllic scene was picture perfect.

Up ahead the trail narrowed to a single footpath winding past Bianchini's Pit, a privately owned quarry now leased to the Lincoln Lab at MIT in Cambridge. Here high-tech underwater equipment checks sonar sounds below its still, green surface from aboard a small floating laboratory. The Bianchini quarry was selected for its depth and ease of accessibility, both of which fit MIT's criteria for the operation. Bianchini's Pit is the only quarry on the Cape conducting such tests. All the rest have been abandoned; most are now privately owned, others serve communities as reservoirs. Once teeming with busy men and powerful equipment, the quarries now lie dormant, part of Cape Ann's silent, rugged landscape.

The trail along the old railroad laces through the uplands from Pine Pit at Curtis Street in Pigeon Cove to Bianchini's Pit on Leverett Street in Gloucester, a distance of about two miles. The neighbors along this section of Leverett Street have had very famous people living in their midst.

Long-time resident Sylvester "Hoolie" Ahola, reputed to be the best trumpeter in the world—ever—lives here. Ahola came out of the Finnish community which migrated to America in the 1800s to labor in Gloucester's dust-filled quarries. Along with others of his station and culture, he joined musical groups as a jazz musician in the temperance halls and social centers of that time, practicing his music while tending the family's herd grazing in nearby Dogtown. He went on to become a distinguished performer in the 1920s and '30s. Following highly acclaimed appearances in his native Finland and in England, he was soon borne upon a shooting star which took him to heights of international fame. After a long and very successful musical career, he retired to Cape Ann where he and his wife live quietly among family and life-long friends.

Walker Hancock is another distinguished resident, as was the late Paul Manship, both internationally-famous sculptors. Born in St. Louis, Mr. Hancock has lived most of his adult life on Cape Ann, creating award-winning works of art. Among his most famous are busts of Robert Frost; John Barrymore; John D. Rockefeller; Stephen Foster and James Madison (the latter two on display in the Library of Congress in Washington, D. C.); *The Sculptor's Daughter*, a portrait in marble of his daughter, Deane, then a seventh grader, and the Gloucester Mariner's Medal, designed for his adopted city. On one side of the bronze medallion is a schooner; on the other, lettering which reads "The Mariner's Medal of the City of Gloucester, given for courage on the sea."

Mr. Hancock's most challenging work was the completion of the Stone Mountain Memorial, featuring the figures of Jefferson Davis, president of the Confederacy, General Robert E. Lee and General Stonewall Jackson. Located 16 miles west of Atlanta, the football-field-size carving, called the Eighth Wonder of the World, is the world's largest work of sculptural art. Begun by Gutzon Borglum in 1923, it was blasted away two years later by Augustus Lukeman who began his own version. After 12 years, funds ran out and for more than a quarter of a century, the work remained unfinished. In 1963, Mr. Hancock returned to America from Rome, where he was sculptor-in-residence at the American Academy, to win the international competition to complete the memorial. For the next 15 years, he worked tirelessly on the project, redesigning the theme, revising Lukeman's models which were out of proportion, and supervising the carving. On May 9, 1970, the memorial was dedicated by Vice President Spiro Agnew but work continued long after that date.

Paul Manship (1885-1966), a native of St. Paul, Minnesota, spent much of his early life learning his craft in New York, London, Paris, Holland and Rome. Studies included drawing, portraits and human and animal anatomy. Later, he lived in Manhattan where he bought five brownstone tenements, converting one into a high-style, palatial home for his family, with a studio in the backyard. The others became apartments and studios for artist friends and students.

Most of the sculptor's large art pieces were created there, among them

Duck Girl, displayed in Rittenhouse Square in Philadelphia; *Little Brother,* on exhibit at the Cincinnati Art Museum, *Centaur and Dryad* at the Metropolitan Museum of Art, New York and *Salome* at the National Museum of American Art at the Smithsonian Institute. Another important work was the Memorial Gateway at the New York Zoo, designed after ornate iron grilles in Spanish cathedrals. European works include the *Woodrow Wilson Memorial Celestial Sphere* in Palais des Nations, Geneva, Switzerland, and the *Soldier's Monument* in the American Cemetery at Thiacourt, France. Widely known for his works, Manship contributed "The History of Sculpture and Decorative Sculpture" to the *Encyclopedia Britannia.*

In later years, the artist took up summer residence in Lanesville, again buying an old house and renovating it into a comfortable home at the edge of Bianchini's Pit. A weathered oxen barn was moved to the site and became his studio, where he worked on smaller pieces. But, because pollen irritated his asthma, he would stay for only two or three weeks at a time, returning from New York frequently to finish projects. While most of the masterpieces created during his lifetime are in public and private collections throughout the world, several pieces are on display in his Leverett Street studio, now managed by his artist son John. Others, along with those of Walker Hancock, can be seen at the Cape Ann Historical Society.

Leaving the neighborhood of these gifted artists, we returned to the woodlands.

"Most trails made by the early settlers went east to west as they built further inland," Ted explained. "Later, as more people moved onto the Cape, foot and oxcart traffic increased and new trails were blazed from north to south."

As we crossed the Gloucester-Rockport line, a road went off to the right. "That's the Luce Trail," Ted noted, adding, "We'll take that on the Cape Walk."

He was referring to the walk across the Cape which he leads each Columbus Day at the peak of the fall foliage. The walk is usually five hours long and covers a distance of 11 miles, beginning at Cape Hedge Beach and ending at Halibut Point, with a stop at Whale's Jaw in Dogtown for a picnic lunch. The strong-hearted meet at 9 o'clock for the full tour, others join them at various points along the route which Ted announces in advance. This is the only walk during which the group is allowed to tarry—to photograph the gorgeous autumn scenery along the way.

The Luce Trail he mentioned was named for Dorothy Luce, an avid birdwatcher who summered on the Cape for many years, leading bird-watching groups until age 70. An original member of the Conservation Commission, she brought members of her Brookline Bird Club to these woods to study the many birds that migrate here in the spring and fall: purple sandpipers, guillemots, dovekies and kittiwakes, and the more common species such as thrushes, and warblers to name a few. Very active in land conservation on Cape Ann, she was responsible for the preservation of much of the trail that today bears her name.

Pointing to a pile of granite stone along the trail, Ted suggested that because of its isolated location, it could have been a dynamite shed.

"Powder magazines," he explained, "were placed in sheds with heavy granite walls and light wooden roofs. As a result, there used to be a lot of splinters, but not much stone around after a blast."

The footpath forked here and we turned to the right, past beautiful large oaks and patches of bracken fern and catbrier just donning their autumn plumage. Ted and some in the group stopped to pick late blue-berries, stretching to gather large succulent ones on the crowns of high bushes. As others crowded around him, reaching above his head to get at the choicest ones, he jokingly warned them off, "Actually, they're poiso-nous and I have the only antidote."

The path opened onto a broad grassy lane which led past Woodbury Farm. Unlike the small cozy designer-perfect farm setting we had seen earlier, here acres of dense woodlands had been painstakingly cleared to make way for a real working farm. Following the example of those early colonists who were forced to work the rocky terrain into clearings for homes and gardens, this busy farmer had labored diligently to render his land suitable for pasturing a large flock of sheep. Several long, wide stone-walled pastures bordering both sides of the main house were again partitioned into smaller grazing fields. All was in readiness; but the sheep had not yet arrived. When they do, they'll find their shepherd well prepared.

A short distance further was Gronblad Quarry, its quiet waters shad-owed by surrounding damp gray walls and dense woodlands whose full green leaves had not yet turned. The one dramatic exception was a small lone maple growing out of a crevice in the layered granite on the fore-ground of the wide chasm. The maple's bright, salmon-colored foliage contrasted sharply with the dark scene playing in the background. This was the home of many exotic wild plants before the area gave way to quarrying, Ted informed us. Bayberry, which survives in any soil, was scattered across the ledges and on the knoll to our right, where it met up with sweetfern and low-bush blueberries.

Also on the ledges were a number of painted markings readying the site for aerial photographs to be used in a Geological Informational

Survey of Cape Ann. Because these pictures are very precise, they help in defining property lines, as well as obtaining other valuable geological information. They are extremely important to city planners in all four townships which must continually balance the protection of natural resources against the social needs of their communities.

Cape Ann's beautiful wilderness crosses the boundaries of Rockport, Gloucester, Essex and Manchester. All these areas—woodlands, marshes, bogs, swamps, coves, harbors and coastlines—are overseen by commissions and agencies sworn to preserve these beautiful natural resources for future generations. Unfortunately, that's not always possible. Business interests sometimes override conservation efforts, affecting the quality of life of families and communities, in both the short and long term.

As we left Gronblad Quarry, Ted introduced us to "reindeer lichen," a crusted gray leafy substance growing alongside a patch of emerald green hairycap moss.

"It's a combination of fungus and alga," he explained, "and likes to live on rocks and other hard surfaces throughout fairly sunny woodlands."

There were lots of ruts on the wider trails, caused by cars driving in the woods after rainfall. For this reason, large boulders have been placed across most pathways throughout the trail network to prevent access by automobiles and motorized bikes. Too, in times past before land conservation became an environmental necessity, woods and quarries were favorite dumping grounds for unwanted cars and discarded household appliances.

We continued our walk along a broad, grassy road shaded by large, arched oaks and red maples. Tall, leafy staghorn sumacs were just beginning to turn; a few more days of sun would change their pale yellow leaves to flaming crimson. A little further on striations—minute grooves—could be seen on several large boulders, tracing them back about 12,000 years when the last glacier passed over the region. The beautiful wilderness we hike through each week has long since emerged from that far-off glacial meltdown, but not so the ancient stone. Those telltale narrow lines are battlescars, bearing silent witness to the fact that they were part of the geological evolution that gave birth to the land we now call New England.

We soon came upon yet another in Cape Ann's labyrinth of wooded trails, this one leading to Pigeon Hill Road. A great barberry bush, favored among early pioneers for making jelly, loomed large beside us along the path. Most of the houses of those early settlers had two bushes flanking their front door—a pretty lilac and a barberry. It was one of the many community customs they established in their struggle to settle the new land. This trail was homeward bound, taking us to the parking area at Pine Pit.

10. PIGEON COVE
RAILROAD

1. Old Castle Museum
2. The Paper House
3. Pine Pit
4. Old Granite Railroad Bed
5. Gronblad Pit
6. Woodbury Sheep Farm
7. Bianchi Pit

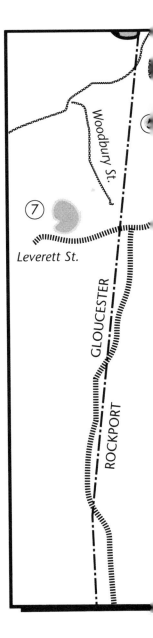

Leverett St.

KEY

ⅲⅲⅲⅲⅲ	Trail
.. .. .	Sub Trail
⎯⎯	Street or Highway
· · ·	Railroad Tracks
▓	Ocean
▒	Pond or Lake
▨	Swamp

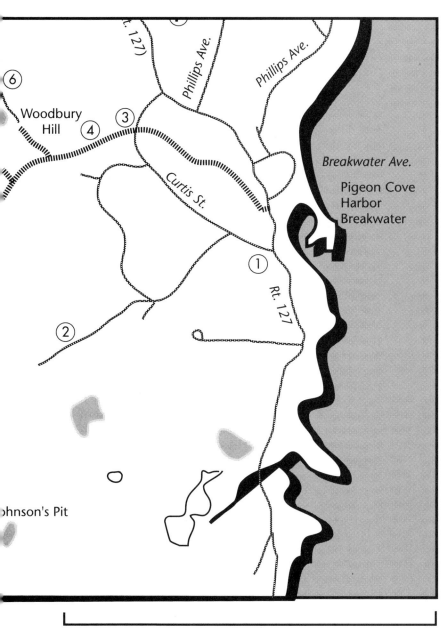

Phillips Ave.

Phillips Ave.

(t. 127)

(6)

Woodbury
Hill

(4)   (3)

Curtis St.

Breakwater Ave.

Pigeon Cove
Harbor
Breakwater

(1)

Rt. 127

(2)

ohnson's Pit

1 Mile

Manchester Woods

"If you delight to view beautiful scenery, summer homes equally as beautiful, fine equipages, and all else that signifies immense wealth, great culture and 'smart' social life, drive to Manchester and you will find it there," wrote an anonymous traveler in 1896.

Today, almost a century after that description was penned by a fanciful travel guide, Manchester-By-the-Sea is still considered one of the most beautiful seaside communities in all of New England, in fact, in all America. Its magnificent homes and natural beauty have made it the envy of other coastal towns. It's difficult to think of this lovely Boston suburb as Jeffries Creek, which it was called originally. Somehow the name just doesn't belong to the beautiful community it has become. Like Atlanta—first called Marthasville, then Terminus—the name finally settled upon suitably captures its true persona.

Agassiz Park

Agassiz Rock and Swamp Agassiz are two huge glacial erratics, deposited by the great sheet of ice more than one mile deep which covered New England thousands of years ago. Identified in the 1870s by Louis Agassiz, Harvard University's famed Professor of Natural History. Vegetation is hemlock, beech and maple, mosses, lichens, bearberry. Top of Beaver Dam Hill view of Massachusetts Bay

... reads the sign at the entrance of Agassiz Park, located one-half mile west of Route 128 on School Street. The focal point of this lovely forested reservation is Agassiz Rock, which measures about 6,000 square feet. Both the park and rock are named for Louis Agassiz. After his death in 1873, his widow, Emma Cary Agassiz, helped found Radcliffe College in 1882 and served as its first president for ten years.

From the summit of the immense Agassiz Rock, one gets a splendid panoramic view of the surrounding Manchester land and seascape. It's unusual to see large trees growing out of huge boulders. But there are several on Cape Ann, including one in Rockport on Route 127, just past the American Legion Home on the left side of the road. Another—which is much more dramatic—is here in Agassiz Park, in the valley to the north of Agassiz Rock, where an ancient, gnarled birch is embedded on its side in a soily cleft. A younger cedar has also taken root within a wider ledge on top of the rock. Both trees sustain life and nourishment from the soil found deep within the crevices of the massive boulder.

CEDAR SWAMP • BLUE HERON POND • MILLSTONE HILL

Ted decided to leave the trails through the park for another day. Instead we entered the woods on Old School Street across from the park's entrance and a few hundred feet east. Here we would explore Cedar Swamp, Blue Heron Pond and Milestone Hill. Parking is permitted in a little turn-around off School Street near a sign that reads:

> Conservation Area
> For Foot Travel Only
> Please Do Not Remove
> Plants or Disturb Wildlife

A barrier placed across Old School Street provides privacy for the few residential homes adjacent to the conservation area. Following this broad open road, we headed into the woodlands, vibrant with luxuriant forest growth on this sunny October morning.

The trail took us through Cedar Swamp, a large wetland one mile long and one-half mile wide, where moist soils and cool air provide the ideal habitat for cinnamon fern, tupelo, beeches, red maples, water-tolerant alders and high-bush blueberries. Everywhere we looked the tree swamp was aglow with colorful autumn foliage amid dark-green hemlock.

Huge boulders line Old School Street, built in 1817 to accommodate horse-drawn traffic between Manchester and Essex. But, in the name of progress, the street gave way to development and modernization in the ensuing years. Today a paved highway joining these two villages has taken the original School Street name, and the old path it replaced has become a well-worn nature trail relegated to being "Old School Street."

At the first intersection, Ted turned off the old historic road onto a single footpath which leads to Heron Pond, a 10-foot deep, man-made lake named for the great blue herons which feed in the vicinity. This elegant shore bird, the largest of American herons, is comfortable in both salt and freshwater habitats. Extremely patient, it stands motionless for long periods of time, then thrusts its bill into the water to catch unsuspecting prey.

Heron Pond had its beginning in the 1960s when Cedar Swamp was considered as a source of drinking water for the towns of Gloucester and Manchester. Between the swamp's surface and bedrock flooring is an "aquifier," a storage area between 15 and 30 feet thick into which water from surrounding hills seeps, filling tiny spaces between the sand and gravel—resulting in an enormous "underwater storage tank." In an attempt to determine if Cedar Swamp's underlying natural resource might add to the public supply, geologists performed tests which revealed the water to be of good-to-excellent quality. The project soon got underway. However, it was quickly found that the plan worked better on the drawing board than it did in practice. As the dirt was removed, the gravel pit would immediately fill with ground water. In the end, the operation was abandoned, leaving behind the man-made waterfill today known as Heron Pond.

Following closely at Ted's heels, we came upon a clearing in the woods which opened onto one of the most spectacular fall scenes imaginable. As if peering through a candy store window at displays of luscious sweets, we gazed transfixed across the deep purplish waters of Heron Pond into a woodlands scene which was indescribably beautiful. Completely encircling its dark, rippling waters was a forest of lustrous pink and salmon-colored maples blazing against a cloudless blue October sky. Low shrubby bushes, still draped in variegated greens, lined the water's edge, creating an artist's masterpiece in the unspoiled sylvan setting. The dramatic effect mirrored itself in the pond's raisin-colored waters, radiating a rosy glow from the crowned trees above. Sprouting up from a tiny island in the center of the pond was a bouquet of sedges, rushes and white waterlilies whose wide, flat leaves floated nearby.

Awed at the startling beauty that lined the bank across the water, we lingered longer than usual, completely mesmerized by its captivating splendor. It was truly the most gorgeous fall scene any of us had ever seen.

But leave it, we must. Hopefully, others would be along soon to enjoy it as we had. Turning aside, Ted pointed out a number of common wetland plants surrounding the pond: horsetail—a primitive plant that looks like ground cedar clubmoss—royal fern, sphagnum moss, the pitcher plant, and ladies' tresses which resemble tiny delicate wild orchids.

Returning to the footpath, we walked along the edge of Heron Pond, gaining another perspective of its length—as well as its extraordinary autumnal display. Soon we ascended a small, rocky ridge that connected with the blue dotted Cedar Swamp Trail, taking us deeper into the forested swampland. We came upon a bedrock valley shaded by large pine trees. Ted urged caution as we climbed over huge, moss-covered boulders, then stopped to point out the steep cliff of ancient granite ledges to our left. Cascading down the rocks from the rich, dark soil deep within its cracks and crevices were large rooted hemlocks, ferns and mosses.

"In the winter, this is a beautiful spot," he remarked. "Water coming down over the rocks freezes into long icicles. You can see the fern and moss reflected in the glistening ice, and with the dark green hemlocks, it's a very pretty winter scene.

"There used to be lots more hemlock in the Manchester woods," he continued, "but in the 1970s the old trees were destroyed by hemlock looper, a small yellow transparent worm-like caterpillar which eats hemlock needles."

We proceeded to the junction of Prospect Ledge Trail, marked on a tree with a pink dot. Here we left the swamplands and began our ascent to Millstone Hill. The path intermittently rose and dipped while continuing to wind its way upwards. There was not much color along this stretch as flaming red maples gave way to hemlock and beech. The ground was covered with polypody fern and partridgeberry.

"There's lots of deer in these woods," Ted informed us, as we continued our climb. "You don't often see them, but you'll notice their droppings along the way."

It's good having a naturalist lead our Sunday walks. Ted is that, and much more; a good sense of logic and intellect, combined with a great love for nature and people, make him a very special person. His warm personality and quick wit enhance the enjoyment of our weekly outings. We learn a great deal from him during our walks while enjoying every minute of the learning process. His lectures on botany and ecology are often laced with amusing anecdotes and witticisms as he drives home a well-made point, just as his colorful historical sketches breathe life into otherwise boring historical facts. There is so much to see and understand about today's world, who we are and how we arrived here, and how all this impacts the balance of nature in our fast-paced, global environment. From Ted we learn that life—*all life*—is precious and everyone traveling its pathway should take time to stop and renew themselves spiritually from time to time.

As the trail plodded along a hillside, we found ourselves the unwelcome intruders upon a romantic rendezvous involving garter snakes.

Coiled together in the warm sunshine on a leafy embankment were a large female, which Ted thought might be pregnant, and three amorous young males.

Snakes, the most feared and perhaps despised of all reptiles, evolved from lizards 130 million years ago through the burrowing process. Powerful muscles and numerous ribs—up to 140—support their graceful serpentine movements, allowing them to travel up to four miles per hour.

"Some snakes carry their eggs inside," Ted explained, examining the fullness of the female more closely. "They give birth in the summer. This one looks like she's pregnant," he noted, "which is surprising for this time of year. And the amorous attention of the males is a little late, too."

Picking up one of the small males, he coiled it around his forearm, citing a few details about the mating habits of reptiles. The rest of us listened from a respectful distance, amused and interested but not quite as comfortable in the presence of snakes—even harmless garter snakes—as Ted appeared to be.

We decided henceforth we'd call the hillside "Betty's Knoll" for the woman who led our Eastern Point walk several weeks earlier, but who was not with us today. We were being a bit disingenuous in doing so since Betty, like many of us, is petrified of snakes.

Our pace resumed onward and upward along Prospect Ledge Trail. White pine made splashes of green in the woodlands, in contrast to the red maple's autumnal flames and the yellow of witch hazel and white oak. Rock tripe, that spreading leafy alga-fungus, covered many of the boulders along the ledge. An edible wild plant, this lichen is a soft, grayish green when moist, but becomes brown and brittle when dry—as it often is atop rocks and boulders exposed to sunlight.

Arrows painted on a ledge pointed the way to Millstone Hill, the highest point in Manchester at 220 feet above sea level. We continued the rocky, steep climb. Up we went, over huge boulders, around many more. It took strenuous effort, forcing us to stretch to pull ourselves up, higher and higher to the ledges above. At one point the trail dipped, rounding a curve at a 90-degree angle, then continuing down the slope for another short distance before turning upwards again. After a particularly rigorous stretch-and-pull exercise which caused many in the group to fall behind, Ted stopped to gather in his flock.

"If you're not here, speak up," he yelled down to us.

A few more painful pulls and we finally reached the top of Millstone Hill, spent and exhausted. Only 220 feet above sea level, said he—it felt more like 2,200 to most, even the seasoned among us! But reach it we did, greatly elated that we met the challenge. Atop the summit was a huge flat rock, serving as an overlook from which to view the surrounding woodlands. Most of the trees were white pine and oak, though uncharacteristic in their growth. Oak is usually a tall hardy tree; these reminded me of small dogwoods. Pines are also straight and slender but here the extreme sun and wind cause them to have stunted, distorted trunks. Atop the rock itself low-bush blueberries, goldenrod and tufted moss grew out of gaping crevices.

Asked to explain the reason a large patch of low shrubs seemed to be growing out of the lower slope of the rock, Ted summarized the cyclical pattern of rock growth. "First lichen attaches itself to rocks in exposed, sunny spots like this," he explained as the group came closer to inspect the hilltop shrubbery. "Then the lichen is overtaken by moss, which enriches the soil and provides nutrients for small plant growth. These are bearberry plants which is a common groundcover in a situation like this."

Later he told us, "There used to be a tower up here, but unfortunately, it was vandalized some time ago and they gave up rebuilding it. We used to be able to see the ocean from here," he continued, gazing out toward the Essex marshes, "but as you can see, the growth has built up so much that even when the leaves are gone, the view is somewhat limited."

Too soon it was time to leave. Taking the lead again, Ted led us down a narrow, rocky path which soon brought us back onto Old School Street. Here the roadway was lined with greenbrier, low-bush blueberries, Virginia creeper, red maples and staghorn sumac—all "prettied up" in their autumn colors. Further down the way patches of sweetfern, goldenrod, meadow grass and cinnamon fern ran along the ancient stone walls bordering the lane. Wrapped around a tall oak was a colorful poison ivy vine, prompting a warning from our leader: "leaves of three, let them be." The leaves of the blueberry and poison ivy are gorgeous in the autumn. The blueberry is mostly variegated reds—crimson, magenta, scarlet, and brick; while the poison ivy's cover a broader spectrum: blotches of red, orange, yellow, and purplish brown. Both wear their brilliant colors for several weeks.

The walk along lower Old School Street was intriguing; the right side was darkened by tall, shadowy hemlocks and large sprays of cinnamon fern. By contrast, the left was a sea of brightly speckled hardwoods, tall yellow hawkweed and wild blue asters. The arrangement made for a rather curious set of circumstances, since the hemlock grove stretches up to drier land (along the new School Street Highway) and the hardwoods—maple, tupelo, oak, and water-tolerant alder—descend into a tree swamp. Usually the reverse is true: hemlocks like damp, moist soil, while hardwoods are mostly found on hillsides and dry ground—except those which inhabit a tree swamp, as these do. But such is the way of nature in the beautiful Manchester woods.

When we returned to the parking area, the hands on my watch were straight up—12 o'clock. It never ceases to amaze me how Ted always seems to plan our walks, no matter the distance or terrain, to arrive back at our cars at high noon. I wonder sometimes if he calculates the time by the length of our walks, which he surely knows almost to the footage, or if perhaps he has an inner sense that tells him when it's time to go home. A combination of both, I suspect. He's been researching Cape Ann's landscape and mining its historical lode all his life. As a result, he knows his subjects well, including flora, fauna, and trails, as well as people, places and events. And *always* on Sunday, a tempting family dinner awaits...

11. MANCHESTER WOODS

1. Agassiz Rock
2. Cedar Swamp
3. Millstone Hill

KEY	
‖‖‖‖‖‖	Trail
-- -- .	Sub Trail
⎯⎯	Street or Highway
• • •	Railroad Tracks
▓	Ocean
▒	Pond or Lake
▨	Swamp

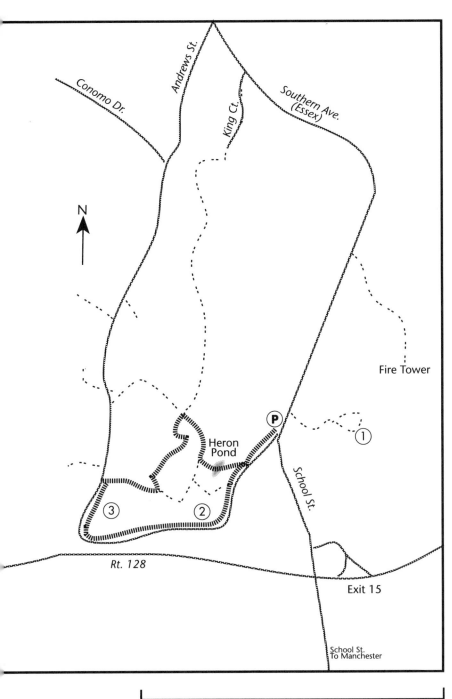

N

Conomo Dr.

Andrews St.

King Ct.

Southern Ave.
(Essex)

Fire Tower

Heron
Pond

P

(1)

(3)

(2)

School St.

Rt. 128

Exit 15

School St.
To Manchester

1 Mile

South Woods

It was cold and cloudy and "spitting snow" in early November when we set out to explore the woodlands surrounding the Rockport Golf Course. As we gathered at Whistlestop Mall bundled up in warm woolen jackets, pulldown hats and mittens, we happily greeted the first snowfall of the season.

"It looks like we're going to have a traditional white Christmas," a cane-carrying gentleman in his 70s called out as he joined the group.

"I hope so," we chorused in unison, sharing his penchant for nostalgia.

We were as excited as little children at seeing the dancing white flakes swirling about us. We knew that old man winter would soon be making his way down from the Canadian provinces to pay his annual visit—a visit that could last well into late April. Having recently returned to New England after spending all my adult life in the sunny South, I was anxious to recapture the magical wonder of winter so eloquently depicted in films and on Christmas greeting cards. Ted had often described with great sensitivity many old-fashioned frosty scenes along Cape Ann's wilderness trails which teased my senses. I could hardly wait to see for myself the frozen landscapes he had mentioned during our many Sunday outings. We all shared his great love of nature in all seasons, and I'm sure the expectancy of seeing Cape Ann's enchanted forests covered with snow was the cause of the merriment with which we greeted today's prancing flurries.

WARING FIELD • CRANBERRY BOG • ROCKPORT GOLF CLUB

To begin our journey on this cold wintry morning, we drove to Waring Field on South Street, about one-half mile south of the village. In 1980 Lloyd B. Waring, one of the town's leading benefactors, donated two parcels of land to the good citizens of Rockport. The first, Waring Field, is a five-acre grassy meadow bordered on three sides by natural woodlands, and marked by a large boulder in centerfield. The other is a cranberry marsh of slightly lesser size, located behind the field between the golf course and the DeLamater Bird Sanctuary. Both gifts serve to enrich nature lovers who enjoy hiking and observing birdlife.

South of Waring Field is a broad pathway leading past the Rockport Golf Club into the peaceful South Woods. Formerly the old road to Long Beach, it wanders past a storage barn, down alongside the fairways to the south water tower, then along what are now Ridgewood and Frank streets, and across Thatcher Road to Saratoga Creek in Gloucester.

Turning from South Street onto the historic lane, we came upon another breathtaking scene. Tunneling its way far into the distance was a dazzling canopy of spreading maple trees, aglow with bright green and luminous yellow leaves. Its radiance transformed the quiet wooded trail into a magical fairyland 'neath the flurrying snow flakes. Blanketing the wide tree-lined path and its bordering stone walls was the same textured brilliance. We took our time walking slowly through the long, glowing alcove, golden leaves crunching softly beneath our feet, entranced by the beauty surrounding us.

Emerging from the bright archway into an open clearing beside the barn, we again felt the showering snow upon our faces. Following the curves of a perfectly formed S, the path took us alongside the third fairway, from which we could see the Rockport Golf Club on a knoll in the distance to our right. Built sometime in the 1920s on land purchased by Ted's grandfather and a few like-minded friends, the large, comfortable white-frame clubhouse overlooked the sprawling grounds of the sporty nine-hole golf course. A proviso in the deed allows expansion to 18, but does not permit construction of additional buildings on the 80-acre site.

On the day we explored the South Woods, Rockport's volunteer firemen—all, except Ted, that is—were braving the elements to play their annual golf tournament. Their laughter sparked the frigid air with sounds of spirited competition and camaraderie.

Walking the lane beside a hedgerow separating the fairways, we could see fall's beautiful earthtones crowning the trees across the greens. Most were gray beech whose leaves had turned to a coppery bronze, while red maples still held onto various shades of green, yellow, pink, orange, and flaming red. These and many other deciduous hardwoods provide the beautiful autumn landscape for which New England is known and loved.

To the left of the third fairway, a huge ancient rock stood where the glacier tossed it thousands of years ago. Surrounding its base were shrubs and fading wildflowers. Mr. Waring's cranberry marsh beckoned from nearby.

Stooping to pick a few, Ted informed us, "This is where I get my

Christmas cranberries. Just a quart last year," he confessed, adding that it was "pure symbolism" on his part.

We followed the path past the fruited marshland where it met up with the old Long Beach Road. Our trek along this section was brief; we soon left it to return to the woods where we set upon another narrow, leafy trail. Our hike then began in earnest. Shuffling briskly through large crisp brown leaves—mostly oak and beech—past low green junipers and under a canopy of bushy sweetpepper trees, we no longer felt the bone-chilling temperature; in fact, the weather now seemed quite comfortable.

The woods were taking on the look of winter Along the trail were several spotty patches of sheep laurel, looking downcast and sorrowful as if weeping forlornly in the cold. Beneath their droopy green leaves was a tiny forest of ground cedar clubmoss, from whose soft, lacy pine limbs sprouted dust-like, inch-long spores. For many years, thrifty New England housewives decorated their front doors with simple Christmas wreaths made from this delicate pine. In Massachusetts, however, this long-time tradition was brought to an end several years ago with the adoption of a state law protecting endangered wildlife plants. Princess pine, lady's-slippers and Jack-in-the-pulpits are among them.

The winding, dipping trail passed through a thicket of barren catbrier vines. Like the southern kudzu, this barbed creeper is considered quite a nuisance to Cape Ann nature-lovers. Its colorful names bear witness to its ill-favored reputation: greenbrier, bullbrier, hellfetter, tramps' troubles and blasphemy vine, all spell beware, as anyone who has had the misfortune to venture into its midst will agree.

At one point, several old-timers trooped ahead since they knew the trails as well as anyone, having walked with Ted for many years. Approaching a T, they unhesitatingly turned right and continued merrily along their way. It was not often that he called back those who assumed the lead, but he did so now as he turned in the opposite direction. With good-natured chiding, the errant stragglers obediently retraced their steps and rejoined us along the path across Saw Mill Brook. The clear, cold waters of this quiet valley stream flow gently through the Cape's woodlands, meandering far and wide while providing back-up for Rockport's over-burdened water supply. But its waters are not always peaceful. Characteristically a "flashy brook," it flows heavily after rains, often causing flash flooding, and then must be cleaned out before flowing into town reservoirs.

As a log bridge came into view, our valiant leader left the trail and dashed quickly into the woods. He returned dragging a large log which he carefully placed across the chasm. Earlier several women had voiced anxiety about this particular crossing because the logs became slippery when wet. Ted had assured them that there was no danger. Strengthening the bridge with another strong, wide log was intended to reinforce its safety, as well as dispel any fears the ladies might have. Taking the lead, as was his custom in questionable situations, Ted held onto an overhead branch and gingerly "walked the plank." Checking its "structural integrity" as he went, he proclaimed it safe when he reached the other side. Feet planted firmly on the opposite embankment, he stretched out his hand to help the rest of us, patiently guiding our uncertain footsteps over the damp logs. I could see why the ladies had been concerned, but care on everyone's part brought us all safely across with only one minor mishap. Ted's simple acts of thoughtfulness in helping others enjoy the beauty of these nature walks reflect his care and concern for people in general.

Once safely on the other side of the brook, we relaxed as snow flurries continued their exotic dance overhead. Evidence was everywhere that autumn was waning, but a great deal of colorful foliage could still be seen. Crunch, crunch, crunch sounded the harvest of russet, leathery leaves beneath our treading feet. Occasionally the red spark of a fallen maple appeared in their midst. Royal fern, now a fading ivory, also stood out on the brown forest floor. The trail crossed the old Horseshoe Road, now a bridle path, running from below the fourth tee, around back of the golf course, crossing Frank Street and looping around the other side of the course where it becomes part of the Dorothy Luce Trail. Several icy puddles forced us onto higher ground, which proved hazardous in places because of wet, slippery leaves along ridges and embankments.

As we skirted the water-soaked ruts, Ted remarked with a slight tinge of annoyance in his voice, "This used to be a good trail before it got washed out by bikes."

Nevertheless, we pressed on, passing another large erratic covered with the same clinging lichen blisters we had been seeing on rocks and logs along the trail. In one section of woods, numerous clumps of small mountain laurel, sheep laurel, and a number of young, tender white pine were just coming up after a recent fire. Along another stretch the mountain laurel lining both sides was tall and bushy, having been in full blossom when it peaked the previous June.

High Rock • Saw Mill Brook

Walking through the new tender growth in the area of the fire, we came upon High Rock, the highest point in the South Woods. Detouring briefly, we drew upon every ounce of energy to master the steep, rugged climb up the wall of stone. It proved to be more of a challenge than we realized. Again, wet leaves in creviced ledges posed a hazard. But, being an adventurous lot, we forged ahead, pushing and pulling each other up the small rock mountain, inch by slippery inch. Finally, we all stood at the summit, eagerly searching for familiar landmarks below. Unfortunately, crowns of billowing brown trees blocked our view, and we had to rely on Ted to tell us what we could not see.

"If the trees were not in the way, we'd have a sweeping view of the ocean and Briar Neck, as well as the south end water tank," he explained, pointing to the 1 o'clock position. "The fairways are over there," he added, again pointing into the distance. Disappointed, but having enjoyed the little side trip, we returned once again to the trail.

Rounding a bend, we came to a large red oak leaning across our path. At one time, it had stood proud and tall next to a huge boulder. Having no support on the other side, it was blown over during a storm and came to rest at an angle across the trail. Still firmly rooted in the soil, it continued to grow. But now, instead of spreading gracefully in their normal horizontal position, the branches reached skyward from a massive prostrate trunk. Walking underneath it, we marveled at its strength and resilience.

Shortly we passed what was intended by Ray Smith to be a red spruce tree farm. Unfortunately, it never fully developed as the local lumberman had planned. The woodlands in this section were open, allowing us to view remnants of stone left behind by the glacier. The stone stood silently in the forest of hardwoods where coppery brown leaves of beech clung tenaciously to straight, gray branches.

Up ahead we came to another log bridge crossing the ever-wandering Saw Mill Brook. Here the stream flowed straight, under two wooden bridges in the middle of the fifth fairway, and made its way across the green to the edge of the woods, from which we now emerged.

Stepping carefully over the damp logs, Ted once again tested them for safety before allowing us to follow. When he reached the other side, he again extended a helping hand.

"This is another chance to fall in if you didn't do it the first time," he joked.

When we were on solid ground, he directed us to stay close to the woods on our way back along the golf links to prevent damaging the turf. More characteristic thoughtfulness.

High-bush blueberries, shadbush and maple leaf viburnum could be seen climbing the hillside on the other side of the fairway.

"It's wet where those red maples are," Ted noted. "They were beautiful this year, and they're still holding on," he said, gazing across at the flaming red trees in the distance.

"Still spitting snow," he observed as we passed the sixth fairway and climbed up over a wooden bridge. (We were pleased to have a solid flat surface beneath our feet instead of all those rolling wet logs!)

Returning via the hedgerow, we met up with the path beside Mr. Waring's cranberry bog, then followed a gravel incline that passed through large rock deposits. Up we climbed alongside the raised Number 4 tee, constructed shortly after the Rockport Country Club was incorporated in 1914. Today it resembles the deck of a lookout tower, its base of rough granite blocks hidden beneath handsome natural wood latticework. From here we walked for a short distance along the paved golf cart path, noting an old "wolf tree" whose diseased trunk continued to produce healthy, graceful branches.

We retraced our steps back along the old Long Beach Road, through the long, brilliant archway, savoring its extraordinary beauty and knowing that in a week's time, maybe less, it would be gone. Those of us who walked with Ted that crisp November morning will remember many things about our exploration of the woods surrounding the Rockport golf course, but mostly and forever, we'll remember our enchanting walk through that leafy arcade of autumn brilliance.

In mid-January we returned to the golf club for a winter excursion through the South Woods. The thermometer read a mild 30 degrees, but the windchill factor dropped the temperature to 17.

Parking beside the clubhouse this time, we crossed the service road to the barn, beyond which are the remains of an old ice house in what is now pastureland for prized Morgan horses, owned by Ted's neighbor, Marshall·Winkler. Heavy snowfall had blanketed New England during the previous week, depositing three to five inches on Cape Ann. In places along the hedgerow between the fairways, drifts measured eight to 12 inches, bringing out a host of cross-country skiers to enjoy the favorable ski conditions.

As we began our walk, Ted led us up a small incline past the Number 3 winter tee. From here we followed ski tracks along the snow-covered cart trail as it twisted through a wooded section for a short distance to the elevated Number 4 tee. We continued along this path only briefly, then left the fairways and headed into the woods.

Pointing to a group of large oaks, Ted said, "Great horned owls nest here. I can hear them hooting from my house" (which is located not far from Waring Field).

As its name implies, the great horned owl, also known as the big hoot owl, cat owl, Virginia Owl, and Virginia horned owl, is large—twice the size of a crow. Because of its tolerance of man, this awesome creature nests in parks and close-in woods, and is often seen in neighborhood communities throughout Cape Ann. Its color pattern is sooty-brown or dusky, mottled with grayish-white horizontal stripes. Although they span to 60 inches, its wings are silent as they gracefully pilot the owl through the air. Its ears are tufted and toes fully feathered. Breeding begins early in the year, producing two or three white eggs. Nesting habits vary: generally the female takes over a deserted hawk or crow's nest, adding a few twigs and feathers as a personal touch. Both parents fiercely defend their domain once it has been established. Called "the tiger of the air," this bold, blood thirsty raider is powerful and destructive, especially around domestic poultry. Its call is typically four to seven low hoots, the sound that Ted hears when the great horned owl is nesting nearby.

According to Ted, there are other wild animals in residence at the golf club.

"Historically, there's been a red fox den near the corner of the first tee in the undergrowth. The foxes and their pups didn't seem to mind us and we didn't bother them," he said, "but since the area was cleared, they haven't been around."

In the soft, chalky snow, we saw the first of many animal tracks that day.

"Small mice tracks," Ted pointed out. "See the tail marks? We'll see a lot of mole, squirrel and rabbit tracks today."

A short distance ahead, five deep-black American crows circled low above the treetops, their shrill caws piecing the still, cold air.

"Those crows screaming like that could mean they are yelling at an owl," Ted said. (Perhaps one of the great horns he mentioned earlier.)

The trail took us onto the old Horshoe Road, and for a short distance we walked in the wake of cross-country skiers who, like us, were enjoying Cape Ann's beautiful snowfall on this bright, sunny winter day. Along a section of the white-lined woodlands, both sides of the path were privately owned, and legislative action had been necessary to retain the town's right-of-way for nature walks. Thanks to our leader and like-minded officials, residents and visitors alike are able to enjoy the seasonal beauty of the entire Cape, from the vast shoreline panoramas of the Atlantic Ocean to dark piney dells in remote wilderness spots.

The frosty forest was peaceful and silent. Skeletal hardwoods, deep green hemlocks and shiny-leafed mountain laurel crowded each other to become part of the muted, snow-capped landscape. Soft, white powdery mounds blanketed ancient boulders and frosted tree branches, capturing the wintertime beauty Ted had often described during our summer walks.

Rockport's south water tank, an enormous barrel-like cylinder reaching high into the sky, is situated on this path. Having an 850,000-gallon capacity, it is the largest of the town's three tanks. The other two each store less than half that amount.

Tilting his head backward to survey the huge tank, a man asked in amazement, "Ted, is that full of water?"

Tireless in his efforts to keep his hometown adequately supplied with purified water, he didn't hesitate to assure his questioner, "It better be."

The trail then took us behind Ridgewood Road, crossing the end of Frank Street coming up from Thatcher Road. The pump station at Saw Mill Brook was on our right, surrounded by several tall, spindly alders, their red berries now shriveled and covered with snow. We walked a short distance up an incline to a cul-de-sac, once part of a beautiful two-acre meadow filled with wild lupine before being bulldozed for the new homes now lining the circle.

Here we entered the woods again, returning to the old Horshoe Road which took us over to High Rock. Mice and squirrel tracks scampered along the narrow footpath which wandered up a snow-covered, rocky hillside, and over the bedrock ridge. Several times as I struggled to conquer craggy granite spurs, I felt firm hands on my backside pushing me up the hazardous incline—for which I was very thankful.

A huge, lichen-blistered boulder appeared on our right a short distance from High Rock. We continued to follow the footpath, almost circling completely the massive rock mountain, then plowed through an area dense with white-capped mountain laurel.

Looking ahead, Ted called out, "Use the bannister on the left," jokingly referring to a tall, slender tree shorn of all its limbs which had fallen beside and slightly above a large rocky formation blocking the steep hillside path. Following his suggestion, we supported ourselves by use of the convenient "railing" and climbed up and over the stone almost effortlessly.

Reaching a tabletop, we walked along the "solid hunk of rock," bordered on both sides by craggy pitch pine. As the snow-packed trail became more challenging, dipping and rising, winding around and between rocks, someone asked, "Who designed this path, Ted?"

Having told us the previous week that his method of trail blazing was to follow paths made by wild animals, he quipped, "We just followed a rabid fox."

The winter landscape throughout the four-mile trek continued to delight our senses as soft, white powder blanketed hill and dale. Only the tips of hardy, cocoa-colored beechdrops could be seen poking through the mounds of drifting snow which covered rocks and boulders. Mountain laurel wore jaunty white caps, and long, slender fingers of frosty white icing coated branches and whipped around tree trunks. Hemlock boughs bowed low beneath soft pillows of snow. Through the shadowy pines and somber hardwoods, an occasional gray beech brightened the landscape with delicate orange leaves.

The forest grew dark as we tramped through a dim, damp valley of towering hemlocks, prompting Ted to comment, "This is called Dark Woods Road. That's not its formal name, but old-timers know it by that."

Running toward us in the snow were the ghostly footprints of a sprinting fox out hunting for his breakfast. Later, we came upon the aftermath of the kill.

"He caught something here," said Ted, noting that there was "lots of tooth and fang."

Hidden beneath the snow-covered trail were deep, water-filled ruts. When we attempted to stay on the path, our boots sank deep into cold slush, making the going slow as we carefully guided each step to avoid sinking or worse, falling. Some kept up, others fell behind, all trying to stay as dry as possible. In the lead, Ted stopped to "wait for survivors."

Further along the trail, he pointed out a "muskrat house" in a marsh near Saw Mill Brook, a dome-shaped mound of twigs and aquatic vegetation rising out of the water. Once we learned what to look for, we counted five in the swamp on our left.

From a nearby tree, we heard the fluttering of a lone songbird which Ted recognized as a cedar waxwing. Also called the Southern waxwing, Carolina waxwing, Canada robin and cherry bird, this gentle little bird is happy as a permanent resident of the northern woods, wintering throughout the United States when there's a storehouse of berries. If, however, food becomes scarce in late fall, it will migrate southward to the Bahamas, Cuba and Jamaica. Scores have even been observed flocking to the West Indies, through Mexico and Central America to the highlands of Costa Rica.

This affectionate songbird has been observed by experts to be as polite as it is handsome. Why "gentle, polite and affectionate?" According to Edward H. Forbush, who wrote a paper on ornithology for the National Audubon Societies, members of the cedar waxwing's harmonious little families often show their affectionate nature by "billing" each other and grooming one another's plumage as they perch in a row on tree limbs, fences and wires. Half a dozen of them sitting close together on a limb—which they often do—will pass a cherry along from one to another, down to the end of the line and back again, none of the birds making the slightest attempt to eat even part of the fruit. If not politeness and generosity, this bird expert asks, what then?

Leaving South Woods' snow-capped primeval forest, we returned to civilization by way of the ninth tee. Our approach onto the golf course brought us in sight of gaily clad skiers pushing themselves across the glistening fairways and gliding gracefully down the slope to the driving range. Walking beside the hedgerow at the edge of the course, we studied the dormant trees and shrubs: staghorn sumac, honeysuckle, shad, red cedar, crabapple, a large, gnarled poison ivy vine strangling a wild cherry in contrast to the benign woodbine gently climbing a small sumac, bittersweet, and the Chinese beauty bush which, according to Ted, "is taking over the world."

We all agreed that today held its own special flavor, as we ended our winter walk at the clubhouse enjoying the happy shouts of children whirling down the hillside on large plastic discs. To us, all seasons on Cape Ann are enriching—for their pleasures, peacefulness, and above all, their inherent beauty.

164

12. SOUTH WOODS

1. Barn
2. Cranberry Bog
3. Third Tee
4. Water Tank
5. High Rock

KEY	
ⅢⅢⅢ	Trail
-- -- -	Sub Trail
——	Street or Highway
▪ ▪ ▪	Railroad Tracks
▓	Ocean
▒	Pond or Lake
⊠	Swamp

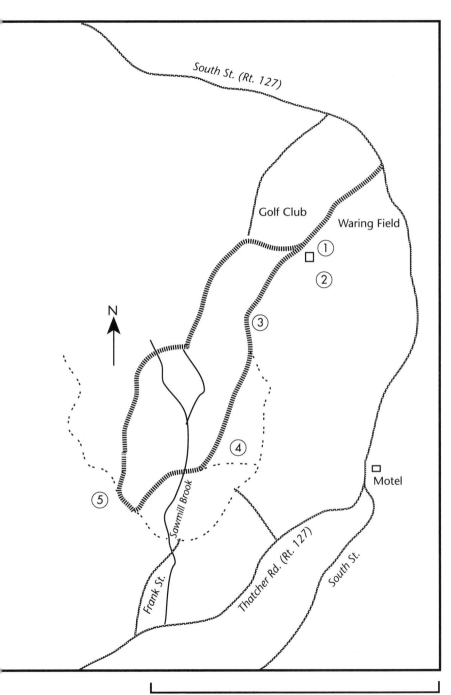

South St. (Rt. 127)

Golf Club

Waring Field

① ②

③

④

⑤

Motel

Sawmill Brook

Frank St.

Thatcher Rd. (Rt. 127)

South St.

N

1 Mile

Cape Pond

New England's landscape becomes magical in the fall when the foliage heightens in color and drama. People come by the thousands to view its spectacular beauty. They travel by foot, trail bike, car, and even low-flying airplanes to gaze entranced at the brightly crowned heads of beech, maple, oak, birch, chestnut, hickory, sassafras, tupelo, and witch hazel. With cameras clicking, they strive to capture the essence of what we like to think is "New England's gift to the world," seasonally speaking.

But this prettiest of seasons is not without its pitfalls. The danger of walking trails, climbing hills, crossing stony brooks and, in general, enjoying the splendor of nature in the autumn can pose a hazard—one that can be avoided by carefulness and an understanding of woodland conditions during this time of year.

The many rocks that make up Cape Ann's geological terrain hinder the outdoorsman when the ground is covered with fallen leaves, especially after a few days' rain. Leaves do not dry in dense woods and bottomlands as soon as the sun shines. It takes several days of dry, breezy weather before their layered dampness absorbs enough light and fresh air to dry out. Moist leaves and pine needles hidden beneath dry surfaces can be a source of mishap when walking rocky trails, climbing and descending hills, and crossing log bridges. A beautiful, ankle-deep red maple flooring can conceal damp rocks, depressions, and fallen obstructions along a sylvan pathway. "Slippery when wet" applies to Cape Ann's labyrinth of wooded trails, as well as its paved highways during this beautiful season.

We encountered such hazardous conditions during several October and November walks. One such experience was on the morning we explored the woods around Cape Pond, following five days of cold, rainy weather. "Raw" and "chowder weather" are the ways New Englanders describe it.

In mid-November, the temperature was in the low 40s, but the sun shone brightly as we headed for the Cape Pond Reservoir, located behind the Rockport Information Booth on Route 127. Joining us on this crisp,

chilly morning was a retired railroad man from Alaska and a young touring couple from Granby, Connecticut.

From the mall we drove to the Town Water Works facility behind the
visitor's shack where Ted had arranged parking privileges. During the
summer, all-day parking is permitted here for a nominal fee. Parking is
also available beside the visitor's booth. We walked along a paved service
road which curved down to the pump station at the water's edge.

Walking across the broad, grassy dam that spanned the reservoir's
deep, dark waters, Ted commented about the town's water system.

"Cape Pond provides Rockport's main water supply," he explained.
"It's backed up by Carlson Reservoir, which is backed up by Flat Ledge
quarry."

Pointing to the shallow water line along an embankment of blackened boulders, he voiced concern about the system's troubling deficiency.

"Those exposed rocks should be covered with water," he said. "We
intend to raise the water level by another 13 feet one of these days. But
I'm not sure I'll live to see it."

On the other side of the dam, our thoughts turned to the waning fall
foliage along the path: bayberry, sweetfern and black alder which is actually a deciduous holly (and looks like a holly, with its red berries).
About this colorful bush, Ted said, "It's getting to be an endangered
species around here because people pick it at Christmastime and during
the fall."

Leaving the broad roadway at the shoreline, we headed into the
woods and up a long, sloping hillside. As we climbed, our botanist trailmaster pointed out sweetpepper, red oak, hemlock and a pretty terrarium fern (polypody).

The late fall scenery along the route was unmatched by earlier trails.
Because fall was descending into winter, most of the hardwood trees were
now leafless—with the exception of oak and gray beech. The color and
texture of oak leaves change to a curly, leathery brown in the fall and
many remain on trees throughout the winter. But the leaf pattern of the
beech is different. Its pretty oval-shaped leaves, almost translucent in the
summer, become soft yellow in early autumn and turn luminous coppery
bronze as the season advances. Today their bright, tawny lucency
gleamed in the morning sunlight. The bark of the beech, at times pur-
plish gray, almost glows. Even as the tree ages, its texture remains
smooth. It was on a large beech in Washington County, Tennessee that
Daniel Boone carved his folksy missive: "D Boone cilled a bar on tree in
year 1760."

Passing between two large, craggy rocks covered with pine needles
and fallen leaves, we followed the trail along a ridge above the reservoir,

also sparkling below us in the morning sun. To our left a moss-covered embankment descended into a valley of young hemlocks. The woods, having returned to their dormant wintertime slumber, allowed a broad view of the rocky terrain. Within a short distance, the path met up with an old forest road that once led from Dogtown to Blackburn Circle in Gloucester. It was here that Ted left us to attend an early luncheon and another member of our party became guide for the rest of the morning.

A stone-wall fence of rather large rocks cascaded down a slope to greet us as we hiked along the trail. Another interesting-looking rock to our left captured our attention: huge and triumphant in the shadows of a towering hemlock, it resembled the backside of a mammoth humpback whale. Unlike Whale's Jaw in Dogtown which appears to be looming skyward out of the water, this rocky specimen was swimming lazily in an ocean of orange-brown leaves.

The rock formations seen throughout Cape Ann, like the white billowing clouds in Florida's tropical skies, spark the imagination of those who take the time to look. High in the heavens above the Sunshine Parkway, a flock of wooly sheep have pranced before my eyes; likewise adorable white French poodles, the stern face of Abraham Lincoln, the Leaning Tower of Pisa, and an army helmet—to name but a few of the many delightful images I've fancied during my travels along that long, desolate highway. All one needs to enter this enchanting world of make believe is sensitivity—and a child-like imagination. While the group was shuffling through crunchy brown leaves in Cape Pond's stark woodlands on that cold November morning, for a moment in time this landlubber was far away—whalewatching on the choppy open sea.

In the distance, denuded white birch and leafy gray beech—their colors ranging from pale yellow to blush pink to deep coppery tones—and a few white pine were scattered throughout the woods. Further on, again to our left, a small vernal pond, darkened by surrounding boulders and hemlock, mirrored their shadowy reflections in the still, black waters amid fallen, matted leaves.

The trail dipped and curved down a rather steep, rocky hillside, necessitating careful, deliberate steps. At the bottom, it opened onto a wide grassy plain, then split into a fork. We turned right which brought us along the northern tip of the reservoir beside at an old granite wall, part of the foundation of a circa 1853 icehouse. New Englanders today don't often experience the "old fashioned" winters their forebears suffered—the closest to one in modern times was in 1977 when snow drifted up to kitchen window sills. The Blizzard of '92 also hurled a hefty punch, dropping three feet of the white stuff on the Berkshires, but on Cape Ann heavy rain accompanied the howling wind and snowfall. In two days all was gone, then a few days before spring arrived, we experienced the winter "Storm of the Century."

In Cape Ann's early years, heavy snowfalls, blizzards and sub-zero temperatures were the norm for everyday life from November to February. This caused severe hardship for even the roughest of fishermen who made their living from the blustery winter seas—but profited the enterprising ice industry during those days before refrigeration and the home freezer. Large blocks of ice were carved out of the Cape Pond lake bed and stored in stone icehouses at the water's edge. The granite foundations of these structures can be seen today along the shoreline in the northwestern quadrant of the reservoir.

Returning to the broad service road, we continued around the pond for a short distance, then took a right onto an undefined footpath leading up another steep wooded hillside. Teaberries and moss-covered rocks greeted us as we entered the area. The leaves were damp and slippery, making climbing difficult, but by grabbing onto tree limbs to steady ourselves and hold our positions, we were able to dig in and inch forward. Up, up, up we scrambled, most of the group laboring in their effort; others, more practiced, proceeded almost effortlessly.

About three-quarters of the way up, our leader turned and walked laterally in a westerly direction for a short distance before turning again to climb straight up the hill. The long line behind her, sporting colorful jackets and sweatsuits, made bright splashes along the trail as they sought to keep up. At the tail end of the line some distance downhill, I lingered for a few minutes at the elbow curve to gaze at a row of small gray beech trees lining a stone wall. Their branches were full with tangy-orange foliage. Three dark, skeletal pillars stood on watch nearby: two old gray birch and a withering oak, all shorn of leaf and limb. Beneath them, a large round rock bore signs of its long-ago trouncing by the marauding glacier: split into two pieces, the larger stone hovered over the smaller one nestling beneath it in the leaves—like a doe sheltering a baby fawn.

I paused for a moment to savor the autumn splendor surrounding me on that quiet hillside. The others had gone ahead, but I could see their colorful forms through the leafless trees above me. They were cresting the hill and heading toward Babson Museum on Route 127. I shouldn't tarry any longer. Pointing my Minolta at the row of delicate young beeches, I wanted to take their exquisite beauty home with me. In another month, these woods would be covered with snow. The energized buds of last spring which blossomed into summer's green leaf, then burst ablaze with autumn brilliance, would soon become leafmold beneath a frosty blanket of white. In this decaying condition, they'd undergo further recycling, enriching the soil with valuable nutrients. Next spring, their tireless rejuvenation will bring forth another spirited season of growth upon the good earth.

At the top of the hill, the path became the Dorothy Luce Trail, bright orange double-dotted trees clearly marking its route through the uplands. The trail dipped lower into a section of woods dominated by medium-sized copper-leafed gray beech. Along the way, we passed a tall ageless red maple, which drew my attention because of the unusual formation of its bark. Slightly above eye level facing the trail, its leathery skin displayed a natural "cut away," forming an almost perfect design of an armored breastplate similar to those worn by ancient Roman soldiers. Or was this, too, a figment of my child-like imagination?

Descending further, the Luce Trail continued through an opening in a moss-covered stone wall, then curved to the right where a log bridge took us over a marshy section. The path then rose slightly, over a gentle brook, and turned right at a dead end. From this point beside an ancient red cedar, we could hear traffic along Route 127 near the Babson Museum.

"That's called Nugent Stretch," someone informed me, referring to the long, straight road in front of the museum. "All this property at one time was the old Nugent Farm. When it was sold and opened to traffic between Gloucester and Rockport, this was the only section that allowed cars to go fast, so they dubbed it 'The Nugent Stretch.'"

This whole area, in fact, was once known as "the Farms," because a number of farmsteads bordered the one-time country lane, including not only the large Nugent Farm, but also a piggery and several other smaller farms.

Here the Dorothy Luce Trail crossed Route 127 and joined the Dogtown network. But we stayed in the woods on the east side of the road, following a rugged footpath for a short distance, then turned right. Passing what appeared to be a children's campground, complete with a floored treehouse, we continued on with Route 127 now at our backs. Then I realized the reason for the circuitous route as the Cape Pond Reservoir came into view.

The woods along the trail were brown leaf, mostly gray beech and a few oak, except for several green mountain laurel, spindly white pine, and moss-covered logs. Again, rocks along the leaf-covered pathway mandated a sure foot. On an embankment overlooking the water stood an old, gnarled laurel which looked more like a Japanese bonsai tree than the healthy, full Calico bush it's known to be. Down we descended through the laurel, both mountain and sheep, to the water's edge where we hugged the shoreline north to the pump station. Walking over and around the blackened rocks, we came upon a storm strewn bird's nest and numerous seagull feathers. The latter surprised me, although the site was not too far from the ocean.

Sweetpepper lined the shoreline to the gravel pathway which brought us back to the winding service road. Raspberries, barberries, bittersweet and dried fall bouquets followed along beside us as we walked back to our cars.

We missed Ted's friendly lecture and witticisms on that sunny November morning but, because we've learned so much about Cape Ann's wilderness under his tutelage, the trails in and of themselves held much interest for all of us.

We returned to Cape Pond on a bright, sunny morning during a January thaw, a warm spell which traditionally welcomes in the new year after several weeks of snowfall and raw, wintry weather. But these pleasant conditions would be short-lived as an Alberta Clipper was heading our way. This is the intriguing name given to a blast of cold, arctic air originating in Siberia. It blows across western Canada, swoops down through the Great Lakes and the Midwest, then takes a final punch at New England before dissipating in the Atlantic.

It had snowed for most of the previous week on Cape Ann, following days of bone-chilling temperatures which, with the windchill, dropped thermometer readings to 8 below zero. The Cape became a spectacular winter wonderland when three to five inches of snowfall blanketed the area, and whirled into drifts measuring a foot or more. On this crisp Sunday morning, it had warmed to 37 degrees with a projected high of 52. The 30 walking enthusiasts who hit the trail around Cape Pond considered it a heat wave.

With only a slight detour, we followed the same trail we had taken in late fall. Today Ted led us, offering a running commentary on the wintry conditions of the woodland. The beautiful snowfall that lent added enchantment to the South Woods the previous Sunday was almost gone. Then, the trail was powdery white with freshly fallen snow and, for a time, we followed the tracks of cross-country skiers. Today's pathway was brown with pine needles and leafmold, frozen in places of shadow, in others moist in the sunny aftermath of the winter thaw. Only a few small patches of snow remained along the trail and throughout the woods.

Scanning the landscape through tall, leafless hardwoods, we now had a broad view of the wintry woodland terrain—ancient glacial stone, fallen trees, molding stumps, decaying leaves, ravines, slopes and small icy ponds beneath a forest of red maple, yellow birch, red oak and a few pines.

Trees are as interesting in winter as in other seasons of the year we learned that pleasant January morning. Stripped of their essentials, the broad-leafed trees stood tangled and bare-boned against the clear blue sky. In wintertime it's possible to study the characteristics of different buds, twigs and bark, as well as a tree's shape and form—to see how a trunk divides some distance from the ground and divides again and yet again as it reaches toward the sky. Barks vary in color and texture from light, silvery gray and parchment-like to dark, fibrous and furrowed. The twiggy crowns of trees are also noticeably different. During the winter season, some take on rich tones of raisin brown and rose; others are drab and dull in somber shades of gray.

As Ted continually points out during our seasonal explorations of Cape Ann's wilderness, soil, temperature and rainfall play a vital role in the condition and growth process of trees and shrubs. Several weeks previously while walking in the South Woods on a very cold day, we heard several trees "popping." He explained at the time that trees absorb water through roots (and leaves in season) which freezes and expands during frigid weather. This expansion causes limbs and branches to crack and break under the pressure.

On this day, we continued along the old forest road we had taken last fall, passing several familiar sights: the long stone wall that came out of the woods to greet us, the huge rock resembling a humpback whale, the old ice house foundation, the pretty gray beeches along the ridge above the reservoir, the centuries-old oak sporting a Roman breast-plate. And new ones that Ted pointed out: a large swamp that spills over to Thatcher Road and down to the marshes behind Good Harbor Beach, a narrow footpath leading to the old Joppa section of Gloucester, and several pretty vernal ponds that are so important to amphibians that winter over and lay eggs in the spring.

As we stood at the water's edge at the site of the old icehouse, a woman in the group gazed across the ice-covered "great pond" (any pond over 40 acres is called a great pond; Cape Pond is about 86), and pointed out the former site of the Abbot icehouse, a thriving business in the early 1800s. A novelist from Vienna, she and her husband now own the beautiful old Abbot house, an imposing Greek Revival built on the slope of Pleasant Street. In an effort to recapture its earlier charm and grace, she restored her backyard "necessary house," a two-seated model, to its original fine finish. The building considered necessary in those days is now simply an interesting conversation piece.

As we walked, Ted cited another chapter in Rockport's history which took place along Nugent Stretch across from the Babson Museum. Wild overgrowth now covers the ground that once held all the boisterous excitement of Webster Field, a popular baseball park that drew fans from near and far to cheer their favorite semi-pro team. They came by foot, trolley and train, the latter stopping at Bass Rocks Station, a short distance from the museum. Both the baseball field and the railroad station are gone now.

Along the wooded trail beside Nugent Stretch, the lesson changed from history to botany as Ted drew our attention to an unusual fungus attached to a large decaying red oak. Known botanically as rusty-hoofed foam fungus, this parasitic plant is really very beautiful—mahogany in color, singular in form, and shaped like a turreted seashell. It grows on the trunks of oaks and beech trees—giving the appearance of colorful seashells decorating a bathroom wall.

Our walk on this mild January morning was indeed pleasant. Others seemed to agree; later in the afternoon, Rockport village and Bear Skin Neck were teeming with Sunday visitors enjoying the unseasonably warm weather—if only for the day.

13. Cape Pond
RESERVOIR

1. Visitor's Information Booth
2. Rockport DPW
3. Observation Ledge

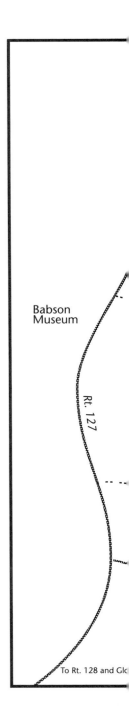

Babson
Museum

Rt. 127

To Rt. 128 and Glc

KEY

ⅢⅢⅢⅢⅢ	Trail
-- -- .	Sub Trail
‿‿‿‿	Street or Highway
▪ ▪ ▪	Railroad Tracks
▓	Ocean
▒	Pond or Lake
⊠	Swamp

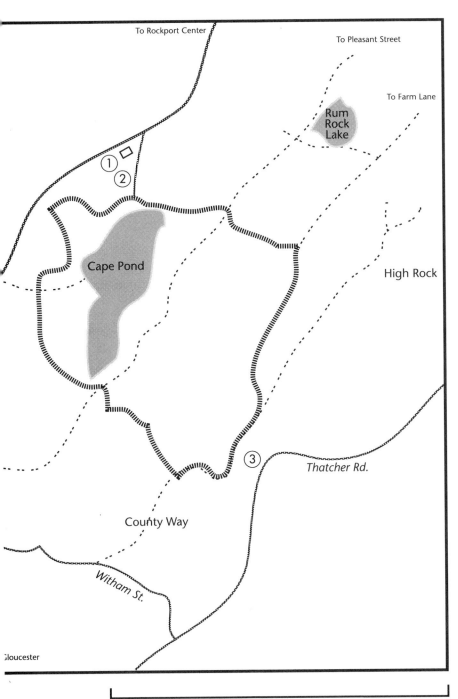

To Rockport Center

To Pleasant Street

To Farm Lane

Rum Rock Lake

① ②

Cape Pond

High Rock

③ Thatcher Rd.

County Way

Witham St.

Gloucester

1 Mile

THE DUNES AT WINGAERSHEEK BEACH

Wingaersheek Beach is one of Gloucester's most enjoyable summertime attractions. Here, thousands of visitors each year become beachcombers for a day, a weekend or a season, strolling its white sandy beach and sandbars, swimming its gentle bayside surf, and exploring the windswept dunes at its back. Cape Anners, nearby residents and tourists alike, return season after season to enjoy sunny, fun-filled, family outings on this picturesque New England bay. In March and April, a spectacular display of colorful kites of all shapes and sizes fly high above the waters of Wingaersheek, marking the onset of spring. Kept aloft by gusts from the sea, these high-flying acrobats dip and wing with the grace and ease of the curious shorebirds that join their flight.

To reach this beautiful stretch of sandy beach, take Route 128 north from Gloucester to Concord Street (Exit 13), then right on Concord for one-half mile to Atlantic Street. Follow the signs to Wingaersheek Beach, past the ice cream stand (on the left), the Long Wharf Public Landing and Boynton's Island (on the right) and the new Castleview community just before the stone gateposts at the entrance to the private summer colony. Bear right around the sharp curve and continue to the end of the road, which terminates at a waterfront parking area. The distance from the Atlantic Street turn-off to the beach is exactly one and eight-tenths miles. A friendly word of caution: most of the dramatic hillocks of sand—the dunes—are located within Wingaersheek's private community. The best time to explore this area is in the off-season—late fall through early spring, or Columbus Day through Memorial Day. The Essex County Greenbelt Association, which maintains the dunes and much of the surrounding marshland, permits off-season expeditions to these conservation sites (through the private gate), requesting—always—that visitors respect the privacy and property of the colony's residents in order that others may continue to enjoy this privilege.

The origin of the name Wingaersheek remains a mystery. Some feel it's Indian. But more likely it's a corruption of the German-Dutch "Wyngaert Hoeck," the name originally given to the area, according to Cape Ann maps published between 1630 and 1670. Wyngaert was possibly the German word *weingarten* meaning vineyard and "hoeck" the

Dutch term for "hook." The latter was dropped when it became known as Wingaersheek Beach. If one recalls New World history, the Pilgrims who settled in Plymouth had lived for many years in Holland, a fairly short distance from Hoek van Holland. It's easy to see that early map-makers of Dutch persuasion could have spelled the term "Hoeck" instead of the anglicized "hook." Hook, by definition, is a "sharp bend or curve, as in a stream, or a spit or narrow cape of sand or gravel turned landward at the outer end, as Sandy Hook." That seems to describe the Coffin Beach sand spur jutting into the Essex River, which is now considered part of Wingaersheek.

Whatever the origin of this unusual name, Wingaersheek Beach is one of the prettiest strands found anywhere. What makes it so extraordinary is its miles of natural, unspoiled shoreline, its white sandy beach, its clear, warm water and gentle surf, and sandbars that extend far out into the channel and Ipswich Bay. Adding to its charm and beauty are the swirling tides of surrounding inland waterways—the channel of the Annisquam River, Ipswich Bay and the Essex River.

"Hooking" into the Essex Bay is the aforementioned Coffin's Beach which fronts the private summer colony. While both beaches are open to the public, Coffin's is accessible only by boat or by wading around a rocky promontory east of Wingaersheek. This is a pleasant venture at low tide, but the rocks provide the only route back for landlubbers when the water rises. Some have been known to walk the sandbars to Coffin's Beach when the tide was out and found themselves stranded there when it came in again. With a little forethought, it's possible to enjoy both beaches on a hot summer afternoon.

Coffin's Beach has an interesting history unto itself. The area, known as Tuppeny Loaf, was originally bought from the Indians for a tuppence (twopence). Later it was granted to shipwright William Stevens by the town of Gloucester and came into the Coffin family of Newbury in 1688. They developed the farm started by Stevens. Generations later, in the eighteenth century, it became the largest farm on Cape Ann—five hundred acres—owned by Peter Coffin who took to raising sheep. At one time, sand from the dunes was a source of family income for the Coffin heirs. This fine-grained sand found a market among early settlers from Portsmouth to Boston who used it for scrubbing unpainted kitchen floors long after carpets were laid in "front rooms."

These sand dunes also played an unexpected role in the Revolutionary War when the British warship *Falcon* sailed into Ipswich Bay on August 5, 1775. Captain John Lindsey, spotting sheep grazing in Coffin's pasture, dispatched a pinnace with about 30 men to bring back the makings of a hearty meal of fresh mutton for his hungry crew. But

Major Coffin and his farmhands were also on watch that day. Mustering a surprise attack, Coffin and his men fired such a fusillade of musket balls from behind the dunes that the besieged Redcoats thought Coffin's defense was much larger than it actually was. Looking through his glass from the ship, Lindsey saw reinforcements running to Coffin's aid from both ends of the beach. He ordered his men back. They quickly put about without touching shore, and once again the fiery revolutionists overcame the mighty force of the King's Royal Navy—who found themselves without mercy, and without the tasty mutton they had hoped would grace their dinner table that night.

The day Ted chose to visit the dunes at Wingaersheek was bright with warm April sunshine, following months of cold wintry weather. It was an occasion we had all been eagerly awaiting—the first hint of spring, and a walk through Wingaersheek's famous desert world. These shifting sand hills are a natural resource more often associated with the heat mirages of the Mohave Desert than the rocky New England seacoast that only a few weeks earlier had experienced the snowstorm of the century.

Those of us who were new to the experience of sloping sand dunes on Cape Ann wondered aloud how they had come to be here at all. Ted satisfied our curiosity by explaining about underwater mountains of sand and the forces that shape them into the bleached hummocks seen along desolate coastlines that lack heavy forestation.

"The sand washes in from the ocean floor with incoming tides," he said. "These grains of sand are very fine and don't hold water. Also, they lack nourishment which means they don't produce vegetation to stabilize the soil. Wild plums grow here, along with beach grass (called eel grass) and sea lavender. But much of the growth is trampled or ripped up by storms, leaving the sands exposed and easily blown around by the wind. As a result, their shapes change constantly, creating these hills and ridges of sands."

Sand dunes are a critical resource of barrier beaches. They defend against flooding, shelter wild animals and dramatize the scenery of the beach itself. Acting as a natural buffer zone, the dunes absorb wind and wave energy of the ocean, protecting the mainland behind them.

We parked on a private road beside a posted Essex County Greenbelt conservation site and climbed a steep sandy hillside. Reaching the top, we were dazzled by the sheer beauty of the natural seascape surrounding us. At our back was the Annisquam River, straight ahead the mouth of the Essex and beyond that, Crane's Beach, Castle Neck and Steep Hill hugged the shoreline of Ipswich Bay. Plum Island was a speck on the distant horizon. The closer view punctuated white beaches and sandbars from the vivid blueness of placid inland waterways, the Atlantic Ocean and Shakespeare's "majestical roof fretted with golden fire . . . that separates day from night."

Off to the right, on the Upper Beach section of Wingaersheek, the turrets of two turn-of-the century castles poked through the pines. "Tuppenny Towers," located at the western tip of Two Penny Loaf, was originally the 12-room summer home of Edward Hawks, a successful Buffalo attorney. Not to be outdone, his brother-in-law, W. W. Bailey, built "Red Gables" close by—so close, in fact, that it appears the two structures are joined, but they're not. At about this time Edward's brother James, a railroad tycoon from Detroit, bought land nearby and vowed he, too, would own a castle-by-the-sea. He selected the ideal spot—on a high ridge a short distance inland overlooking Ipswich Bay with a magnificent view all the way to Boston. Plans were drawn and the foundation laid. Next, granite orders were placed with nearby quarries—gray from Gloucester and rust from Rockport.

All was going as planned—until Mrs. James Hawks arrived one day to survey her new summer homesite. This would not do, she declared, much to her husband's chagrin. It was too isolated; she wanted to live closer to the bay. Being a devoted and dutiful spouse, Mr. Hawks again tramped the land and found another spot more to his lady's liking. On a bluff at the east end, he constructed a modest one-story fieldstone English cottage which they called their "Bungalow." There they lived happily ever after—during the summertime. The small beach house stands today at 19 Bungalow Street, named for the famous Gloucester landmark. A rare story, indeed—a woman of wealth who preferred a small bayside bungalow over her very own castle—and a loving husband who sought to please her in every way. Ah, the age of romance and gallantry!

In time, the land owned by James Hawks increased to 1,000 acres. In an effort to develop the area by shading the dunes, the farsighted ecologist imported 10,000 Austrian pines which he planted throughout his vast land holdings. On his deathbed, he instructed his son to protect his strikingly beautiful trees for future generations. Sadly, this was not done. When the pines grew tall and straight, almost all were cut for lumber and hauled off to Essex shipbuilders across the bay. Just as the native pines of Dogtown went into ships for the British Navy; a century later, the stately Austrian imports gave rise to America's fishing industry. In any event, because the point was no longer forested and reseeded by these beautiful conifers, the dunes once again took over Wingaersheek Beach. Only a precious few of Mr. Hawk's prized legacy remain today.

As is the case with many of Cape Ann's interesting historic land-marks, Ted was no stranger to the interior of "Tuppenny Tower," having attended a political reception at the imposing granite stronghold hosted by the present owner.

"It's very Victorian inside," was his usually brief commentary on such things.

Walking along the ridge within sight of the two castles on the point, we stumbled upon the foundation of what was to have been the third of such regal Cape Ann summer homes. Now abandoned and overgrown with beachgrass and wild plum bushes, it bore silent witness to the age-less power of love.

Beachgrass helps stabilize the dunes and slow their migration. Tolerant of saltspray and wind, it has the unique ability to grow after it has been completely covered with sand because of its network of under-ground stems and roots (sometimes 6 feet deep). These characteristics make it a valuable dune builder, but despite its tough, sharp-pointed leaves, beachgrass is very fragile. When shoots are broken by foot traffic, they die.

From the sandy heights, we descended the opposite hillside. Almost a sheer drop, it made the plunge rather challenging. Holding onto the branches of a budding shad and a nearby apple tree, we dug in our heels and made our way down to the bottom—into a patch of sea roses. With his trusty shears, Ted, in the lead, quickly cleared a path which brought us to another ridge of shifting sand. There were no trees along this downward slope and no briers at its base, just a gradual descent of clean white sand which made travel easier and fun. Some slid, others dug in and "waddled like ducks" down the sandy hillside, this time land-ing in a bed of poverty grass, also called beach heath, a low shrubby plant with scale-like leaves growing close to the stem.

"It's one of the few plants that can survive in these sands," Ted informed us.

Crossing the street, we then took a brief hike through the roadside marshes. Cutting through a thicket of American beauty shrubs—the China import that is "taking over the world"—Ted led us along a trail that almost immediately brought us back to the cars. Someone stopped to examine a sea star, a small buff-colored papery ball whose star-shaped petals pulled back like wedges of an orange peel, revealing a cluster of spores, the type of seeds found in mushrooms and other fungi.

Leaving the hilly dunes, we drove to another conservation area to explore the marshes near the old Stella Maris Catholic Youth Camp. Abandoned for many years, the camp's isolated cabins now provide real-live-action training for the Gloucester and Rockport fire departments. A sign painted on the long, straight wire-fenced blacktop needling through the Greenbelt wetlands warns that "No Hunting" is allowed.

It was a pleasant morning walk, peaceful and relaxing. Bordered by a sweeping vista of meandering marshes and an unspoiled swampy area, we sought signs of early spring wildlife after the long, harsh winter. We didn't wait long. From the swamp came the loud shrills of spring peepers (small frogs about an inch and one-half to two inches in size), and a snowy white egret took hurried flight, pursued by a cawing black crow. Nearby two plump black-bellied plovers splashed in a pool in the marsh. The egret, a member of the heron family, is a regular visitor to New England. It had been brought to the verge of extinction by plume hunters, a situation the National Association of Audubon Societies rectified, fortunately. Soon the persistent and jolly *o-ka-lee* of a red-winged blackbird filled the air and, although we scanned the area carefully, we failed to spot the illusive feathered optimist of bogland.

"They love the cattails and nest in them," said Ted. "The males are here, but I don't think the females have arrived yet."

High-bush blueberries, alder, shad and viburnum of various kinds dotted the swamp on our left. And something new along the roadside caught my eye—mullein, a tall hairy Eurasian herb which has become a well-established weed in pastures and fallow fields throughout the United States. Its simple leaves form a rosette, alternating on the stem, and its flowers terminate into spikes. Mullein foxglove is a pretty variation found mostly in the South.

To the right, beyond large stands of cattails and phragmites, a commanding view of the soft, wet marshes opened a window onto its earthy milieu. Wetlands are usually not a cheerful place, but if there's a songbird singing, peepers peeping, plovers playing and other wildlife stirring, nature lovers enjoy this watery habitat.

At the end of the fenced-in roadway was the abandoned youth camp. Here we turned left and followed an unpaved road that took us to higher ground where the soil was drier. We passed a grove of red cedars, a long lichen-covered rock which to one "looked like an upside down alligator," and the remnants of a tennis court. Further into the woods were more red cedars and various other pines—pitch and Scotch and a few of Mr. Hawk's beautiful Austrian imports.

The broad dirt road curved to the right and climbed a rise where sections were divided into lots and staked with pink ribbons.

"The word 'develop' always scares me," sighed Ted, whose profession is land management with a strong emphasis on conservation. He then reported on the status of the development that had begun long ago in these pretty wooded heights.

"This land is owned by a development company which has been trying to build houses here for about ten years," he explained, "but they've had difficulty resolving the sewage problem. They originally planned to install a private water treatment plant, but the question was how to pay for it—and who would maintain it. They haven't found answers yet. In the meantime, the lots remain unsold and the land, thankfully, is still undeveloped."

Walking through the abandoned home sites, he led us to a large flat rock at the edge of a ridge which provided another spectacular view of the surrounding waterways and shorelines. Below, attractive beach houses dotted Wingaersheek's summer colony. A tiny red buoy (of the whistling kind) floated in the channel at the mouth of the Annisquam River, today as smooth as a millpond, separating the beach from the community of Annisquam. Its lighthouse on Wigwam Point is one of the most picturesque scenes on the Cape, drawing scores of artists and photographers each year to capture its ageless charm. Lovely waterfront homes, from villas—one a towering Spanish hacienda—to modest shingled cottages, tier down to the shore from rocky ridges silhouetted against the sky.

It was then time to leave this idyllic spot, perhaps to return again after the crush of summer. We retraced our steps back to the Greenbelt sign and our cars, having explored the exciting world of lordly castles, desert sand dunes, and British warships off Coffin's Beach—all of which are part and parcel of the saga of Cape Ann.

14. THE DUNES AT WINGAERSHEEK

1. Entrance Gate to Private Community
2. Essex County Greenbelt Land
3. Old Hawks Castle Foundation
4. Tuppeny Towers
5. Red Gables
6. Old Camp Stella Maris
7. Rock Overlook

Twopenr

KEY

︙︙︙︙︙	Trail
-- -- .	Sub Trail
﹏﹏	Street or Highway
• • •	Railroad Tracks
▨	Ocean
▧	Pond or Lake
▨	Swamp

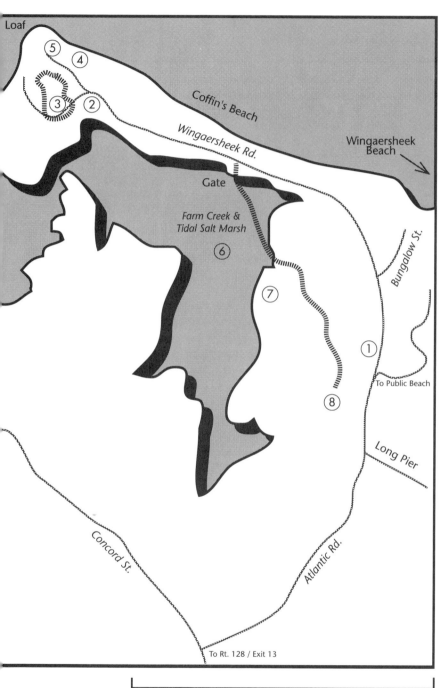

Loaf

⑤ ④

③ ②

Coffin's Beach

Wingaersheek Rd.

Wingaersheek Beach

Gate

Farm Creek & Tidal Salt Marsh

⑥

⑦

Bungalow St.

①

To Public Beach

⑧

Long Pier

Concord St.

Atlantic Rd.

To Rt. 128 / Exit 13

1 Mile

Essex

Have you seen the waste of salt marsh
When the fog has left its haze
On the winding, blue-gray river?
Have you seen it on such days?

From *The Marshes*
By Agnes Choate Wonson

Essex County Greenbelt Association • Cox Reservation

The Essex County Greenbelt Association is a private land trust dedicated to the preservation of natural resources throughout Essex County, which includes Cape Ann. Its aim is to save open space having ecological, agricultural or scenic significance. At the present time the organization oversees almost 6,000 acres of land, with additional properties coming under its protection annually through donation, restriction rights and direct purchase. As its name implies, the group places special emphasis on protecting corridors or "greenbelts" of land for natural resources, as well as for the enjoyment of nature lovers, birdwatchers, wildlife photographers, educators, hikers, and people who simply want a few hours away from the busyness of everyday life.

The topography of Essex County is varied and includes rocky shores, granite ledges, coastal thickets, forested uplands, salt marshes, tidal flats, tidal ponds, swamps, barrier beaches, inland waterways and offshore islands. Of the 6,000 acres protected by Greenbelt, approximately 1,000 are salt marshes, extending from Gloucester to Salisbury at the New Hampshire border. Its many reservations are open to the public free of charge every day from sunrise to sunset. They can be found in an excellent booklet published by the Association called *Passport to Essex County Greenbelt* which includes directions, general description, special features and a trail map of all locations. A list of birds and amphibians is included, as well as a calendar indicating what can be seen on Greenbelt properties—and when and where. It's a practical naturalist's guide to Essex County—one every nature-lover should tuck inside a convenient pocket. Inasmuch as this book is about Cape Ann, we will confine our Greenbelt walks to the communities of Rockport, Gloucester, Essex and Manchester-By-The-Sea, but all the other properties are well worth exploring.

On the first Sunday in May the sun shone brightly over every acre of Essex County Greenbelt land so Ted decided this would be a good day to explore the marshes and farmlands in Essex (before the mosquitoes and greenheads "arrived by the millions"), with a side trip to Watch Hill. Because the weather was gorgeous—temperatures reaching the 70s by afternoon—a growing number of newcomers joined us for the walk. Carpooling from Whistlestop Mall, we headed for Route 128, taking Route 133 to Essex. Just beyond Farnham's Restaurant (exactly two and six-tenths miles after leaving Route 128), we turned right at the first drive and continued up a long, straight, unpaved road leading to a historic white saltwater farmhouse nestled against a hillside, part of the scenic Cox Reservation and headquarters for the Greenbelt Association.

For 50 years this historic Essex landmark was the country home of a famous muralist, Allyn Cox, and his wife. Upon her death, Mr. Cox left the 18th century colonial farmhouse and gardens, his studio and 31 acres of marsh, meadow and woodland to the Essex Greenbelt. The interior of the house has many classic features of lasting charm and dignity; lovely red reeded dado on the mantel in the upstairs living room and patterned wainscoting throughout were popular themes in homes of that period.

Complementing the residence in style and character are beautifully landscaped gardens, adding to the portrait of comfortable rural living. Here, in the heart of the marshes, a patch of its rich black soil has been transformed into a Garden of Eden, bordered in fieldstone and splendid in every detail. Stone walkways wander through a bed of old and rare roses, one an ancient rosa mundi from the garden of Governor William Dudley's ancestral home in Exeter, England. Nearby a 200-year-old red mulberry tree has become a favorite nesting place for songbirds hidden in the shade of its heart-shaped leaves and thriving on a bounty of tasty berry-like fruit. Small, well-designed plots draw attention to an extensive collection of perennial flowers and shrubs, among them peonies, irises, blue and white wisteria, lilacs and forsythia—a truly magnificent bouquet of spring freshness. Pretty meadow violets with deep blue flowers and dark green, heart-shaped leaves lend harmony and simplicity to the old-fashioned dooryard.

The meandering stone path opens onto an orchard of ancient apple and pear trees, among the former a Ben Davis, a variety nearly 200 years old, a Rhode Island Greening, originated from seed near a Rhode Island tavern, and a Thompkins King, which first appeared about 1800 in New Jersey. But the Roxbury Russet is perhaps the oldest of them all, coming from Roxbury in the mid-1600s, about 100 years before Johnny Appleseed set out from Leominster with a sack of apple seeds (gathered from cider press refuse) to plant apple orchards wherever he met early settlers clearing their land. Another eye-pleaser is the grape arbor, well-tended and robust as is the orange tree which grows nearby—the latter, like the magnolias of Ravenswood, a rarity in climates like New England.

The parking area rises above the tiered gardens, next to a sturdy, shingled New England barn which long ago had been renovated into a modern art studio by the gifted Allyn Cox. It was here in the quiet of the Essex marshes that Mr. Cox did the preparatory work for murals that at once became treasured masterpieces. Among his widely acclaimed works are three mosaic murals he created for Grant's Tomb in New York City; *Moses with the Law*, a mural decoration painted at the University of Virginia; and *All for Love*, another mural painting artistically rendered on the ceiling of the W. A. Clark, Jr. Library in Los Angeles. Shortly before his death in 1982, the artist completed a major restoration of the ceilings and walls of the nation's Capitol in Washington, D. C. Among the eight historic scenes he mastered skillfully in fresco, while balancing himself high atop the scaffolding, were George Washington laying the Capitol's cornerstone in 1793, Andrew Jackson's inauguration on the Capitol steps, John Quincy Adams speaking in the Old House Chamber, and the Capitol rotunda being used as a hospital during the Civil War. It took him a year and a half to prepare the full size drawings of these and other mural designs he created for the Capitol renovation. Some of these preparatory works are now on display at the Smithsonian Museum; several of the frames he used for large canvas panels can be seen just as he left them hanging in his Essex studio. To the sensitive artist, his presence lingers.

During the summer, an "Art in the Barn" festival provides local artists an opportunity to work and exhibit in the studio where this great artist labored so diligently for most of his remarkable life, inspired by views of Ebben Creek, his beloved fruit trees and bronze-gold stretches of marshland seen through the glass north wall. The studio also features a 30-foot-high, roll-around staging which he had constructed to handle large pieces of artwork.

The Cox Reservation includes two parcels of land: 27 acres of upland and marsh, rendering magnificent views of the salt marsh, Essex River, the back of Crane's beach, Castle Hill and Hog Island, and a four-acre woodlot on nearby Lufkin Street, which each spring and summer becomes a naturalist's delight in its prevalence of wildflowers and birdlife.

To begin our exploration of the marshes, we followed a wide grassy path separating an alley of woodlands from the Anderson Meadow, a pretty green field of huge, golden King Alfred daffodils sloping down to the river bank. The meadow is named in honor of the late George Anderson, a man who stood tree-top tall among conservationists. While living in Magnolia in the early 1970s, he became involved with the Greenbelt Association. Later he joined the organization as resident care-taker of the Cox Reservation and became the Greenbelt's official walk-master, responsibilities he embraced with great vitality and loved pas-sionately for 13 years. He served on the board of directors for many years and as vice president prior to his death in January 1992. Among the pleasures he gained from his work at the reservation was creating many of the gardens and walkways visitors enjoy today. Over the years he contributed endless hours and personal resources planting thousands of bulbs, like the King Alfreds in the meadow, and hundreds of perennials and annuals. He came from a family of avid gardeners and at age 10, received the first of many gardening awards. Under his tutelage, the Cox Reservation became an annual stop for many garden clubs and flower lovers, as well as those who wandered in to enjoy the simple beauty of this very special place. All who came were always warmly welcomed. In addition to the Anderson Meadow, a bench with a memorial plaque has been placed along the path in his honor. Cox Reservation, like Halibut Point State Park, will forever cherish the memory of this sensitive, gentle man whose legacy to nature lovers provides nourishment for the mind, body and soul.

As we continued along the path between the woodland and the meadow, a song-bird serenaded us from a nearby tree—a mockingbird or cardinal, we couldn't see which. In the distant marshes, two snowy egrets fluttered along the top of the channeled marsh waters.

On a rise jutting into the marshes was a small private clearing on which a large contemporary house was in the early stages of construc-tion.

"There used to be a little summer cottage there tucked in between apple trees, with lots of wildlife in the woods," Ted reminisced; "but now someone's building that casino-like structure and taking every inch of land to do it," he said ruefully. The site did indeed appear to be a com-mercial venture, with several new detached buildings underway, stretch-ing to the very edge of the owner's property lines. Large blue plastic sheets were draped over unfinished sections to prevent dust and debris from getting into the marshes. Watching Ted as he surveyed yet another assault on nature's ecosystem, I wondered if I were going to see a grown man cry. But he continued on with only a shake of his head—and, I'm sure, a troubled heart. We learned later the owner was 80 years old and wondered why he would want to build such a large home at this time in his life.

Once we left the *terra firma* of the meadow, walking closer to the marshes became more difficult.

"It'll be a little wet, I'm afraid," Ted told us. He was right. Cushioned by layers of dry marsh hay, we thought we'd be dry, but soon found ourselves sinking deep into wet mucky soil. But we plodded on. Picking up two shells, Ted identified them as blue mussels, pointing out the difference between their smooth and ribbed shells. "You'll find the smooth shells attach themselves to rock by a thin thread, but ribbed mussels work their way into the mud."

In explaining the marshy habitation, he said, "Small fish breed in the marshes to feed big fish. These salt marshes provide the base for the fisheries, so preservation is extremely important. One acre of salt marsh provides ten times the biological activity of a good corn field of the same size."

He continued, "The greenhead flies which are so prevalent in these marshes provide food for both fish and birds, but they do a lot of damage to animals and people because they live off protein which they get from blood."

In the 1930s, ditches were dug to drain the marshes as a means of mosquito control. Horses equipped with wooden platform shoes pulled wagon after wagonload of rich black earth to nearby embankments, but it proved to be a fruitless task. Water from the Essex River immediately flowed into the trenches, forming channels which are now eroding and falling in. Later, a new method of mosquito control was developed—the digging of retention ponds with shallow ditches leading out of them. These ponds have no outlets to the river, which enable small fish to survive in the pools at low tide. Other advantages of this method are more protection from eroding currents and better filtering of man-made pollutants into the main marsh channels and clam beds. But, walking along the river bank, we saw evidence of erosion caused by weather, tides, and prop wash from powerful pleasure boats. The end result is that both the river and the channels are becoming very shallow because areas once covered with thick grass are now gutted.

As a research biologist, Ted is keenly attuned to Cape Ann's ecosystem, discoursing on a wide range of interesting topics during our times together. His down-to-earth, no-nonsense lectures and witticisms delight listeners of all ages who hang onto his every word. Sometimes those in the back miss something but are never hesitant to ask, "What did he say?" and the lesson is passed along until everyone catches the drift of his remarks.

We stood for a few moments drinking in the wonder of the scene spread out before us. The tall thatch extended for acres and acres. How many? someone asked. Later, we learned that our panoramic view swept about 1,000 acres of marshland, taking in the waters of the Essex and Castle Neck rivers, Hog Island, Cross Island, Conomo Point, the dunes at Cranes Beach and the tip of Annisquam. Later, from Watch Hill, we would see it from higher ground and it was every bit as stupendous.

Two common salt marsh grasses are native to the Essex wetlands: *spartina alterniflora* and *spartina patens*. These plants provide a good visual map of changes in the height of the salt marsh soil. *Spartina alterniflora* grows where the tide wets its roots twice a day. In contrast, *spartina patens* is much finer in texture and grows in flattened whorls like cowlicks. This grass has been harvested for salt hay since the Indian days. The heavier *spartina alterniflora* was used for roof thatching.

Stopping to pick up a hollow reed, Ted remarked, "These were also stuffed into walls to insulate old houses. They were sewn together as mats, like Japanese Venetian blinds ... now that's an odd combination of words," he said, interrupting himself. "The mats made handling easier, but they went up like matchsticks in a fire—so you were either warm or very warm."

On a stretch of rocky shoreline, swirls of damp, dark brown rockweed lay embedded in the dried marsh grass. Ted explained that these seaweeds are algae without actual roots or leaves. However, root-like fasteners secure them to rocks along the shore at the low tide line. During high tide, they rise toward the surface and are kept afloat by air bladders (little bubbles) attached to their rubbery leaves. Two types of this rockweed are common along Cape Ann shorelines: *sea wrack* and *knotted wrack*.

Our next stop was a grove of red cedars which provided a picturesque, park-like setting on a small point sloping down to the river bank. A rustic bench offered the visitor a chance to stop and rest in the shade. Here, too, we found another instance of Mr. Anderson's beautification endowment. "He cleaned this out so people could enjoy the river," said Ted, a long-time friend, who helped him with spring plantings. Together, they shared many enjoyable nature walks over the years, sometimes on Ted's turf along one of Cape Ann's wilderness trails, sometimes on Mr. Anderson's at Halibut Point or here at the Cox Reservation.

Leaving the shady nook of pine, we followed a narrow footpath through an orchard of apple and wild cherry trees, skirting the western side of the construction site which spread to its stonewall boundary. A right curve led down to Clam House Landing, across the river from the historic Cogswell Grant, a rare surviving example of a 17th-century Town Grant recently deeded to the Society for the Preservation of New England Antiquities. This area of sandy clam flats is known for the tasty shellfish it yielded up to Indians and early settlers in centuries past.

Continuing straight, we soon emerged into another sun-splashed meadow with grass that belonged in an Easter basket, its texture and color were so vibrant. Bouquets of jonquils, a cream-colored version of the King Alfred daffodil, grew in patches along the farm road that edged the field.

"That field is good for quail nesting," we were told by our wildlife teacher. "The time of mowing was changed until later in the season so as not to disturb the nests."

The quail native to eastern North America is the bob-white; Northerners call him quail, to the Southerner he's a partridge. Men have always sought this good-natured bird; farmers because he destroys weeds and insects, sportsmen for hunting and dog-training, and the gourmet for fine dining. Severe winter weather and hunters have greatly reduced the population of quail in the northern states, but ornithologists have been very successful in propagating it artificially during the last thirty years. As a result, it's now possible to breed the species in unlimited numbers throughout its entire range.

Along the route a tired old birdhouse looked forlorn in the crook of an equally tired old apple tree. Several more were perched atop poles in a field in an attempt to encourage the nesting of bluebirds whose population seems to be declining each year. Also lining the path were large choke cherries towering high above shrubby viburnum, wild currants and wild onions. The road continued on to the Cox studio, bringing to an end the first part of our exploration of Essex marshland, which took about a half hour. Next we would climb Watch Hill at the north end of town and walk along Island Road to gain another perspective of the marshes.

WHITE HILL (WATCH HILL)

Leaving the solitude of Cox Reservation, we drove across the causeway through the tiny village of Essex, rich in maritime history. Soon after its incorporation in 1819, shipbuilding and shellfish brought world fame to this little New England hamlet. It's still small—five miles long and three miles wide—but today antique shops, historic homes and farms, and seafood restaurants are its main attractions.

Traveling east on Route 133, we passed a large brown colonial salt-box, the John Wise House circa 1701, Hardy Hatcheries, and the golf course, taking a right onto Island Road—a distance of exactly two and one-half miles from the Cox Reservation. Our destination was on the immediate right, atop the James N. and Mary F. Stavros Reservation, 73 acres of woodland, field and salt marsh.

White Hill is a drumlin that built up after the glacier passed. Many refer to it as Watch Hill because of the large, fieldstone Watch Tower built in the late 1800s to observe ground and forest fires. Four decks reached skyward on the original structure, but all have since been removed. Today only the 12-foot base remains, having been capped at the first platform.

With the tower at our backs, we had a magnificent 180-degree view of the brooding marshes—and much more. Sweeping the landscape, we gazed down upon the Essex River lapping at Dean Island, Hog Island, Cross Island, Conomo Point and Dilley Island (in Essex), Castle Hill, Steep Hill and Crane's Beach (in Ipswich) and the distant dunes at Wingaersheek Beach (in Gloucester). Binoculars focussed, cameras clicked and camcorders whirled as we sought to capture the natural beauty of salt marsh, wandering river, islands, and the jagged line of sand dunes in the distance.

Soon it was time to leave. We descended the hill and continued along Island Road, an old paved-over log-based oxen trail that winds down to a public landing. Looking to our right across the marshes, we could see White Hill and the manicured turf of the golf course. Straight ahead were the dunes along the south end of Crane's Beach, the thin blue lines of Annisquam and Lanesville, and the islands in between. Rounding a curve, we came upon a pastured hillside fringed with elms, butternut and wild cherry trees.

When the road straightened again, the long, brown-shingled hen-houses on Hardy's original homestead came into view. "Hen-house" is a good description for these large, three-story, barracks-like affairs, which have rows and rows of small-paned windows. Across the road, the family's old wooden farmhouse still stands hidden by two giant oaks.

A local television station produces beautiful seasonal programs featuring scenes and activities of Cape Ann, shown against a background of classical musical. One piece shown regularly during the Thanksgiving and Christmas holidays is "The Barnyard Opera." Its theme is a visit to the farm; the music the *Habanera* movement by Bizet from the *Carmen Suite*. Each time the chorus sings, huge, white barrel-chested Tom turkeys are shown "gobbling" away noisily, as if in sync with the music. As the soloist continues, peaceful farm scenes depict cows chewing at the trough, horses roaming the pasture, sheep huddling together—and the sashaying rumps of large white ducks waddling across the field. When the credits roll, special thanks are extended to the Essex Turkey Farm "for the use of the chorus."

Another farmland performance features Hardy's feathery broods. In this production, hens and roosters are seen poking their heads out second- and third-story windows. Strains of Gershwin's *Rhapsody in Blue* are heard in the background, choreographed to the movements of myriad of Hardy's prized fowls. It's a scene with which many Cape Anners are familiar—and greatly enjoy—which is why we were delighted to see the actual performers greet us from their high-rise "stage" as we passed along Island Road. But this was no television set, of that we were quite sure. We could tell from the pungent aroma that filled the morning air.

The public landing today is limited to small aluminum rowboats (used by clam diggers), canoes and kayaks because of the narrow, shallow channel. Old clamshells cover the shoreline along banks of rich black peat, and several large rocks rising out of the water at high tide further restrict the size of vessels using the landing. We lingered for awhile, sensing the mystique of this ancient place that long ago saw Indians farming the land, canoeing the river, and digging for clams, ever mindful that the source of their bounty was the Great Spirit in the Sky.

HOG ISLAND

The only way to visit this historic island farm and its neighbors—Dean, Corn, Cross, and Dilley islands—is to drive down to the Essex Marina and climb aboard the Essex River Queen for a cruise through the tranquil waters of the Essex River estuary. Regularly scheduled cruises aboard a comfortable, open, three-pontoon riverboat tour the marshes and islands daily from May to October. Narrated by a naturalist well-informed on the area's history, wildlife and vegetation, the trips are interesting as well as relaxing. I joined several travel writers for the cruise on opening day in mid-May, and returned in the fall with Ted's walking group.

Sailing through the channel past peat bogs and salt marshes estimated to be several thousand years old, we were taken back to a way of life that is difficult for most of us to imagine. Remnants of pulverized clamshells along Clammers' Beach were a lingering reminder of Indian days. Hog Island was their summer camping grounds. Today commercial clammers can be seen, bucket in hand, digging the same ageless clam flats.

As the open riverboat wound its way through the meandering Essex waters to Hog Island, we had a good view of Crane's English Manor House at Castle Hill in Ipswich. This imposing estate, now under the management of The Trustees of Reservations, was the scene of several episodes in the *Witches of Eastwick*.

Hog Island is another classic drumlin, rising 300 feet out of the marshes. Swine were said to have grazed here in the early 1600s, hence its name. However, some say the name comes from the island's large, hog-back shape which gave rise to the ditty, "Hog Island is a whale and folks live on its tail." Whatever one's belief, the history of this beautiful "Emerald Jewel of Essex Bay" is time-worn and richly flavored.

The Agawam Indian tribe owned the island until 1638, selling it to John Winthrop of Ipswich (then Chebacco) for 20 pounds. John Choate purchased common lots in 1667 and the land remained in the Choate family for 250 years, until 1916 when it was sold to Richard Crane. It was presented to The Trustees of Reservations in 1975 by the widow of Cornelius Crane, a descendent, and is now open to the public.

Landing on Long Island (next to Hog Island), we walked the shore-line toward the 1725 Choate house, resting on a slope of the "hog's back." At the river's edge, we tramped over quartz, granite and slate—rubble that had been brought down from Canada by the glacier. From there, we followed a country lane through a thicket of woodland. Long Island appears to join Hog Island at low tide; at high or flood tides (when the moon is full or new) the separation is more pronounced.

A dark hillside of blue spruce, planted by Mr. Crane in the 1930s, was the first of many beautiful scenes we enjoyed during our hour-long visit. Like a tapestry of the Emerald Isle, 26 shades of green were splashed across the landscape—hills and valleys, pastures and meadows, fields and gardens, country lanes and shoreline sweeps—a mosaic of nature's wonders cresting the aged marshes.

The rolling meadows were thick with cypress spurge, a pretty golden wildflower that thrives in open fields and along roadsides. Blue-black tree swallows swooped playfully through acres and acres of these pretty yellow tufts as we made our way along the peaceful farm road.

Time allowed only a quick visit to the main house, a large chocolate brown, two-story colonial, now permanently closed and boarded against storms. One white summer cottage is all that remains of the several attractive guest houses that were once part of the Choate compound at the height of its glory days.

Returning to the riverboat, we continued our journey on the mean-dering Essex River, becoming part of the seascape we had seen from White Hill. Cruising the white sands of Crane's Beach, past "Tuppeny

Towers" and "Red Gables," the English castles we had seen weeks earlier while exploring the Wingaersheek dunes, we then headed back to Essex, passing Cross Island, Conomo Point and Dilley Island, as we plowed through the channel to the marina.

15. ESSEX

1. Farnham's Clam Stand
2. Cox Reservation • Essex County Greenbelt Headquarters
3. Cox Barn Studio
4. George Anderson Meadow
5. Clam House Landing
6. Historic Cogswell Grant
7. White Hill
8. Hardys Hatcheries
9. Public Landing

John Wi
Ave.

KEY	
‖‖‖‖‖‖‖	Trail
‥ ‥ ‥	Sub Trail
⎯⎯⎯	Street or Highway
▪ ▪ ▪	Railroad Tracks
▨	Ocean
▨	Pond or Lake
▨	Swamp

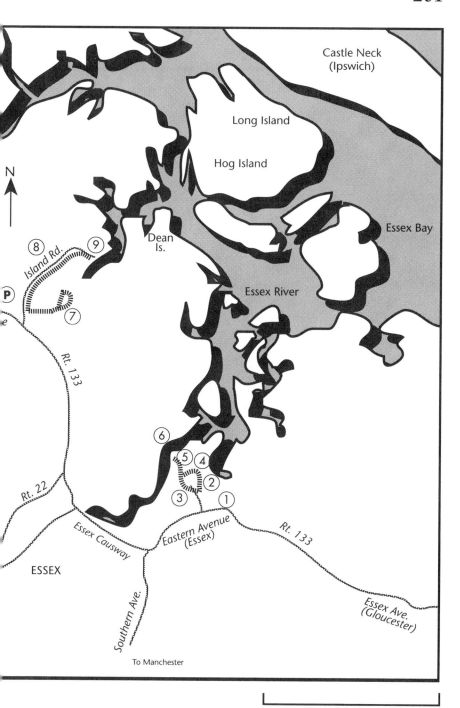

Castle Neck
(Ipswich)

Long Island

Hog Island

N

Essex Bay

⑧ ⑨
Island Rd.

Dean
Is.

P

⑦

Essex River

Rt. 133

⑥

⑤ ④

② Rt. 22

③ ②

①

Essex Causway

Eastern Avenue
(Essex)

Rt. 133

ESSEX

Southern Ave.

Essex Ave.
(Gloucester)

To Manchester

1 Mile

Flower Trails

I long for a Rockport Summer
and roses 'round every door
With white picket fences and gates of blue
that wind down to the shore.

From *A Rockport Summer*
By Dorothy Ramsey Stoffa

Old Garden Beach • Roger's Sanctuary
Keiran's Nature Preserve

In late spring and early summer, by unanimous agreement, trails always lead to "where the flowers are."

The gardens and nature preserves along Rockport's Old Garden Beach section offer a sampling of the beauty and wonder enjoyed at this time on Cape Ann. It was here that we began a garden tour on a sunny morning in mid-May. We started from the Headlands, a flat rocky outcrop jutting into the ocean at the southeastern tip of Rockport Harbor. From atop this scenic overlook, we had a magnificent view of the surrounding area. Looking north, the seascape spans the harbor, village, Bearskin Neck, Front and Back beaches, Pigeon Hill, and the rocky Atlantic coastline to Halibut Point. Gap Head lies to the south, as do the Straightsmouth, Milk and Thachers islands.

Ted led us along the Headlands path to Old Garden Road—and the beginning of our garden tour. Our first stop was a small, pretty English garden on the street side of an oceanfront cottage at the bottom of Norwood Avenue. From early May until "the last rose of summer," this little plot sparkles with a rainbow of colorful flowers— mostly perennials—roses, peonies, hollyhocks, snapdragons and shasta daisies, midst pots of geraniums and patches of pansies, all framed by dwarf fruit trees.

Continuing on, we passed the Old Garden Beach park and turned down the Old Garden Path between two large oceanside mansions at the foot of Dean Road. This cliff walk, a miniature version of Newport's world-famous Cliff Walk, has one shortcoming: it is far too short. But here, too, the view of land and sea is spectacular. On a clear day, Mt. Agamenticus in far-off Maine can be seen on the distant horizon. To the north the rugged shoreline winds into the harbor and north to Andrews and Halibut points; Gap Head juts out into the ocean to the south, the off-shore islands just beyond. Along the walk today, gardens were bright with yellow tulips, red geraniums, pink and white sea roses, and lavender wisteria. On the seaward side, a patch of raspberries tumbled down to the shore.

The narrow footpath all-too-soon opened onto a broad grassy lane and turned away from the sea toward Marmion Way. At the turn, Ted looked over the cliff at the rocks below, pointing out a landing dating back hundreds of years. Despite the storm-tossed rocks, it was possible to see the sandy stretch that had been cleared centuries ago to allow vessels in and out of the water.

"This is a public way," he lectured as we walked along the wide, well-tended green leading to the street. "It's been that way since these landings were built back in the 1700s. There's another public entrance onto Old Garden Path from Sandaba Road, a short distance from Dean Road."

At the end of the promenade, we turned left on Marmion Way and walked about a city block. A private paved drive left of Pioneer Circle took us behind Seaward Inn. Having obtained permission from innkeeper Roger Cameron (which is required for this part of the tour), Ted led us through "Roger's Sanctuary," a small nature preserve established for the enjoyment of guests.

"This is a little paradise," a woman beamed as we crossed a wooden bridge and circled a small, man-made lake. We continued along a path into a secluded natural setting of pines, maples and mountain laurel. Although we were only a short distance from the inn (and the ocean across the street), the preserve was completely hidden from view in the quiet woodlands.

Here we observed a variety of plants and trees, some cultivated, many more thriving happily in their natural setting. Newly planted hemlocks took root alongside bracken fern in shaded areas while further along the trail, high-bush blueberries, a flowering crab apple and wild strawberries were doing nicely in open sunlight. Wild roses, buttercups, peonies, jonquils, Jack-in-the-pulpits, lady's-slippers, and several birdhouses brightened the scene. As we followed along, Ted identified a number of wildflowers—wood anemones, Soloman's seal (both regular and false), Canada mayflowers, wild oats, wood trillium, and starflowers. Of special interest was the ajuga plant, (also called bugle-weed), a pretty violet used as ground cover. This ancient European herb was brought to North America several centuries ago, probably by early tradesmen. Now it grows rather commonly by roads and in fields throughout the eastern half of the United States.

Several paths wandered through the small sanctuary, eventually meeting up with the main trail which took us out to a clearing behind the inn. We followed Ted as he turned right onto a county way, passing under a canopy of viburnum and woodbine before emerging onto a private driveway that intersected with Marmion and the lower end of Straitsmouth ways.

Gazing across Gap Head Cove, Ted said, "That's where seals usually spend the winter, but there was nothing there last year."

"I don't blame them," quipped a wit, "it was a bad winter. They probably went to New Jersey."

(But, remember, we had seen three in Loblolly Cove.)

Turning onto Straitsmouth, we walked the quiet, peaceful lane back into the woods, our eyes continually searching for spring wildflowers. We were not disappointed. Wild geraniums, bluets, wood anemones, wild oats, and columbine dotted the roadway on both sides.

A short distance on the left was the John Kieran Nature Trail, named for the famous Rockport summer resident. A popular New York Times sports columnist, Mr. Kieran also wrote numerous books on natural history, which was his primary interest. He was extremely knowledgeable about other subjects as well, hosting the nationally syndicated radio-television program *Information, Please* for many years. The Kieran Trail slices through ten acres of dense forest between Marmion and Straitsmouth ways, where markers appear at both entrances. The guidepost at the Straitsmouth end replicates that placed in New York City's Central Park in honor of the highly-acclaimed naturalist.

As we studied wildflowers and listened to songbirds, we noted several pieces of carpeting along the trail. As usual, Ted had a ready explanation.

"This section is a big sponge," he said. "It holds water for the entire area."

He then went on to explain that the previous day, he and his volunteers had cut carpeting into three-foot strips and placed them on wet spots as a temporary protection for our walk today. Next week they'll return to wrap the strips in plastic and cover the spots with woodchips. They've found this helps keep the paths relatively dry for visitors to the preserve.

Many of the wild plants and flowers seen earlier in Roger's sanctuary were also thriving well here in the moist soil—cinnamon fern, Jack-in-

206 • Walking Cape Ann

the-pulpits, lady's-slippers and wood violets. But further along the path a Japanese yew and columbine needed a little more sun which brought out Ted's trusty clippers to trim away intrusive branches.

Both these nature preserves are along the migratory route birds fly each year to summer on Cape Ann. Thanks to conservationists like Roger, Ted and the late Mr. Kieran, nesting places and handouts are waiting for the frequent flyers when they arrive.

"The first thing that grows up is greenbrier where warblers and other small songbirds like to nest," Ted noted. Among those flitting about this morning were catbirds, mocking birds, cardinals, robins, sparrows, mourning doves and a purple house finch.

The winding trail soon led out of the preserve onto Marmion Way. Turning right, we walked past Seacrest Manor and turned right again onto Shetland Road, passing several pretty flower gardens. Mid-way down Shetland, which parallels the scenic ocean drive, we looked back across the Kieran Preserve to the lighthouse on Straitsmouth Island. Sloping down to the sparkling sea was a wide sweep of new spring growth capping the trees with tender green leaves.

"They look like soft green pillows," remarked a long-time Cape Anner.

Mingling among the multishaded greens of oak, willows, beech, birch, tupelo and indigenous pine were white shad and pink crabapple blossoms, creating a pretty spring landscape against the blue Atlantic.

Rounding the corner onto upper Straitsmouth Way, we walked along enjoying the pleasant neighborhood—large homes, sprawling lawns, shade trees, stonewall fences, and spring flowers of every kind. Passing through the tall stone posts onto South Street, we headed toward the village—past the Rockport Lodge, the Golf Club, and Den-Mar Nursing Home. Leaving South Street, Ted turned onto Old Straitsmouth Way, a quiet tree-shaded lane behind lovely period homes. Flowering trees and plants blossomed in backyard gardens and nearby fields, but one scene in particular brought a broad smile to the face of our walkmaster, the ultimate conservationist. A clever homeowner—either past or present—needing a shed to store his winter firewood, had the ingenuity to save a huge red oak by skillfully building a lean-to around its trunk. The shed was piled high with fireplace logs ready for winter.

"Now that's the way trees should be treated," Ted beamed, closely examining the structure enclosing the mammoth oak. Needless to say, the sight warmed his heart and made his day.

We continued onto Richards Avenue, bearing left across Marmion Way, then back onto Old Garden Road. Across from the park at Old Garden Beach, a town right-of-way between two large beach houses brought us to Caleb's Lane, a narrow dirt road that continues through to South Street. Midway up the lane, we took a right onto Highland Avenue, where we stopped to chat with a woman tending her garden. Passing the homes of the late John Kieran (on the corner of Highland and Norwood) and his neighbor, Dorothy Luce (for whom the Cross Cape Trail is name), we returned to our cars at the Headlands, the starting point of our garden tour.

LADY'S-SLIPPER TRAIL

One of Cape Ann's prettiest spring wildflowers is the lady's-slipper, also known as the moccasin flower. A member of the orchid family, each plant has only one stem and one delicate, purple-veined flower puffed out to look like the toe of a slipper. The brownish "shoelaces" at the top add to its shoe-like appearance. Unfortunately, because of its unique characteristics and beauty, throughout the years people have uprooted this plant for their gardens. The result is that the lady's-slipper is becoming more and more rare in New England and now appears on the endangered species list.

In late May, when this beautiful wildflower was in full bloom, we headed for the lady's-slipper trail in the quarry uplands. To get there, we left Whistlestop Mall and drove north on Granite Street to Landmark Lane just before the Yankee Clipper Inn. Climbing Pigeon Hill, we parked at the turn-around at the base of the water tank. The distance from the mall to the summit of Pigeon Hill is exactly one and six-tenths miles.

Owned by the town and maintained by the Sandy Bay Historical Society, this hilltop is a popular site for picnics and blueberry picking. The vantage point offers an expansive view of the Atlantic Ocean and the surrounding seascape, including Halibut Point, Rockport Harbor, Thachers and Dry Salvages islands, and to the north (about 25 miles in New Hampshire) the Isles of Shoals.

From the parking area, a footpath led across a meadow and private land to a gravel extension of Rowe Avenue, which runs past Big Parker's Pit and up into the quarry fields. Canada mayflowers, also called wild lilies-of-the-valley, were profuse throughout the walk. This pretty wildflower, with heart-shaped leaves and star-shaped flowers, carpets large areas in forests and under trees along roadsides. When the flowers fade, red speckled berries follow, providing wild birds with a hearty meal.

Wild strawberries were also prevalent in sunny spots along the roadside. Unlike cultivated strawberries, wild strawberries are small and their tastiness depends on the amount of rain and sun exposure they receive, but they can be more flavorful than the larger variety.

We followed Ted toward Steel Derrick Pit, past an abandoned granite powerhouse. Inside the smooth granite walls were remnants of pilings and large granite slabs, the former used for railroad tracks, the latter a base for boilers which made steam for drills. To a fellow walker, the site resembled Stonehenge, the mysterious prehistoric English Stone Age monument.

As we followed the paths around the rims of Butman's Pit, Potato Pit, Little Parker Pit, and several small motions, Ted pointed out many wild-flowers coming into bloom, describing the characteristics of each. Bluets, also called Quaker ladies, are dainty light blue flowers with bright yellow eyes, and grow in with grass, violets and other field wildflowers. Indian cucumbers are related to the lily family, and do well in Cape Ann's rich, damp woodlands. This tall, thin plant has two whorls of pointed leaves and delicate white cucumber-flavored flowers; its fruit is a small purple berry. The fragile starflower belongs to the primrose family. As many as ten pointed green leaves form at the tip of its stem, from which two tiny white flowers with thin golden anthers grow. Buttercups are prevalent in North America—81 known species, about 36 of them in New England. All have the same type shiny yellow blossoms, but leaves differ with each variety. These pretty wildflowers love sunshine and are found in fields, along roadsides and in marshy areas throughout the northern half of the United States. Because the leaves and stems of all varieties have a bad taste, grass-eating animals do not eat them, which is why they are so plentiful in the spring and summer months.

In addition to the many spring wildflowers we saw that day, we also noted the trees and bushes coming into leaf—witch hazel, striped maple, mountain laurel, sheep laurel, sweetpepper, sassafras, maple leaf viburnum, big tooth aspen, and wild hawthorn.

But our focus this morning was on lady's-slippers. And high in the upland woods, we found them.

"There's a nice little group right here where it's open," said Ted, leading us to his favorite spot, midway between Buttman and Potato pits. The reason for his choice soon became obvious. Everywhere we looked, on both sides of the trail and extending far into the woods, were the exquisite plants we had come to see. Some clumps had only single stems, others double, still others many more, each having a perfectly-formed slippered toe. One large spray of luxuriant green leaves had eleven pink flowers, the most any of us had ever seen on a single plant.

Returning to the trail, we continued to find lady's-slippers spread out all along the way, including a few of the rare white species. To many in the group, this was a delightful annual event—somewhat like an Easter egg hunt. But to a Florida visitor who had never seen this beautiful plant, it was a once-in-a-lifetime experience she'll treasure.

"Now I know what all the shouting is about," said she.

It's easy to see why people want to take them home for their very own, but I would caution readers not to remove them from their natural environment. Please let future generations enjoy them, too.

As we turned toward Potato Pit, which is located slightly north of Flat Ledge Quarry, Ted pointed out the tomb of Major John Rowe, a Revolutionary War hero who led a contingent of 59 Rockport Freedom Fighters (including his 14 and 16-year-old sons) to Bunker Hill. His body has since been moved to Arlington Cemetery, and the old granite tomb now lost to history.

On our left, bullfrogs provided music from the swamp.

"I love that sound," said a long-time Cape Anner who has been walking these trails for many years.

The woodlands path brought us to the intersection of Drumlin Road and Rowe Avenue, a short distance from Keystone Bridge. Pointing to a large Italian villa nearby, Ted told us that it had originally been the oxen barn for the Rockport Granite Company (of which his grandfather had been president). An Italian sculptor designed and built the house inside the original stone walls, featuring a formal garden in the courtyard, which was also enclosed within the original walls.

Drumlin Road climbs a long, straight, steep incline to Pigeon Hill, winding into Landmark Lane just below the water tower. Bordered on both sides are attractive homes overlooking the harbor and village with sloping lawns and well-tended gardens and fruit trees. As we walked up the hill on the final leg of our flower tour, we enjoyed the season's kaleidoscope against the clear blue sky—delicate pink and white blossoms of apple, cherry, pear, peach and plum trees; dark purple lilacs, salmon-colored azaleas, magenta rhododendrons, red geraniums, white hydrangeas, orange poppies and tiger lilies, pink and purple lupine and rose-colored peonies. All are part of the majesty of spring on Cape Ann.

MOUNTAIN LAUREL TRAIL

In mid-June, we headed for the South Woods to enjoy the beauty of laurel time, when clusters of the beautiful pink-tinged white mountain laurel come into bloom. In the South, this evergreen shrub grows as high as thirty-five feet or more, often blanketing mountainsides in North Carolina and North Georgia with towering, impenetrable thickets.

However, it is the northern state of Connecticut that claims it as its official state flower. Its maximum height is about ten feet in the North, where its growth on rocky or sandy soil is dense but not as dense as in southern mountain ranges.

But the alluring beauty of this pretty wildflower is deceptive; like other members of the heath family, it is poisonous. Both its leaves and blossoms are harmful, causing convulsions and paralysis to animals that browse in its thickets. Most beekeepers in laurel areas discard honey made during its blossoming period; while the bees seem immune, humans who have eaten honey made from its pollen and nectar have become seriously ill. Burning in the mouth, stomach cramps, vomiting, and heart disturbance are among the reactions. Fortunately, the odor from laurel honey is very offensive and should warn people away.

Returning to the positive attributes of this beautiful shrub, burls form on its roots, especially in the South, which are made into briar pipes for tobacco use. The word "briar" comes from the French *bruyere*, the name for the entire heath family (which, incidentally, includes the poverty grass found in the dunes at Wingaersheek Beach.)

To begin our walk along Rockport's mountain laurel trail, we parked in the schoolyard of the High School-Middle School on Jerden's Lane, and made our way through the playground and across the ballfield to a footpath behind homeplate. This path led to Farm Lane, an old oxen trail in use during colonial days when early settlers were assigned woodlots to build and heat their homes.

It was a beautiful spring day and all was right with the world, we thought, as we walked the peaceful country lane. The fragrance of pasture roses, in abundance everywhere, permeated the morning air. A mourning dove, disturbed by our presence, fluttered out of a nearby locust tree; above a Baltimore oriole pursued a fleeing crow. On our right, cattails stood tall in nearby freshwater wetland. A short distance further was Pascucci's gravel pit, now filled in, making a pretty lily pond. Beyond was Kelly's Pond. A freshly mowed pasture lined the roadway on our left.

Throughout the walk, Ted kept up a running commentary on the plants and flowers we passed. "That's crown vetch, it's a wild pea," he said, pointing to a patch of pretty pink and white wildflowers with trailing stems.

"There's some mapleleaf viburnum in bloom."

"Sassafras is coming in everywhere." Then, for the benefit of first-time visitors from New York, he pulled at a branch and pointed out a small, mitten-shaped leaf. Although he's been leading these walks for more than 20 years, he always takes time to explain unique characteristics of plants and trees to newcomers.

We followed Farm Lane into South Woods, where it soon became a narrow bridle path. Lichen-covered glacial erratics dotted the landscape, along with dark green hemlock. Most of the hardwoods were beech. A northern white admiral butterfly winged gracefully overhead. Common in the northeast, this strong flier is frequently spotted sailing up and down the road and forest edges, or quietly perched in open hardwood forests, high in a tree. Although it visits flowers frequently, it's also fond of carrion and the secretion of aphids.

Before we headed into the forest, repellant was shared and applied to ward off bothersome mosquitoes which frequent moist woodlands in warm weather. As we trekked deeper into the woods, we began to see scatterings of laurel. The further we walked, the more we saw, finally reaching our destination—about 200 acres of tall, healthy bushes, with shiny green leaves. The blossoms were delicate and beautiful, but many flowerets were still seeded.

"If it blooms one year, it puts its energy into seeds the next and blooms the following year," Ted explained to our New York visitors. "But this hasn't been a good year for laurel. The severe weather must have killed the buds; it'd be warm for awhile, then we'd get a cold spell. I think they tried to bloom, then were frozen."

The footpath twisted and turned through the dense thicket, prompting Ted to explain that he intentionally kept it narrow to prevent poison ivy, catbrier and other brambles from invading the mountain laurel. Up we went, through the thick shrubbery, rounding curves and plowing through overhanging branches, the winding trail taking us up a steep hillside then descending almost vertically into a valley below. During the downward plunge, Ted, ever mindful of the safety of his charges, positioned himself in front of a spirited matron carrying a cane. Staying close to block a possible fall, he lent his broad shoulders for support; if she fell, it would be onto his back—and not an inch further. Fortunately, she and everyone else made it safely down the hill.

Our walk along the mountain laurel trail is one the group looks forward to each June. Ted usually allows about an hour to enjoy the blossoms. Because of the laurel's growth cycle, each year there's a wide variety of floral displays, making visits especially enjoyable following its biennial revitalization. Although today's tour lacked the luster of previous seasons, we consoled ourselves knowing there's always next year, when we hoped to see a spectacular show along this trail.

THE MAGNOLIA TRAIL (SEE RAVENSWOOD)

16A. **F**LOWER TRAILS
KIERAN'S PRESERVE

1. English Garden by the Sea
2. Old Garden Beach and Park
3. Old Garden Beach Cliffwalk
4. Roger's Sanctuary
5. Kieran's Nature Preserve
6. DenMar Nursing Home
7. Shed built around huge oak

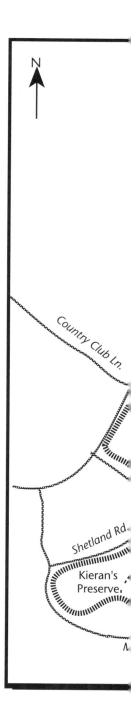

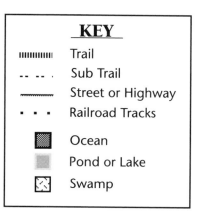

KEY	
ⅢⅢⅢⅢ	Trail
-- -- .	Sub Trail
——	Street or Highway
• • •	Railroad Tracks
▓	Ocean
▒	Pond or Lake
▨	Swamp

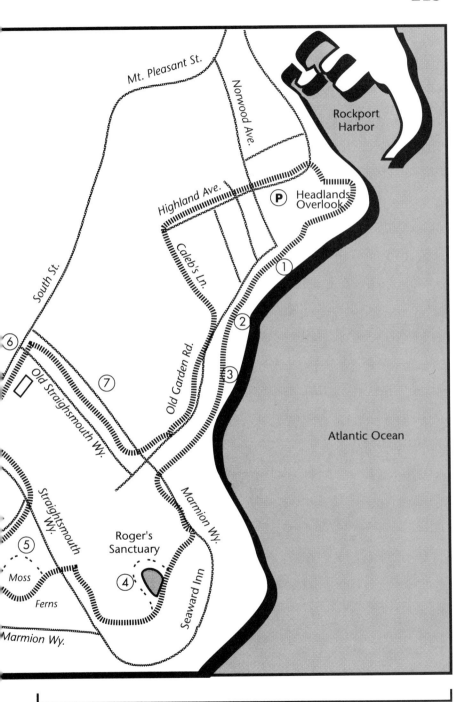

Mt. Pleasant St.

Norwood Ave.

Rockport Harbor

Highland Ave.

P Headlands Overlook

Caleb's Ln.

South St.

①

②

⑥

Old Straighsmouth Wy.

Old Garden Rd.

⑦

③

Atlantic Ocean

Marmion Wy.

Straightsmouth Wy.

Roger's Sanctuary

⑤

Moss

Seaward Inn

④

Ferns

Marmion Wy.

1/2 Mile

16B. Flower Trails
LADY SLIPPER TRAIL

1. Water Tank
2. Lady Slippers
3. Lady Slippers
4. Lady Slippers
5. Italian Villa
6. Magnificent View of Rockport
7. Picnic Area with a View

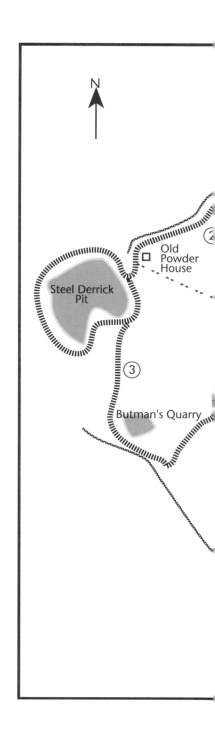

KEY

▥▥▥▥▥	Trail
-- -- .	Sub Trail
‒‒‒‒‒	Street or Highway
▪ ▪ ▪	Railroad Tracks
▦	Ocean
▨	Pond or Lake
▨	Swamp

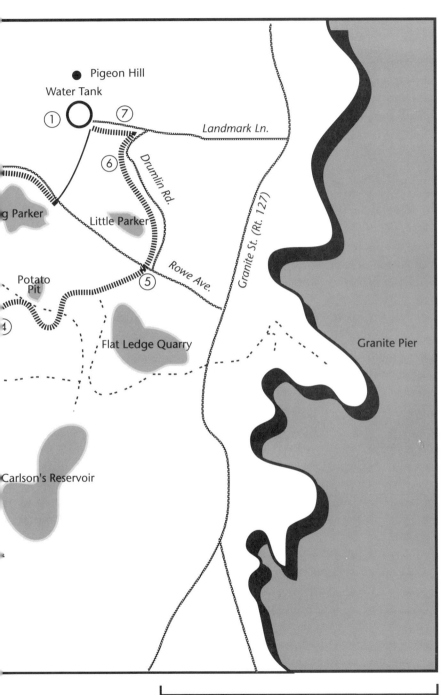

Pigeon Hill

Water Tank

① ⑦

Landmark Ln.

⑥

Drumlin Rd.

Granite St. (Rt. 127)

g Parker

Little Parker

Rowe Ave.

Potato Pit

⑤

④

Flat Ledge Quarry

Granite Pier

Carlson's Reservoir

1 Mile

16C. FLOWER TRAILS
LAUREL WALK

1. Muskrat Swamp
2. Farm Lane
3. Dark Woods Road
4. Triangle Cave
5. High Rock
6. Club House
7. Elevated 4th Tee
8. Horsehoe Path

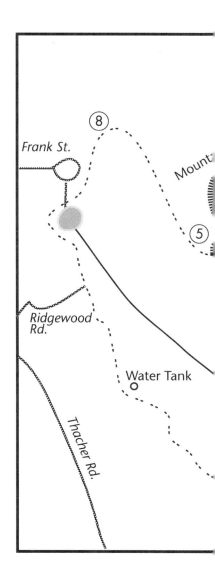

<u>**KEY**</u>

ⅢⅢⅢⅢⅢ	Trail
- - -- -	Sub Trail
────	Street or Highway
● ● ●	Railroad Tracks
▓	Ocean
▒	Pond or Lake
▨	Swamp

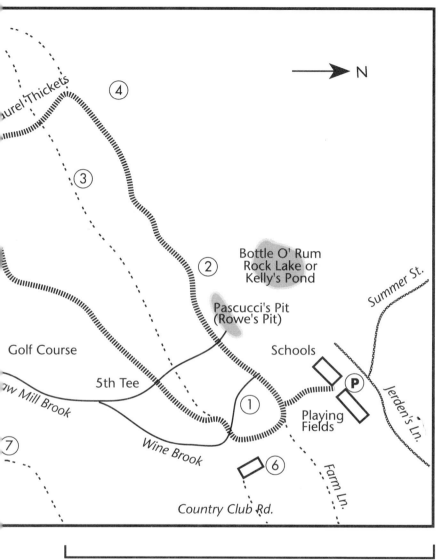

N

Laurel Thickets

④

③

②

Bottle O' Rum
Rock Lake or
Kelly's Pond

Pascucci's Pit
(Rowe's Pit)

Summer St.

Golf Course

Schools

5th Tee

⑩ P

①

ow Mill Brook

Playing
Fields

Jerden's Ln.

⑦

Wine Brook

⑥

Farm Ln.

Country Club Rd.

1 Mile

APPENDIX

OTHER TRAILS AND POINTS OF INTEREST

ROCKPORT RIGHTS OF WAY

(Look for White Posted Signs)

These Rights-of-Ways are maintained by Volunteers to enable residents and visitors to enjoy the natural beauty of this picturesque village by the sea.

Village
1. Way to Old Boat Ramp - Off Dock Square
2. Way to School House Landing - Beside Toad Hall Book Store

North of Village
3. Bay Avenue Public Foot Path to the Sea - Pt.DeChene & Phillips Aves.
4. Way to Atlantic Path (South of Bay Ave.) - From Phillips Avenue
5. Pine Avenue Public Foot Path to the Sea - From Pt. DeChene Avenue
6. Gale Avenue Public Foot Path to the Sea - From Pt. DeChene Avenue
7. Linwood Ave. Public Foot Path to the Sea - From Pt. DeChene Avenue
8. Dawn Avenue Way to Atlantic Path - From Long Branch Avenue
9. Hoop Pole Cove Atlantic Path - From Long Branch Avenue
10. Way to Atlantic Path (Below Haven Ave.) - Corner Cove and Phillips Aves.
11. Reeds Lane Path to the Sea - From Phillips Avenue
12. Thornwood Avenue Way to Atlantic Path - From Phillips Avenue
13. Cedar Avenue to Atlantic Path - From Phillips Avenue

South of Village
14. Way to Headlands - From Atlantic Road
15. Way to Headlands - From Norwood Ave & Old Garden Road
16. Way to Old Garden Path (Cliff walk) - From Old Garden Road
17. Way to Old Garden Path (Cliff walk) - From Marmion Way
18. Way to Steep Bank Landing - From South Street

19.Way to Cogswell Farm Landing - From Penzance Road
20.Way to Flat Rock Point - From Eden Road
21.The Saratoga Creek Foot Bridge - From Thatcher Road

Dogtown Trails - Rockport/Gloucester
(See Dogtown Common Trail Map
Available at Toad Hall Book Store, Rockport and The Bookstore, Gloucester)

1. Art's Trail
2. Babson Boulder Trail
3. Common Road Trail
4. Dogtown Road Trail
5. Town Forest Trail
6. Dennison Trail
7. Luce Trail
8. Moraine Trail
9. Nellie's Trail
10. Adams Pines Trail
11. Squam Path Trail
12. Tarr Trail
13. Wharf Road Trail

Manchester Woods Trails
(See Manchester Conservation Trust Trail Map)
1. Ancient Line Trail - Orange/Red
2. Dug Hill Trail - Pink)
3. Spruce Swamp Trail - Pink
4. Pulpit Rock Trail- Blue
5. Cheever Commons Loop Trail - Blue-Double Dots
6. Millstone Hill Trail - Orange/Red
7. Cedar Swamp Trail - Blue
8. Prospect Ledge Trail - Pink
9. Powder House Hill Reservation
   (Minnie B. Ball Nature Trail) - Unmarked
10. Hemlock Glen Trail - Orange/Red
11. Clara B. Winthrop Nature Preserve - Unmarked
12. Eaglehead Nature Study Area - Unmarked
13. Baby Rock Trail - Orange Red

ESSEX COUNTY GREENBELT TRAILS

(See *Passport to Essex County Greenbelt*
Available from Essex County Greenbelt Association, Inc.
82 Eastern Avenue, Essex, MA 01929 - Tel. 508 768-7241)

1. Alt Woodland - Beverly
2. Beverly Conservation Area - Beverly
3. Boxford Woodlots - Boxford
4. Cox Reservation - Essex
5. Warren-Weld Woodland - Essex
6. Baldpate Hill - Georgetown
7. Goose Cove - Gloucester
8. Stoney Cove - Gloucester
9. Willowdale Mill - Hamilton
10. Julia Bird Reservation - Ipswich
11. Ipswich Riv. Middleton to Topsfield - Middleton
12. Middleton Woods - Middleton
13. Parker River Canoeing - Newbury
14. Pingree Reservation - Hamilton
15. Arthur Ewell Reservation - Rowley
16. Rowley Marshes - Rowley
18. Sawyer's Island Conservation Area - Rowley
19. Ingalls Memorial Wetlands - Boxford

BAY CIRCUIT TRAILS

When finished, the Bay Circuit will be a 200-mile arc of parks, historic sites, and open spaces connected by trails, waterways and scenic touring routes meandering through the Massachusetts countryside, from Duxbury in the south, west through Framingham and north to Newbury. The 52 communities along the Circuit invite you to visit their towns and villages and enjoy the beauty and culture of this typical New England landscape. Following are a few points of interest along the North Shore Scenic Touring Route:

1. Town Center - Rowley
2. Ipswich Historic District - Ipswich
3. Willowdale State Forest - Ipswich, Topsfield, Boxford and Rowley
4. Georgetown-Rowley State Forest - Georgetown, Boxford,Rowley
5. Topsfield Historic District - Topsfield

6. Ipswich River Wildlife Sanctuary - Topsfield, Hamilton and Wenham
7. Bradley Palmer State Park - Ipswich, Hamilton and Topsfield
8. Canoe Rental at Willow Dam - 356 Topsfield Road, Ipswich
9. Julia Bird Reservation - Waldingfield Rd., Ipswich
10. Goodale Orchards - Argilla Road, Ipswich
11. Cox Reservation - 82 Eastern Ave., Essex
12. Castle Hill - Argilla Road, Ipswich
13. Crane Reservation - Argilla Road, Ipswich
14. Essex Town Center - Essex
15. Craft Hill - Essex
16. Appleton Farms Grass Rides - Cutler Road near Highland Ave, Hamilton
17. Hamilton Historic District - Hamilton
18. Wenham Historic District - Wenham
19. Cedar Pond Wildlife Sanctuary - 123 Cherry St., Wenham
20. Phillips Nature Preserve - Route 97, 1/0 mi. south of Wenham-Beverly line
21. The Iron Rail - Grapevine Road at Route 22, Wenham
22. Long Hill - 572 Essex Street (Route 22), Beverly

EMERALD NECKLACE TRAILS

(Information available from Boston Parks & Recreation
1010 Massachusetts Avenue, Boston, MA 02118 - Tel (617) 635-4505)

The Emerald Necklace is a string of nine contiguous parks that include walks, bridle paths, a common, a tidal marsh, ponds, river glens, steep banks, wooded hills, groves, meadows and gardens—all within walking distance of historic Boston Common. Most of this scenic greenspace was designed by Frederick Law Olmsted (1822-1903), the father of landscape architecture who worked in plants, trees, earth and water as a painter works in oils. The parks making up this beautiful, seven-mile linear green ribbon are designated Boston Landmarks and are listed in the National Register of Historic Places.

1. Boston Common - 48 acres
2. Public Garden - 25 acres
3. Commonwealth Avenue Mall - 32 acres
4. Back Bay Fens (The Fenway) -113 acres
5. The Riverway - 28 acres
6. Olmsted Park -180 acres

7 Jamaica Pond - 120 acres (1.5 miles around the pond)
8. Arnold Arboretum - 265 acres
9. Franklin Park - 527 acres

BIBLIOGRAPHY

Copeland, Melvin T. and Rogers, Elliott C.; *The Saga of Cape Ann.* Gloucetser, Mass., Peter Smith, 1983

Bolles, Frank: *From Blomidon to Smoky.* Boston and New York, Houghton, Mifflin and Company, 1894

Chamberlain, Samuel and Hollister, Paul: *Beauport at Gloucester.* New York, Hastings House, 1951

Gibbons, Euell: *Stalking the Healthful Herbs.* New York, David McKay Company, Inc. 1966

Erkkila, Barbara H.: *Hammers On Stone, the History of Cape Ann Granite,* Gloucester, Mass, 1980, Reprinted by arrangement with TWB Books, Falmouth, Maine, Printed 1987

Kenny, Herbert A.: *Cape Ann: Cape America.* Philadelphia and New York, J. B. Lippincott Company, 1971

Massachusetts Audubon Society and The Essex County Ecology Center, Inc., Eleanor Pope: *The Wilds of Cape Ann.* Boston, Mass., The Nimrod Press, 1981

National Association of Audubon Societies, T. Gilbert Pearson, Editor-in-Chief: *Birds of America.* Garden City, New York, Garden City Books, 1936

Parsons, Eleanor C.: *Hannah and the Hatchet Gang.* Canaan, N. H., Phoenix Publishing, 1975

Parsons, Eleanor C.: *Thachers, Island of the Twin Lights.* Canaan, N. H., Phoenix Publishing, 1985

Proctor Brothers, Publishers: *Pleasure Drives Around Cape Ann,* Gloucester, Mass. 1896

Walton, Mason A.: *A Hermit's Wild Friends,* Boston, Dana Estes & Company, 1903

Weed, Clarence M. D.Sc.: *Butterflies*, Garden City, N.Y., Doubleday, Page & Company for Nelson Doubleday, Inc., 1926

Wonson, Mary and Roger Choate Wonson: *Downriver, A Memoir of Choate Island*, Randolph Center, Vermont, Greenhill Books, 1983

Zwinger, Ann and Teale, Edwin Way: *A Conscious Stillness, Two Naturalists on Thoreau's Rivers*. New York, Harper & Rowe, 1982

These are some of the sources that I used in writing my book. The reader should be aware that there are many fine publications on Cape Ann and its history in the Rockport and Gloucester libraries.

ABOUT THE AUTHOR

Long before it was necessary to do so, Helen Naismith embarked on a widely varied career that ranged from government service in Washington (including the CIA) to judging culinary competitons with Julia Child and assisting with the Queen's Bientennial Luncheon in Boston. Whether working backstage at Nashville's Grand Ole Opry researching her best-selling *Country Stars Cookbook* or attending the nation's Bicentennial observances for her book, *Famous Festival Foods*, her domain was America's multicultural culinary heritage.

Born in Attleboro, MA, Helen spent much of her adult life in the South, including 28 years in Atlanta where her writing at that time focused on dining and entertaining. Her syndicated column *Dining with the Stars* and feature articles for *People on Parade* magazine became established showcases.

Returning to her native New England in 1986, she settled in the picturesque seaside village of Rockport and became absorbed in the beauty of Cape Ann's wilderness and rocky coastline, as well as in local history. A volunteer field guide for the Massachusetts Audubon Society at the Ipswich River Wildlife Sanctuary, she combines these interests with her love of walking and writing. *Walking Cape Ann with Ted Tarr* is a reflection of her enthusiasm for life and a career of writing about richly rewarding personal experiences.